IMAGES
*of America*

# SUN CITY

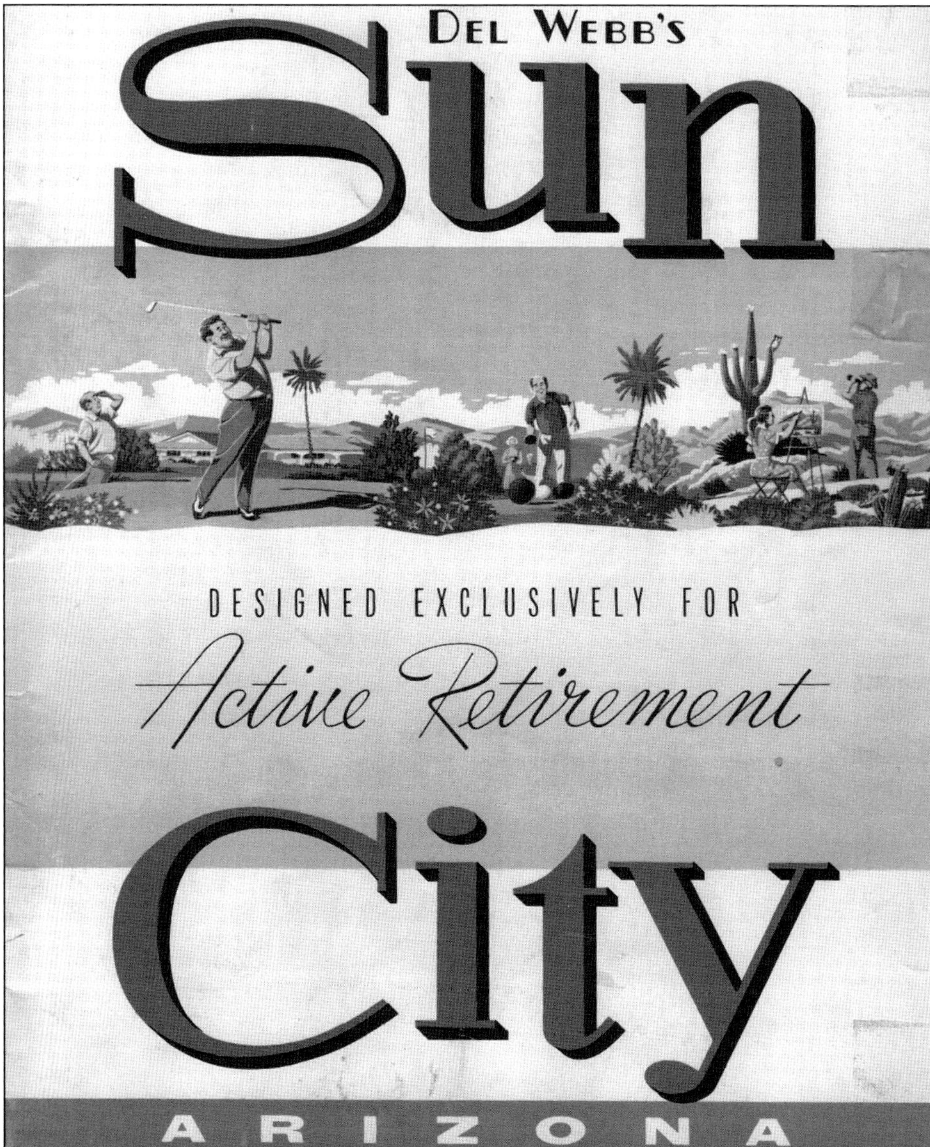


Retirees made the move to Sun City in the early 1960s looking to enjoy "fun in the sun" during their golden years. Many of those early residents were attracted to the new community no doubt thanks to a nationwide advertising campaign launched by Sun City's developer, the Del E. Webb Corporation. Advertisements were published in newspapers and magazines throughout the nation, and the company also created special brochures, postcards, and holiday greeting cards to promote its new community. In the early 1960s, Sun City was even promoted on racing cars competing in the Daytona 500 and Indianapolis 500. (Sun Cities Area Historical Society.)

**ON THE COVER:** From the moment it first opened on January 1, 1960, Sun City has remained a popular choice for active adults looking for a fun place to spend their retirement. Pleasant year-round temperatures provide plenty of opportunities for outdoor activities. This Del E. Webb Corporation publicity shot, taken in 1963, depicts residents enjoying the pool at Town Hall Recreation Center (now Fairway Recreation Center). (Sun Cities Area Historical Society.)

IMAGES
*of America*

# SUN CITY

Bret McKeand and the
Sun Cities Area Historical Society

ARCADIA
PUBLISHING

ISBN 978-0-7385-7951-1

Published by Arcadia Publishing
Charleston, South Carolina

Printed in the United States of America

Library of Congress Control Number: 2010929268

For all general information, please contact Arcadia Publishing:
Telephone 843-853-2070
Fax 843-853-0044
E-mail sales@arcadiapublishing.com
For customer service and orders:
Toll-Free 1-888-313-2665

Visit us on the Internet at www.arcadiapublishing.com

*To the early Sun City pioneers, whose generous spirit, commitment to community, and loyalty to neighbors continue to inspire and set the standard for all those who follow. And to Jane Freeman, whose undying love for her adopted hometown has convinced others that Sun City's history is history worth preserving.*

# Contents

# Acknowledgments

The photographs in this collection are from the archives of the Sun Cities Area Historical Society (SCAHS), Independent Newspapers, Inc., or from my own personal collection of photographs taken over the years. Photographs where no credit is given are from the Sun Cities Area Historical Society archives.

Many photographs were taken by the talented public relations teams employed by the Del E. Webb Corporation and were originally published in the company-sponsored newsletters *SunDial* and the *Webb Spinner*. Credit belongs to the employees responsible for those newsletters and photographs: Jerry Svendsen, Richard Kemp, Don Tuffs, Wes Grant, Al Pote, and countless others who remain anonymous. Sun City historians are indebted to their work.

The Del E. Webb Corporation graciously donated the photographs to the SCAHS when it departed from Sun City, and Pulte Homes continues to support the organization.

The SCAHS has taken on the responsibility of preserving and protecting these photographs. The museum it operates was created in part to serve as a permanent archive to store these and other historical artifacts related to Sun City and Sun City West.

Special thanks are extended to the SCAHS board of trustees, and specifically to the 2009 president, David Verble, and 2010 president, Bill Pearson—all of whom encouraged this project and lent their full support.

I am personally indebted to Jane Freeman, Edson Allen, and Priscilla Fenner. It was Jane who first suggested we consider updating *Jubilee: The 25th Anniversary of Sun City*, the first authoritative history ever written about Sun City, authored in 1985 by Freeman and Glenn Sanberg. This new publication in no way compares to that 1985 masterpiece, but I hope she is pleased with the results.

Ed and Priscilla both continue to impress and inspire me with their knowledge of the community and their constant pursuit of historical accuracy. Their input, guidance, and editorial assistance were invaluable.

I am fortunate to have the support of my employer, Independent Newspapers, Inc. The company hired me as a reporter in 1983 and assigned me to Sun City. I could not ask for two greater mentors than CEO Joe Smyth and Pres. Ed Dulin, both of whom continue to serve as a source of wisdom and inspiration.

The Sun City Independent graciously allowed the SCAHS to use photographs from its files. Special thanks go to publisher Charlene Patti-Bisson for her assistance and to all our reporters and photographers over the years that helped record the history of Sun City.

—Bret McKeand

# Introduction

Sun City's history began January 1, 1960, at the intersection of 107th Avenue and Oakmont Drive. It was on that day the Del E. Webb Corporation unveiled the world's first active-adult resort retirement community.

More than 100,000 curious retirees turned out that opening weekend to see what all the fuss was about. Sun City was an immediate success—237 homes were sold during those first three days alone, and an entire new industry was born.

Today retirement communities and developments are quite common. Senior-only communities and active-adult retirement resorts stretch coast to coast, each one boasting different benefits appealing to different tastes and interests.

But Sun City was the first. It not only launched an industry, but it set the standard for others to follow.

When the Del E. Webb Corporation began work on Sun City, the idea was to go beyond simply building a collection of homes. Sun City would offer everything a retiree would need to make his or her "golden years" comfortable, fun, and invigorating: plenty of recreational amenities, lots of activities, a safe environment, and very affordable homes. Add in 365 days of sunshine and there is a winning formula for success.

The concept worked, and Sun City's growth exploded over the next 15 years. By the time Del E. Webb Corporation left Sun City to concentrate on building other retirement communities, Sun City was the nation's premier retirement community.

But it was not the buildings that made Sun City a household name and a famous footnote in American history. It was the people who lived in Sun City and the lifestyle they enjoyed that made Sun City so attractive, then and now.

Sun City's history can still be found at the intersection of 107th and Oakmont Drive, the place where it all started.

Next to Oakmont Recreation Center (originally called the Community Center when it was unveiled in 1960) sits the Del Webb Sun Cities Museum and the headquarters of the Sun Cities Area Historical Society.

The museum is located at 10801 Oakmont Drive, in one of the first five homes constructed and available for prospective buyers to inspect on that very first day back in 1960.

The museum is home to many of the photographs contained in this book. The photographs selected for inclusion in this volume were chosen not because of their historical significance, but rather because of the manner in which they depict Sun City residents celebrating retirement.

Some are humorous, some are posed, and some merely reflect a moment in time. But all are accurate depictions of life in Sun City. Each one on its own reveals a vibrant community of citizens thoroughly enjoying their retirement years.

Most of the photographs encompassing the first two decades of the community's existence were donated to the museum by the developer, the Del E. Webb Corporation. The photographs were taken for promotional purposes and were meant to show the positive side of life in Sun City.

Most of the photographs from the subsequent decades come from a number of sources, primarily the archives of the *Sun City Independent*, a local newspaper serving the community since 1960. Since these photographs were destined to appear in a newspaper, they tend to be less posed and more focused on the event rather than the people.

The history of the museum and how it came into possession of the Webb photographs is a story worth telling.

Jane Freeman, coauthor of *Jubilee: The 25th Anniversary of Sun City*, paid a visit in 1984 to the offices of the Del E. Webb Development Company (DEVCO), the Del E. Webb Corporation subsidiary responsible for building Sun City. The company was preparing its exodus from Sun City and was planning to move its offices to Sun City West. Employees were clearing out the building and, as Freeman recalls, "literally taking file drawers and dumping them upside down into dumpsters."

Discarded items included old Webb brochures promoting Sun City, newsletters, newspaper clippings, and—most importantly—photographs taken by the company's marketing team during the community's first two decades.

One man's trash is another man's treasure, and Freeman quickly realized the value of the items disposed of right before her eyes.

She and a few friends climbed into the dumpsters and rescued as much as they could. That material served as the basis for the creation of the Sun Cities Historical Society in 1986. The material salvaged that day, as well as future donations by the Del E. Webb Corporation, now rests in the protected archives at the Del Webb Sun Cities Museum.

Many of the photographs were originally published in early Webb advertisements promoting Sun City, or in the *Sundial*, a newsletter published by DEVCO for Sun City residents.

Some photographs reappeared for the first time in *Jubilee: The 25th Anniversary of Sun City*, written by Freeman and Glenn Sanberg. *Jubilee* was published to correspond with the community's silver anniversary and was the first in-depth history ever written about Sun City. It not only highlighted and showcased the community's past, but it was the first to credit Sun City for changing the way Americans perceive retirement.

A few more photographs trickled slowly from the archives over the years. Some would appear in occasional newspaper or magazine articles profiling Sun City or describing retirement in America.

To celebrate the community's 50th anniversary in 2010, the SCAHS published *Reshaping Retirement in America: Sun City 1960–2010* and even more photographs were uncovered and published for the first time in decades. That same year, the SCAHS Board of Trustees began an intensive effort to scan and digitally convert all the photographs in its archives. The project was a massive undertaking and one that would take dozens of volunteers and months of hard work.

The results of that effort are included in this compilation of photographs. Many of the photographs—from the early days of Sun City through its boom years—are published here for the first time since the 1960s, some for the first time ever.

The photographs included here are not meant to necessarily chronicle the history of Sun City. Readers looking for more detail are encouraged to refer to sources listed in the bibliography on page 127. A visit to the museum provides an even better glimpse into Sun City's past and a first-hand look at historical artifacts and mementos. Notwithstanding, the photographs do accurately set forth in vivid detail why Sun City was so successful when it first opened and why it remains popular and relevant to today's retirees.

The people in the photographs are happy to be here. More than just an adopted hometown, these residents appear as if they truly belong here. The plethora of activities found in Sun City, along with an abundance of available friends, combine to create a lifestyle that is secure, comfortable, and worth protecting.

Fifty years after it opened, Sun City remains a popular choice for new retirees. Sun City's attraction extends beyond recreational amenities and golf courses. The people, the lifestyle—and even the community's history—all contribute to Sun City's continued appeal.

# *One*

# Marinette, Arizona

Long before retirees settled in Sun City to enjoy their golden years, prospectors in search of buried treasures visited the area where Sun City now exists.

The Sun City known today is located 14 miles northwest of Phoenix (between Phoenix and Wickenburg), along U.S. 60, the highway known locally as Grand Avenue.

Grand Avenue was once called "Vulture Road" and served as a 54-mile-long wagon route for early pioneers who traveled from Wickenburg to abundant water canals in the far southeastern portion of the Phoenix valley.

By 1866 (a year before Phoenix was founded), Wickenburg had become one of the largest cities in Arizona. Other cities, farms, and ranches began to take hold along Vulture Road.

Water became the new gold, and canals were dug to bring water to the northwest valley. Water companies advertised the cheap, fertile land to people in the East and Midwest. Two businessmen from Marinette, Wisconsin, were among the first buyers, and when a railroad crossed their holding, they negotiated a water stop, naming it Marinette.

Others followed, but few worked the land. R. P. Davie, a land speculator, bought up their holdings and accumulated several thousand acres in what was called the Marinette Ranch when he sold the land to Goodyear for growing cotton in 1920.

It became a plantation, and soon Marinette had a school, two stores, and a cotton gin. The ranch was sold in the 1940s to the J. G. Boswell Company, large cotton growers from California. The farming industry thrived for a few more years, but as water became scare it became less and less profitable to farm the land. The company employed fewer and fewer people, and by the mid-1950s, Marinette was once again little more than a railroad stop.

By the late 1950s, the Boswells were concerned with the diminishing water table and what it would mean to a water-intensive crop like cotton. Fortunately, the Del E. Webb Corporation was looking for a site to build its new retirement community, and the land soon sprouted houses instead of cotton.

Little remained of Marinette by the time work began on the new community in 1959, and within a few years, all signs of the town had completely vanished.

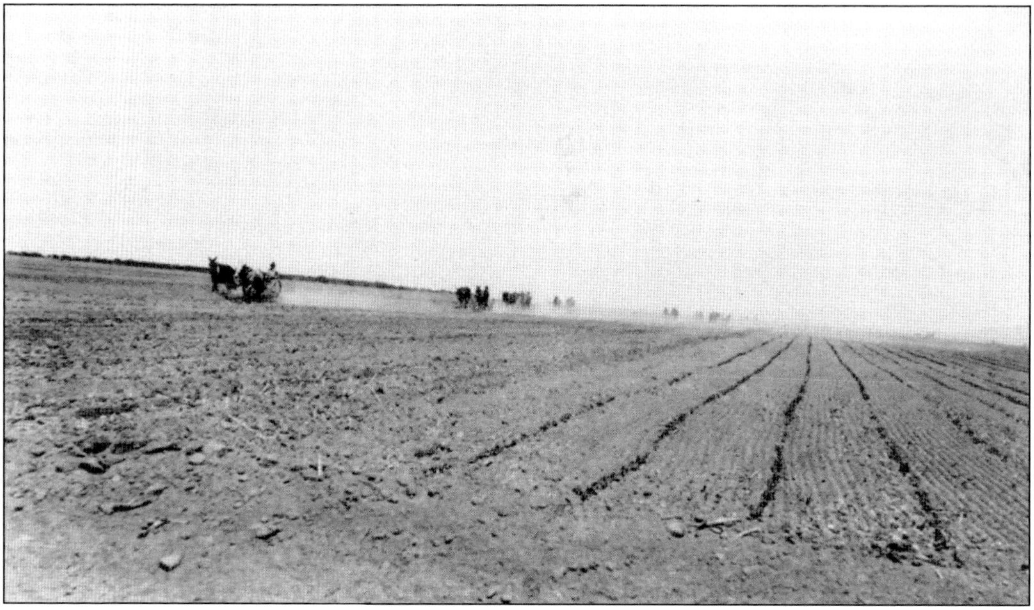

The first mention of Marinette appears in an 1894 Santa Fe, Prescott, and Phoenix Railroad building record, which lists Marinette as a train stop with a pump house and water tank. Developer R. P. Davie bought up tracts of land in 1912 to plat the "Orchard Town of Marinette." Davie sold his holdings in 1920 to the Southwest Cotton Company. This photograph shows the cultivation of the cotton field, sometime around the 1920s.

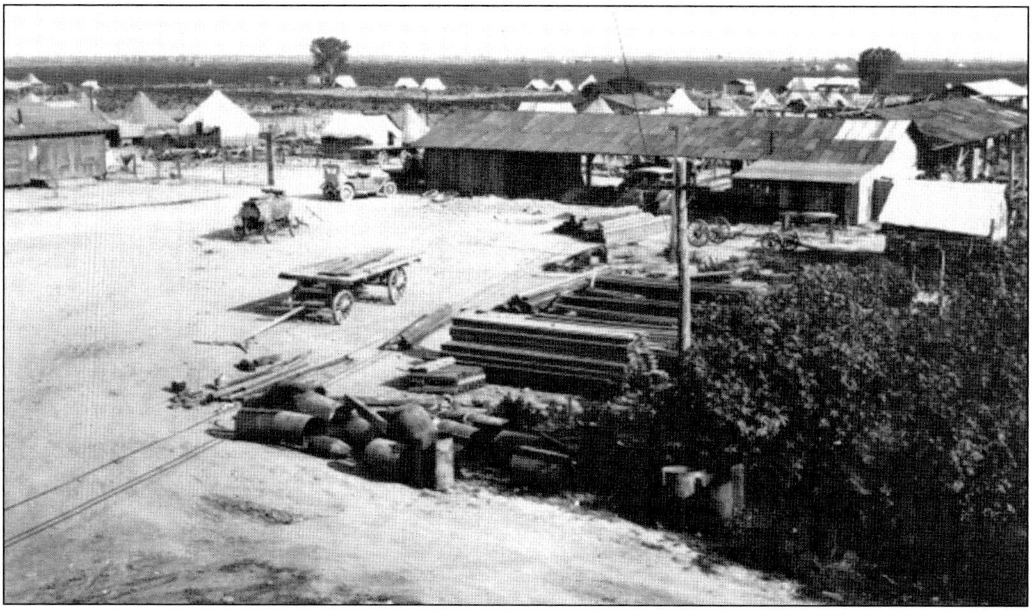

The Southwest Cotton Company, a subsidiary of Goodyear Tire and Rubber Company, purchased R. P. Davie's Marinette Ranch land holdings for $1 million in 1920 and began farming cotton. The affairs of Marinette were administered from the company's headquarters in nearby Litchfield Park. This *c.* 1920 photograph depicts the Las Botas Camp and Compound storage area. Residents, most of whom were immigrants, lived in makeshift tents.

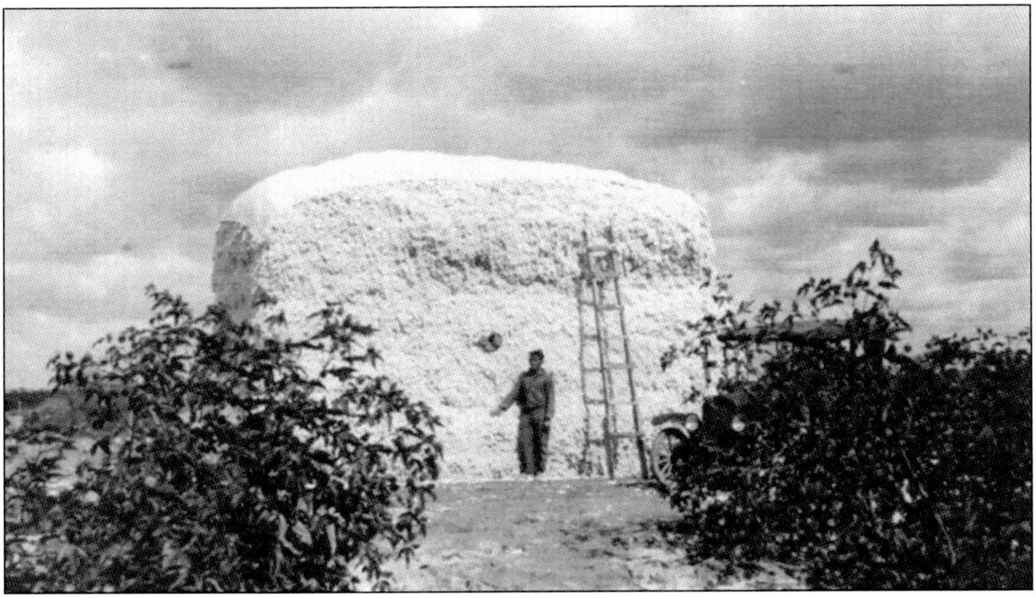

Cotton quickly became a popular crop for owners of Marinette land holdings. Different crops were tried, most notably sugar beets and yuli (a type of sagebrush that produced a substance thought to create synthetic rubber but to no avail). Cotton remained the town's primary industry until the fields were later replaced by homes and golf courses.

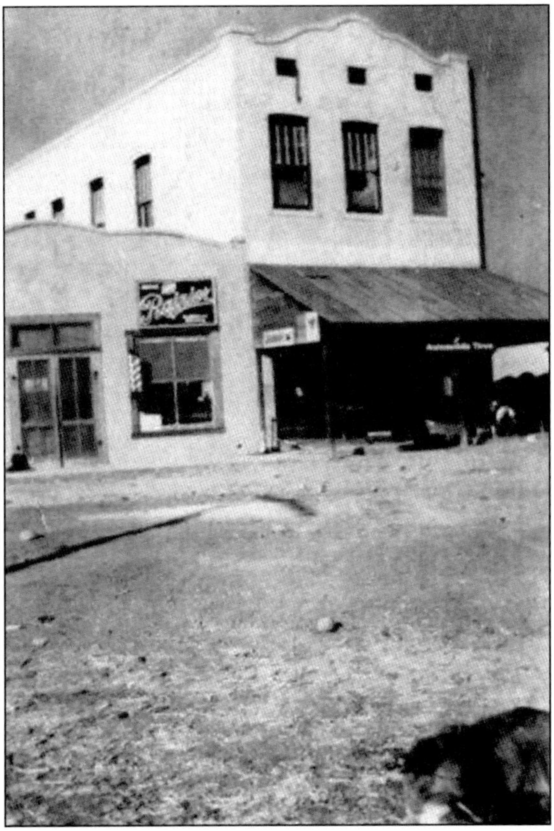

Marinette's general store once stood near the intersection of what today is 105th Avenue and Thunderbird Boulevard. It had a large room upstairs that was a center for dances and other community events. A saloon and brothel were rumored to have existed near today's 112th and Grand Avenues, with a train making periodic stops for "shopping."

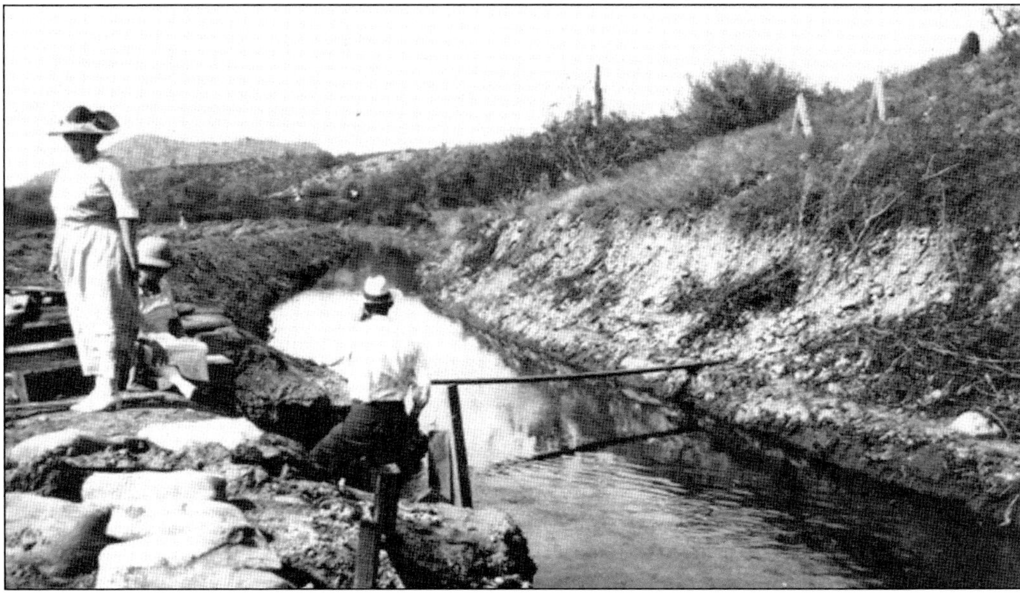

Cotton farmers needed water to irrigate their land, and canals were dug to bring the water from locally drilled wells to the cotton fields of Marinette Ranch. The Marinette Canal, shown here, brought water to the community from wells owned by a water company 5 miles north of present-day Sun City's northern boundary.

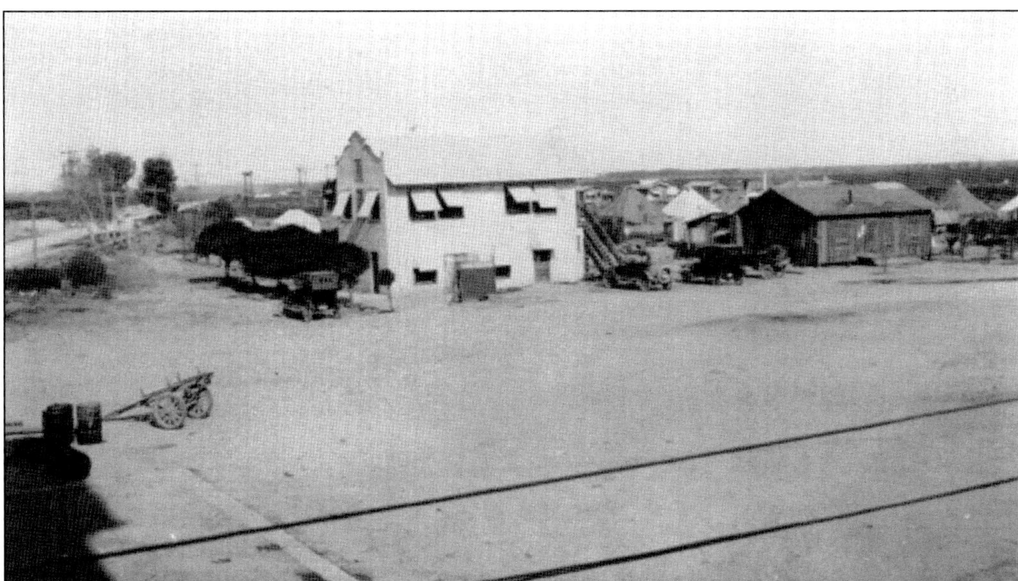

The Southwest Cotton Company's administration building, in the 1920s, was located near present-day 104th and Grand Avenues. Goodyear decided to focus on its core business of tire manufacturing and sold its Marinette cotton holdings to the J. G. Boswell Company in 1943. The Boswells were no strangers to the area. Goodyear had turned over its ginning operations to the Boswells in the late 1920s, and the Boswells began leasing some of the land themselves in the mid-1930s.

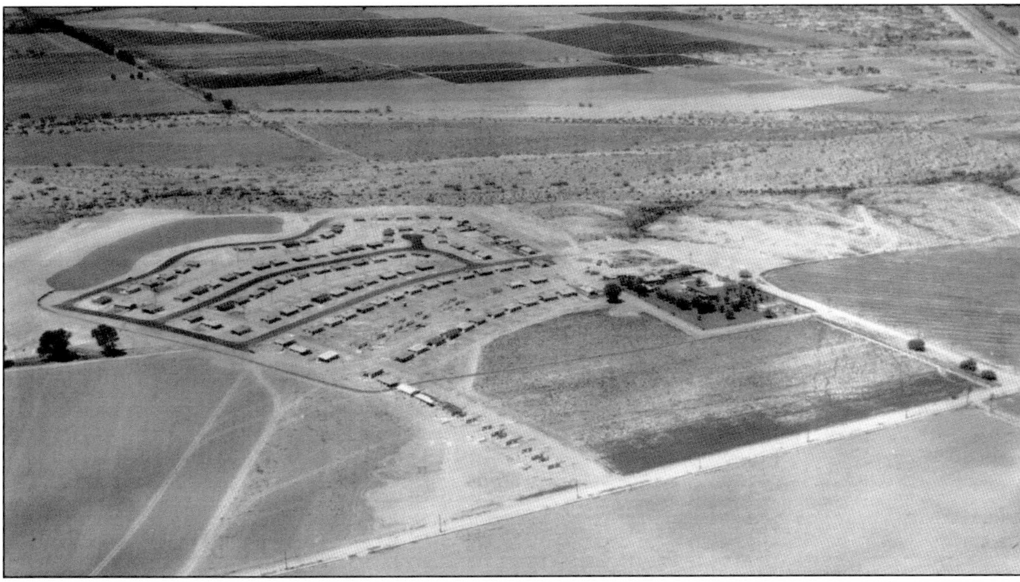

Sun City was the world's first active-adult master-planned retirement community, but it was not the FIRST retirement community. That title goes to Youngtown, Sun City's tiny neighbor to the west. Founded in 1955 by Ben Schleifer and Frances Greer, along with developer Elmer Johns, Youngtown required home buyers be at least 60 years of age. The town caught the attention of Webb officials and served as the inspiration for Sun City. (Independent Newspapers, Inc.)

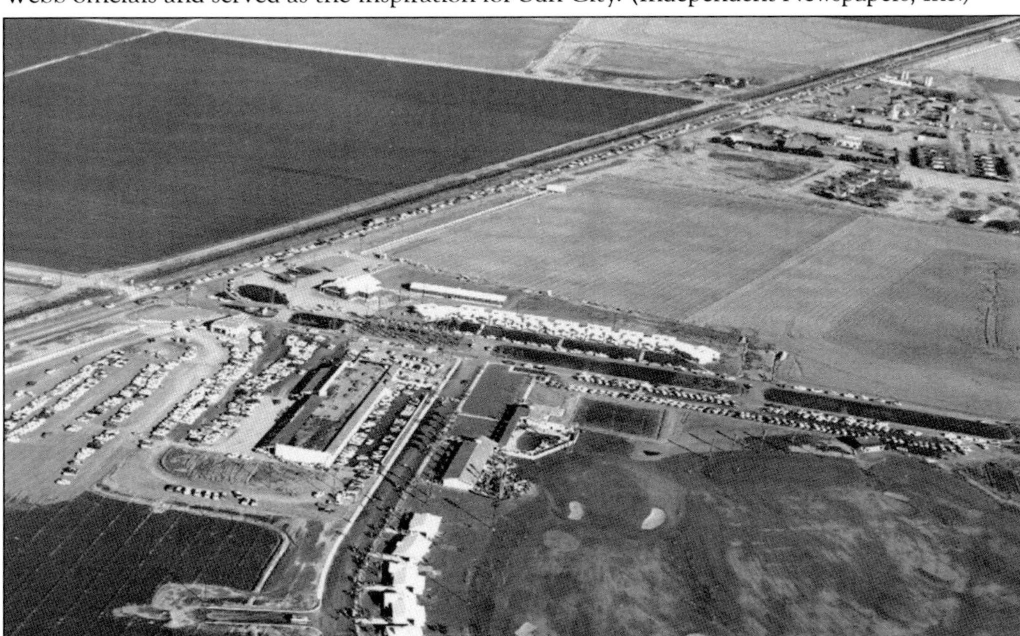

Sun City opened January 1, 1960, and cars stretched several miles east along Grand Avenue as curious retirees rushed to inspect the new community. What is left of Marinette can be seen in the upper right. The last remnants of the town were located near what is now Grand and 103rd Avenues. There is an official marker located at 105th and Grand Avenues signifying the town's original location.

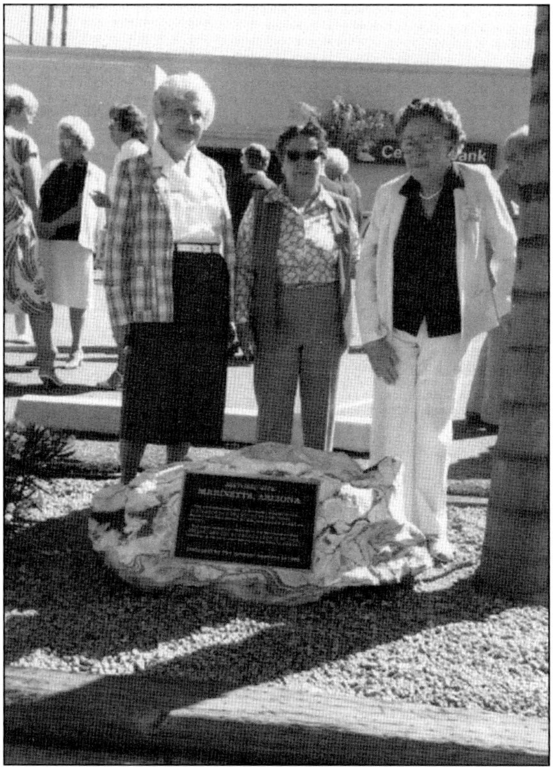

The Marinette chapter of the Arizona Questers, a historical society, dedicated a plaque in 1985 to mark the original location of the town. On hand for the ceremony are, from left to right, Lorraine Baugh, Peggy Squira, and an unidentified member. The marker is next to a church parking lot located on 105th Avenue, just south of Grand Avenue. (Independent Newspapers, Inc.)

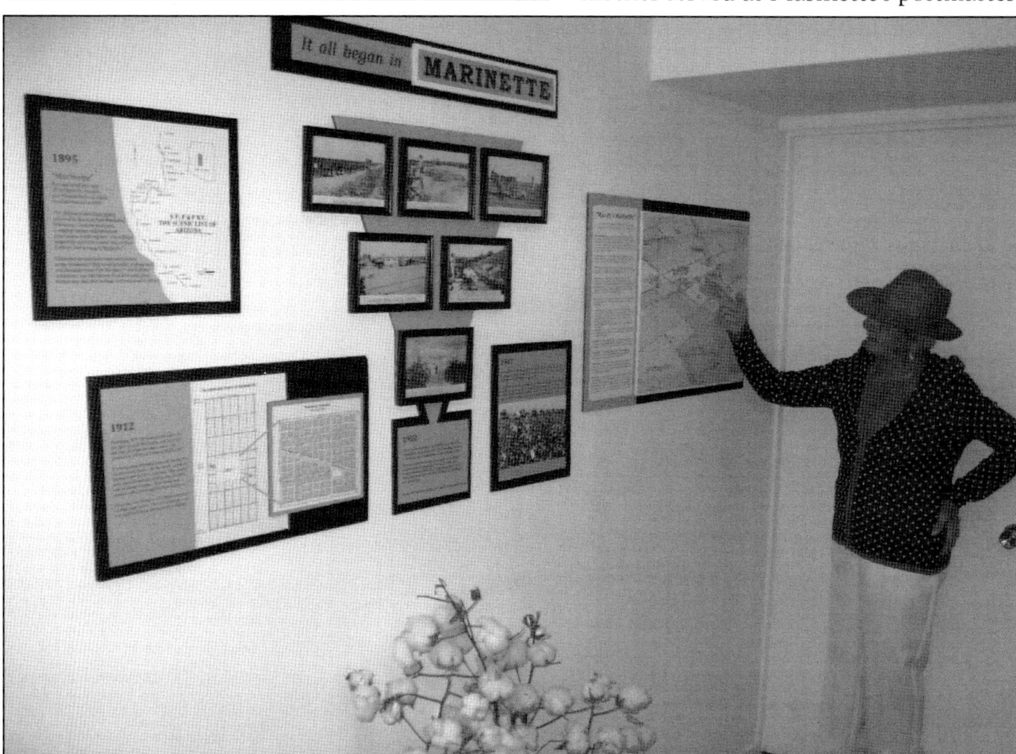


Marinette no longer exists, but its history and memories are preserved at the Del Webb Sun Cities Museum. A first-person account of the town's history was provided to the museum by Amanda Monreal Durant, who grew up in Marinette but now lives in Sun City. Her parents ran a store in Marinette, and her mother served as Marinette's postmaster.

# *Two*

# Del E. Webb

Del Webb's name is synonymous with Sun City and, indeed, with the entire concept of active-adult retirement living. His company's development of Sun City spawned an entire industry that is as robust today as it was back in 1960.

But Webb was more than just the creator of Sun City. His reputation as the nation's premier builder had already been well established by the time the cotton fields of Marinette were cleared to make way for Sun City.

Delbert Eugene Webb was born May 17, 1899, in Fresno, California. His first dream was to become a professional baseball player. A bout with typhoid fever forced him to abandon that dream and prompted a move to Phoenix in 1927 where he opened his construction company.

The Del E. Webb Corporation grew to become one of the world's largest builders of military bases, sports arenas, high-rise buildings, hotels, casinos, and more. Webb's work and influence can be seen and felt in numerous industries, genres, and locales.

As his reputation grew, so did his wealth and fame. He counted presidents, celebrities, and athletes among his closest friends.

Returning to his first love, baseball, Webb co-owned the New York Yankees from 1945 to 1965, a 20-year span during which the team won the World Series 10 times.

The company's foray into building a self-contained community for retirees in 1959 was considered a risky experiment. It would be an ambitious effort, but Webb officials were not the only ones recognizing that senior citizens were the fastest growing portion of the American population.

The venture succeeded far beyond anyone's wildest expectations. Webb died of cancer on July 4, 1974. Shortly before his death, he appeared on a television show hosted by Merv Griffith. Despite all that he had achieved, he proclaimed creating Sun City "the most satisfying thing I've ever accomplished in my life."

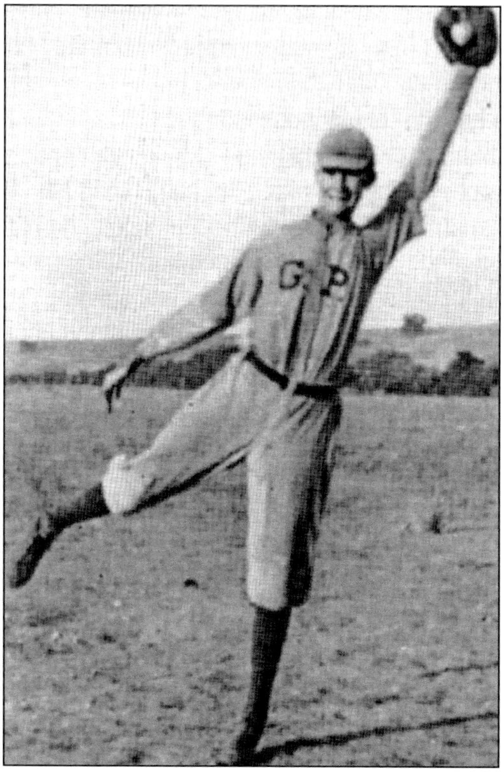

Born in Fresno, California, Delbert Eugene Webb had early aspirations of becoming a professional baseball player. An illness forced him to abandon the dream, although he would remain a sports enthusiast his entire life.

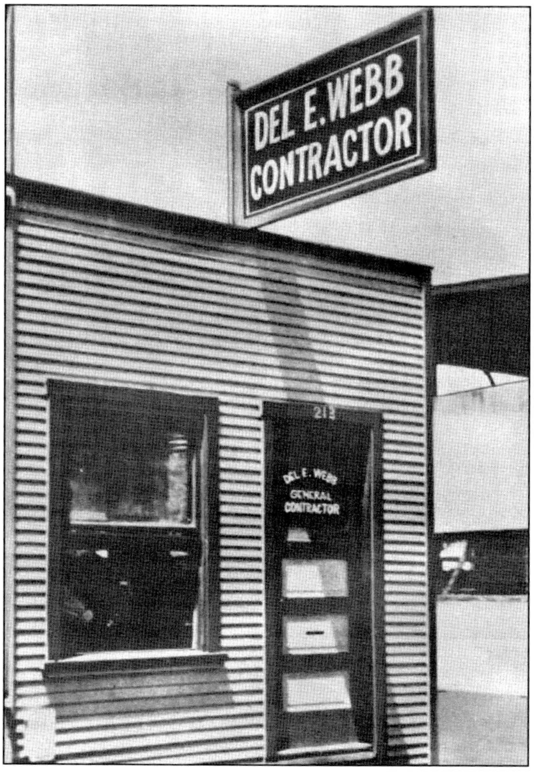


A bout with typhoid fever prompted Webb and his wife, Hazel, to move to Phoenix in 1927. He created his own construction company in 1928. Over the next five decades, his company enjoyed phenomenal growth and its list of projects included military bases, Las Vegas hotels and casinos, high-rise buildings, hospitals, and eventually Sun City.

Webb remained an avid baseball fan his entire life. He and his partners purchased the New York Yankees in 1945 for $2.8 million. The deal included ownership of Yankee Stadium and all the Yankees' farm clubs. During the 20 years he co-owned the team, the Yankees won 10 World Series titles. Shown here, Webb offers hitting tips to Hall of Famer Joe DiMaggio.

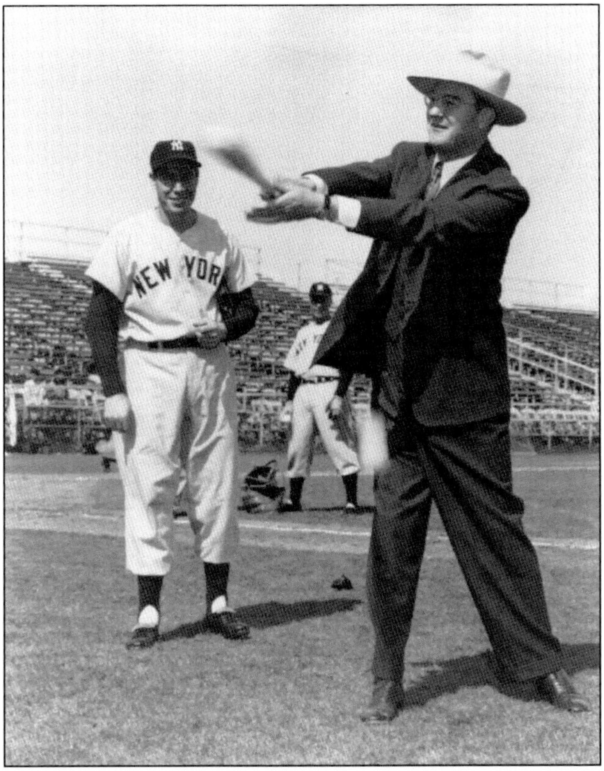


The Del E. Webb Corporation often used sports as a means to promote its newest projects. In the early 1960s, the company sponsored race cars in both the Indianapolis 500 and NASCAR's Daytona 500. Del Webb, right, is shown here with Robert Wilke, owner of the "Sun City Special," a race car driven to third place by Roger Ward in the 1961 Indianapolis 500.

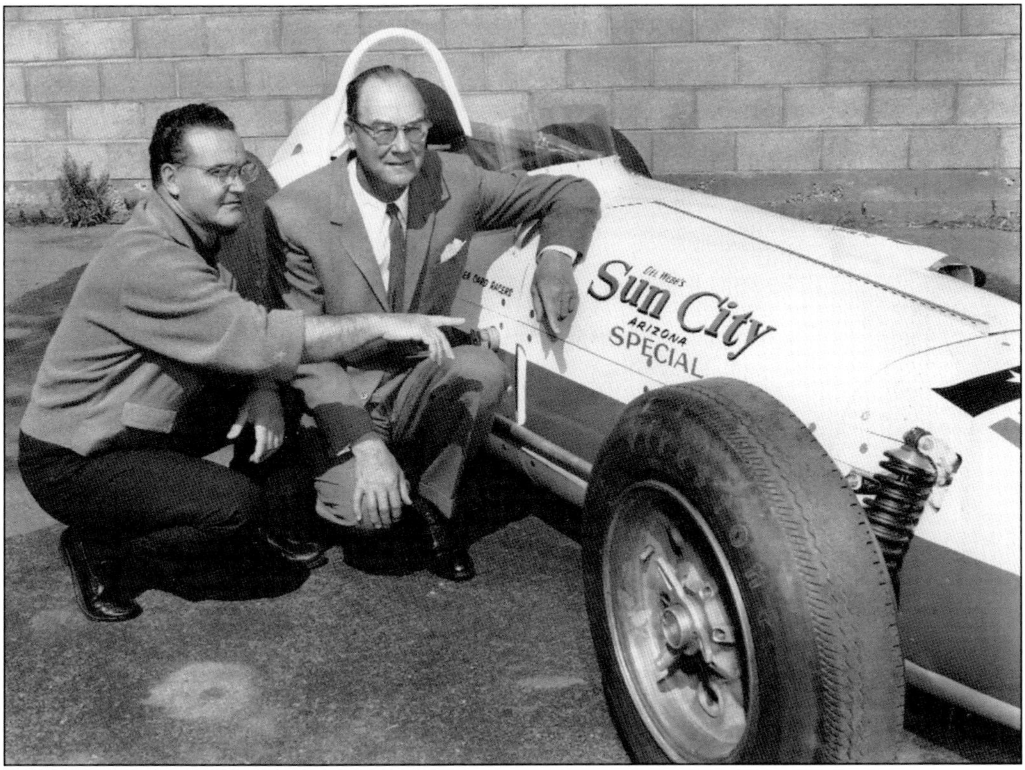

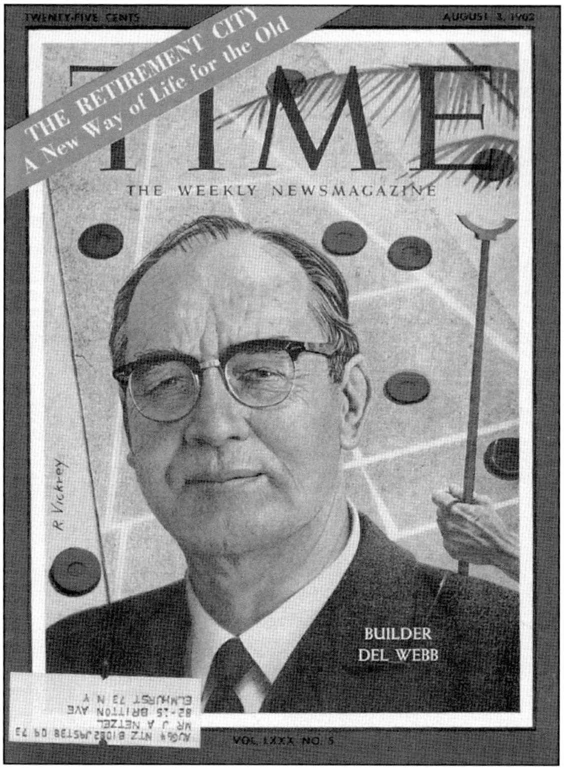


Despite all that he had accomplished prior to launching Sun City, it was development of the community—and the industry it spawned—that landed Del E. Webb on the cover of *Time* magazine. "The Retirement City: A New Way of Life for the Old" was the cover story for the August 3, 1962, issue. By the mid-1960s, the Del E. Webb Corporation had three other "Sun City" communities in Florida and California.

As his fame and fortune grew, Del Webb's circle of friends expanded to include politicians, celebrities, athletes; he claimed to be on a first-name basis with every president since Franklin Roosevelt. He loved golf, and it was not unusual for him to treat friends to a round on the greens in Sun City. Here he and comedian Bob Hope share a laugh in the mid-1960s.

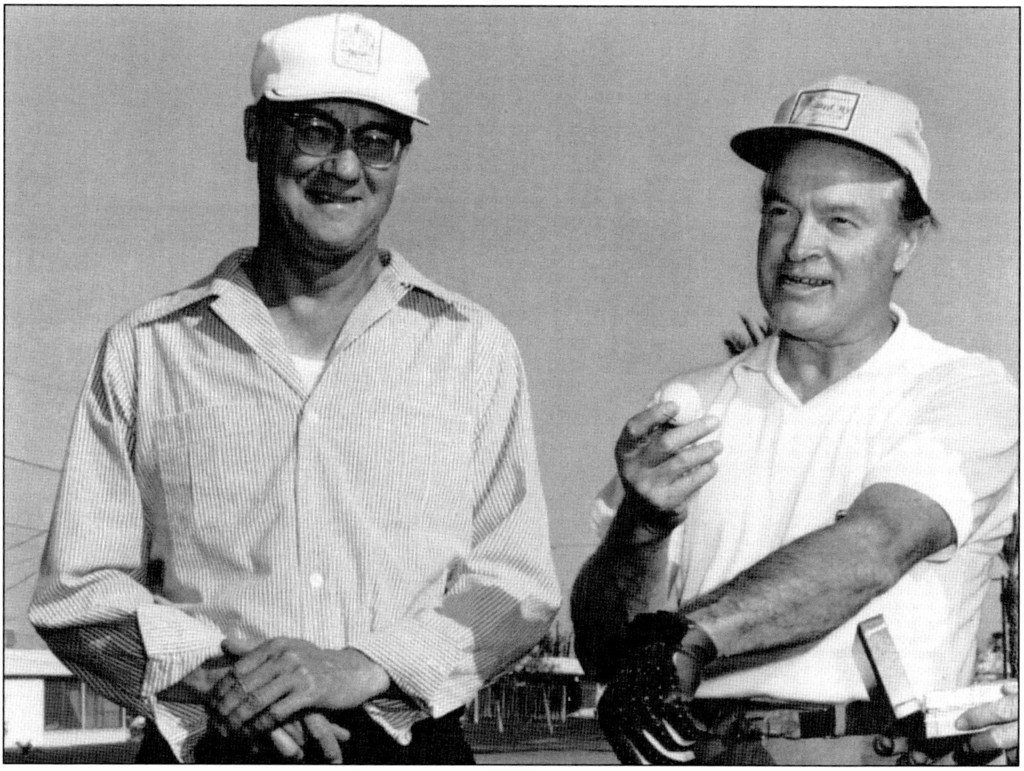

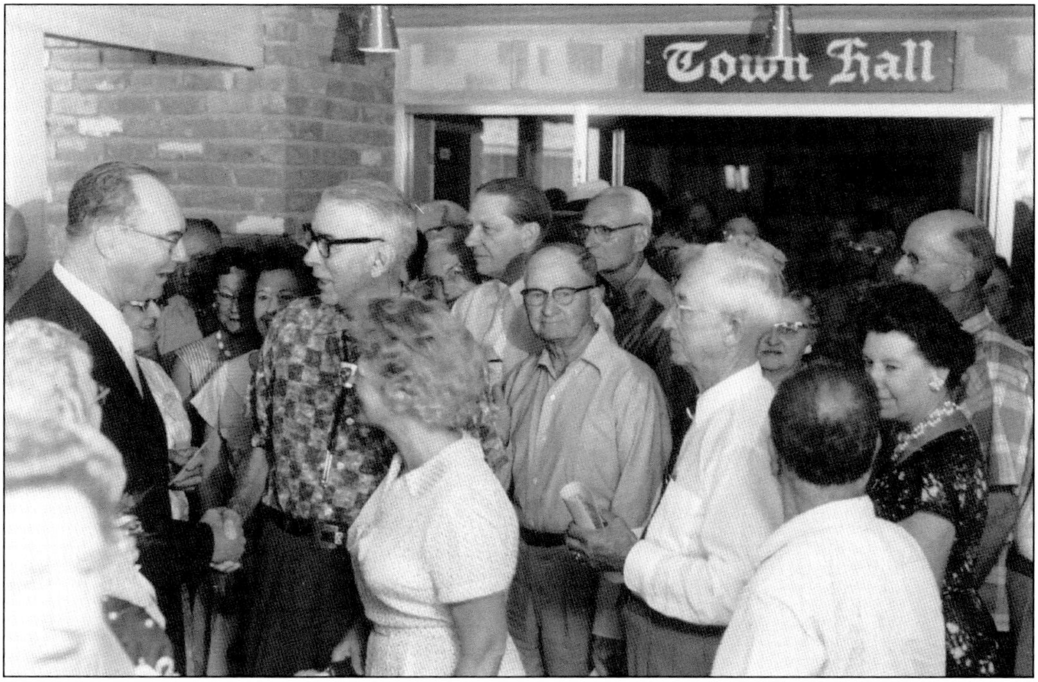


Del Webb was always given a hero's welcome when he visited the community. He spoke to the Sun City Women's Club in 1961 and told the crowd, "I wish I could live here with you fine folks and do nothing but play golf." Club members serenaded Webb with "Let the Rest of the World Go By," which was the community's theme song. He remains to this day a legendary icon in Sun City whose lasting impact can still be seen and felt.

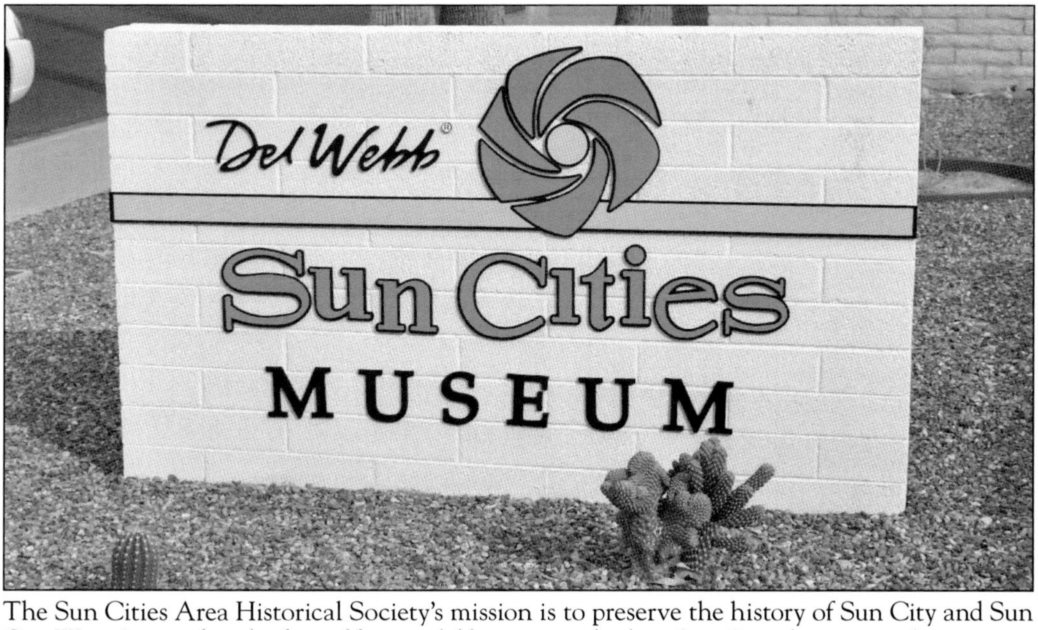


The Sun Cities Area Historical Society's mission is to preserve the history of Sun City and Sun City West. Located in the first of five model homes ever built in Sun City, the society also operates a museum that tells the story of Sun City and Sun City West. To honor the community's founder, in 2009 the museum was renamed the Del Webb Sun Cities Museum. (Bret McKeand.)

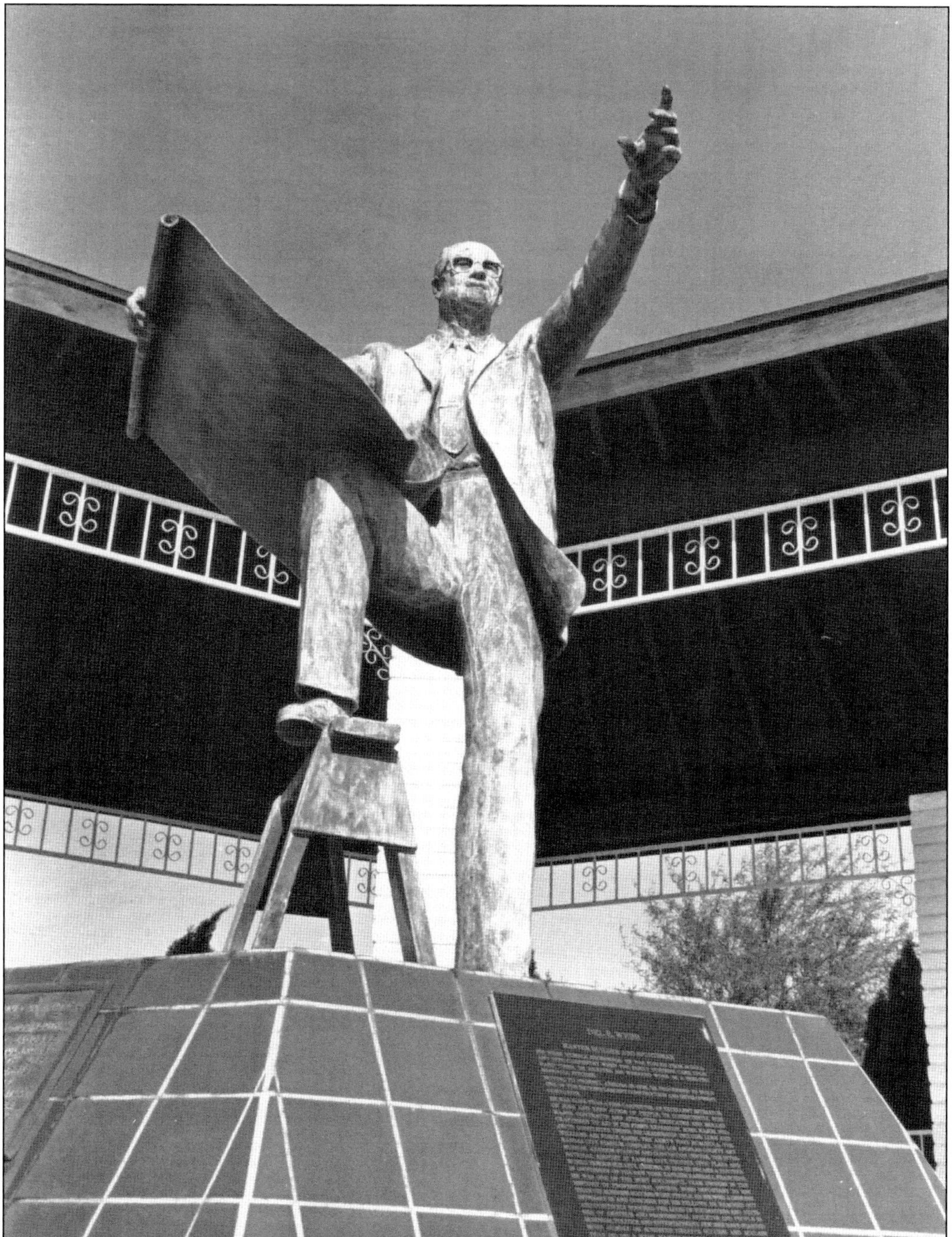

A statue honoring Del E. Webb was dedicated in 1981 in Memorial Garden at Bell Recreation Center. Memorial Garden is also home to a replica of the Philadelphia Liberty Bell and is the site each year of Sun City's Ring the Bell ceremony held on Independence Day. The ceremony celebrates the nation's birthday, but it also honors the memory of Webb, who passed away July 4, 1974. (Bret McKeand.)

# *Three*

# Work Begins on Sun City

In 1955, David Garroway reported on a new community, solely for adults, that was taking shape in the desert northwest of Phoenix. Named Youngtown, it offered retirees modest homes but no amenities or recreational perks.

The Webb people watched this development in their backyard, and initially the concept of a self-contained community specifically for retirees had little appeal inside or outside the Del E. Webb Corporation.

Some company executives questioned the feasibility of focusing on such a narrow segment of the housing market. Experts in aging proclaimed senior citizens simply would not leave their families, and if an adult community was built, "more would die than would move in."

Tom Breen, director of housing for the Webb corporation, felt the idea of a senior retirement community had merit and arranged to interview retirees who had moved to Florida. They loved the climate but were universally disappointed with developers who promised golf courses, clubhouses, pools, and other amenities that never materialized.

With that insight, the Webb people realized the opportunity an adult community could offer if done correctly. As they were laying plans, Jim Boswell offered to sell two 10,000-acre tracts of land in the northwest valley. The water table was dropping, and it would not be long before Boswell's company would no longer be able to farm cotton on the land. A deal was struck that enabled Webb to pay for the land as it was developed, and Boswell could continue farming, knowing he had a buyer locked in.

One tract, known as the Marinette Ranch, became today's Sun City. The other, the Santa Fe Ranch, became a portion of Sun City West, built nearly 20 years later.

Work began on the unnamed community in mid-1959 with cotton fields giving way to a golf course, a recreation center with a beautiful pool, five model houses, a shopping center, and a Hiway House Motor Hotel for visitors.

The goal was to have everything ready for a grand opening in just six months, on January 1, 1960.

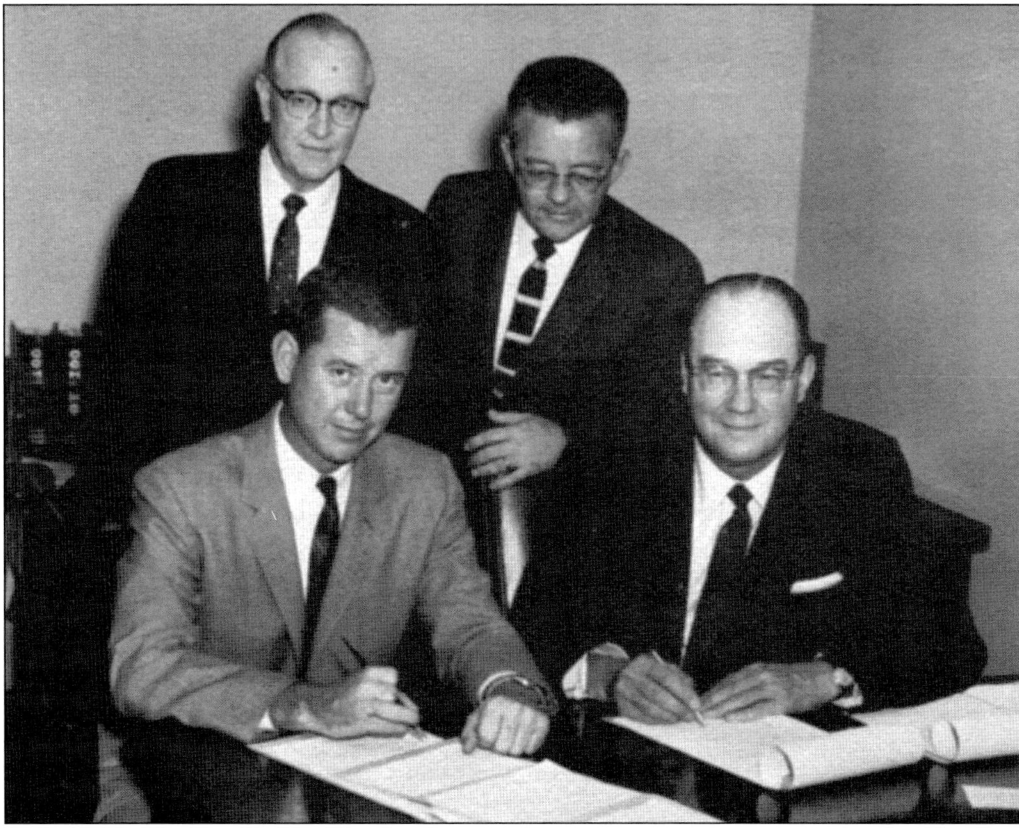

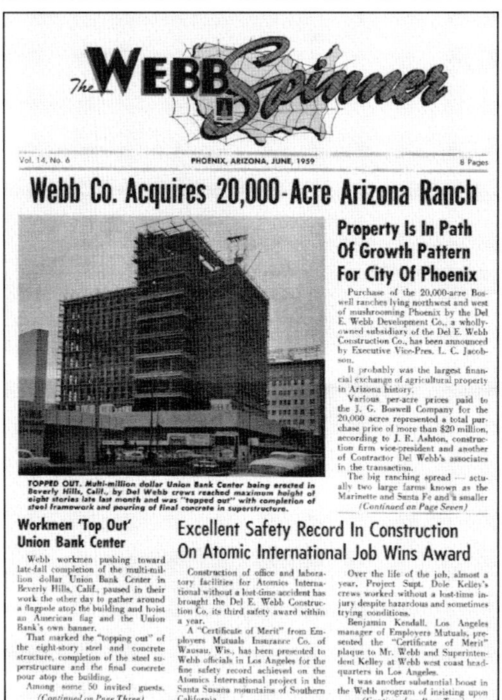

The WEBB Spinner

Vol. 14, No. 6 — PHOENIX, ARIZONA, JUNE, 1959 — 8 Pages

## Webb Co. Acquires 20,000-Acre Arizona Ranch

### Property Is In Path Of Growth Pattern For City Of Phoenix

Purchase of the 20,000-acre Boswell ranches lying northwest and west of mushrooming Phoenix by the Del E. Webb Development Co., a wholly-owned subsidiary of the Del E. Webb Construction Co., has been announced by Executive Vice-Pres. L. C. Jacobson.

It probably was the largest financial exchange of agricultural property in Arizona history.

Various per-acre prices paid to the J. G. Boswell Company for the 20,000 acres represented a total purchase price of more than $20 million, according to J. R. Ashton, construction firm vice-president and another of Contractor Del Webb's associates in the transaction.

The big ranching spread — actually two large farms known as the Marinette and Santa Fe and a smaller

(Continued on Page Seven)

**TOPPED OUT.** *Multi-million dollar Union Bank Center being erected in Beverly Hills, Calif., by Del Webb crews reached maximum height of eight stories late last month and was "topped out" with completion of steel framework and pouring of final concrete in superstructure.*

### Workmen 'Top Out' Union Bank Center

Webb workmen pushing toward late-fall completion of the multi-million dollar Union Bank Center in Beverly Hills, Calif., paused in their work the other day to gather around a flagpole atop the building and hoist an American flag and the Union Bank's own banner.

That marked the "topping out" of the eight-story steel and concrete structure, completion of the steel superstructure and the final concrete pour atop the building.

Among some 50 invited guests.

(Continued on Page Three)

### Excellent Safety Record In Construction On Atomic International Job Wins Award

Construction of office and laboratory facilities for Atomics International without a lost-time accident has brought the Del E. Webb Construction Co. its third safety award within a year.

A "Certificate of Merit" from Employers Mutuals Insurance Co. of Wausau, Wis., has been presented to Webb officials in Los Angeles for the fine safety record achieved on the Atomics International project in the Santa Susana mountains of Southern California.

Over the life of the job, almost a year, Project Supt. Dole Kelley's crews worked without a lost-time injury despite hazardous and sometimes trying conditions.

Benjamin Kendall, Los Angeles manager of Employers Mutuals, presented the "Certificate of Merit" plaque to Mr. Webb and Superintendent Kelley at Webb west coast headquarters in Los Angeles.

It was another substantial boost in the Webb program of insisting upon

(Continued on Page Two)

The J. G. Boswell Company reached a deal in 1959 to sell its Marinette land holdings to the Del E. Webb Corporation. The transaction paved the way for the Webb company to begin work on its new retirement community. From left to right are (seated) J. G. Boswell II, president of the J. G. Boswell Company, and Webb; (standing) Reg Robinson, J. G. Boswell Company's secretary, and J. R. Ashton, Webb corporation's vice president.

The *Webb Spinner*, the Del E. Webb Construction Company's in-house newsletter, announced in June 1959 that the Del E. Webb Development Company (DEVCO), a unique venture owned 51 percent by Del Webb and 49 percent by Boswell, had purchased 20,000 acres of land northwest of Phoenix. The land was purchased from the J. G. Boswell Company for more than $20 million. The newsletter said the land purchase was "probably the largest financial exchange of agriculture property in Arizona history."

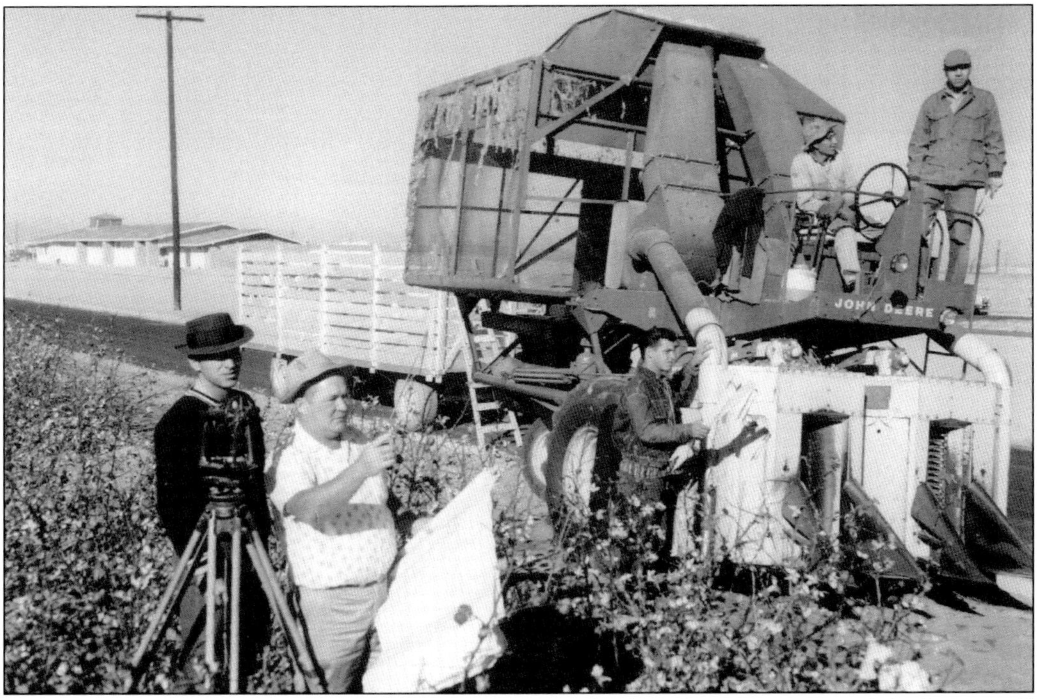


Del Webb architects and surveyors began making plans for their new community while the Boswell family continued to grow cotton nearby. The Webb company began construction of Sun City in 1959, and before the end of the year, the town of Marinette would all but cease to exist. During the initial planning stages, Webb officials were considering calling the project the "Marinette Retirement Community."

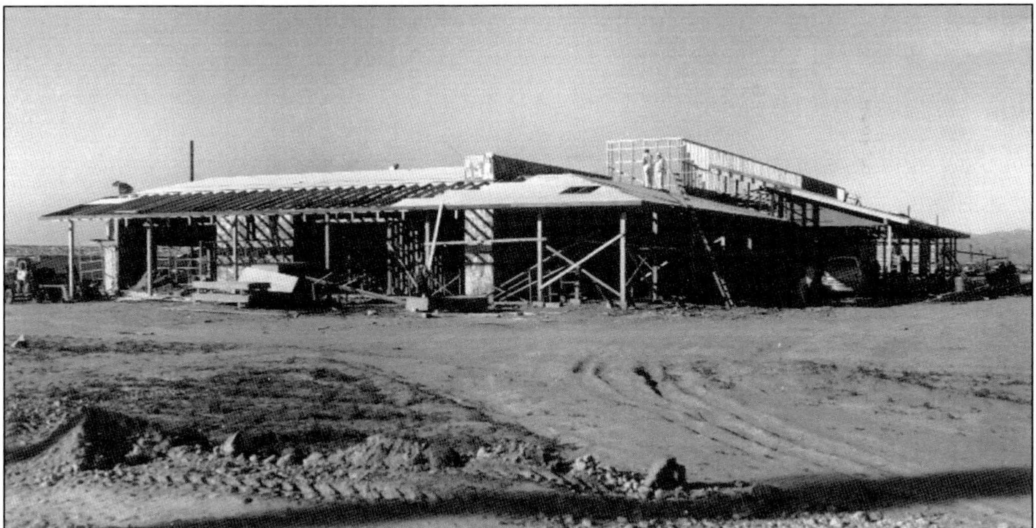

A number of master-planned communities elsewhere failed because developers never delivered on their promises. In a process unique for its time, Webb opted to build amenities first. The process not only created buyer confidence in the developer, but it was also great marketing since amenities were what really convinced people to buy into Sun City. Sun City Shopping Center (today Grand Center), located at 107th and Grand Avenues, was Sun City's first shopping center.

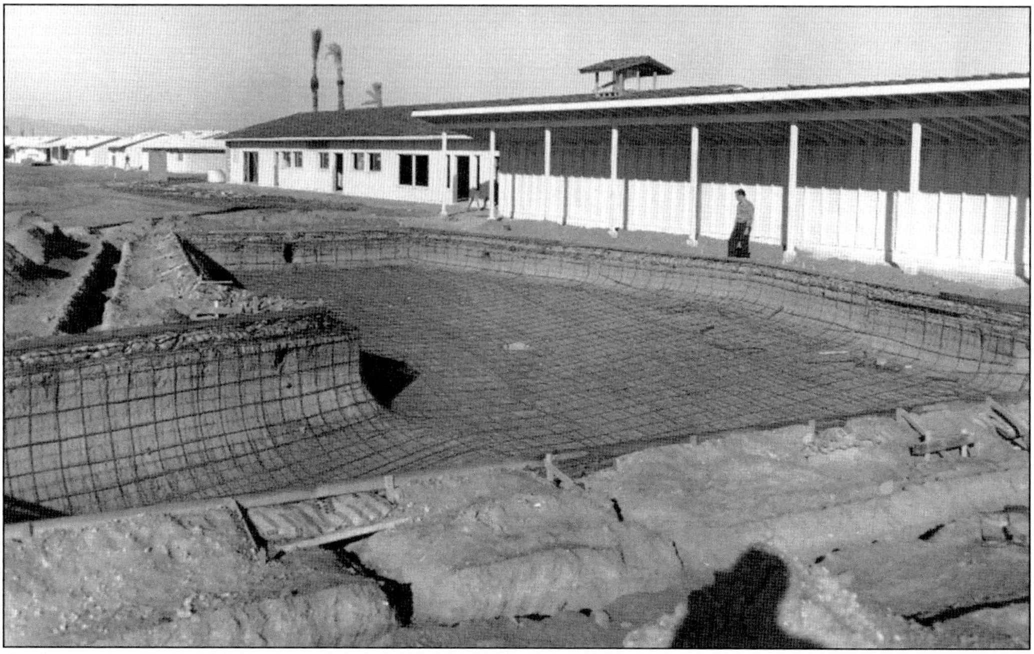

A championship golf course, recreation center, shopping center, hotel, and five model homes were the first to be built in Sun City in 1959. Construction of the swimming pool at what was then referred to as the Marinette Recreation Center (soon to be renamed Community Center) took place in November. The center is located at 107th and Oakmont Avenues. The first five model homes can be seen further down the road.

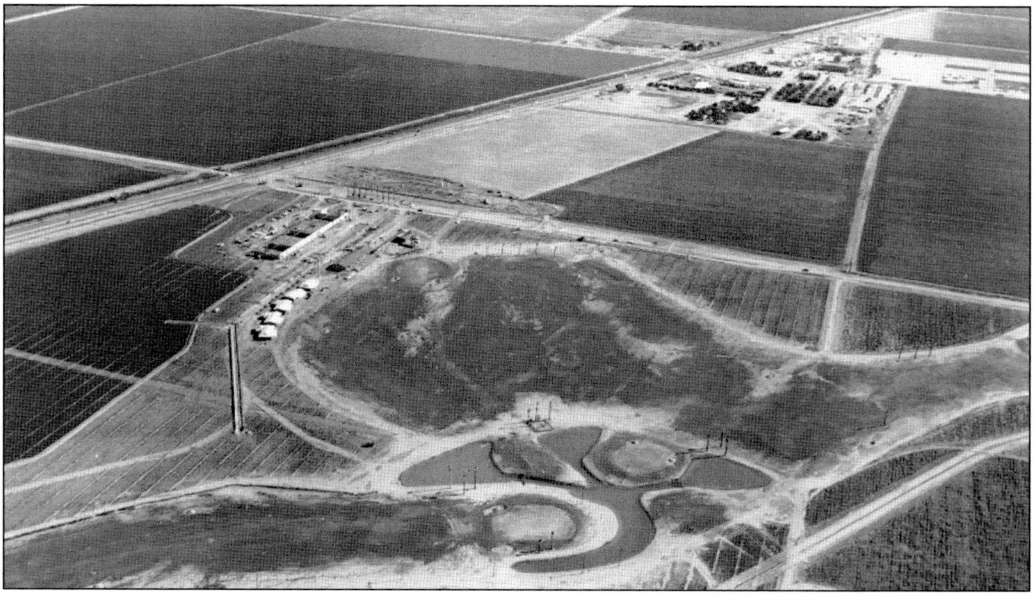

This photograph, taken in November 1959, gives an aerial view of construction progress and the community's first golf course. Left of the golf course is Oakmont Drive, where the community's first recreation center and first five model homes are located. What is left of the town of Marinette can be seen in the upper part of the photograph. At the time of this photograph, less than two months prior to opening, the community still did not have a name.

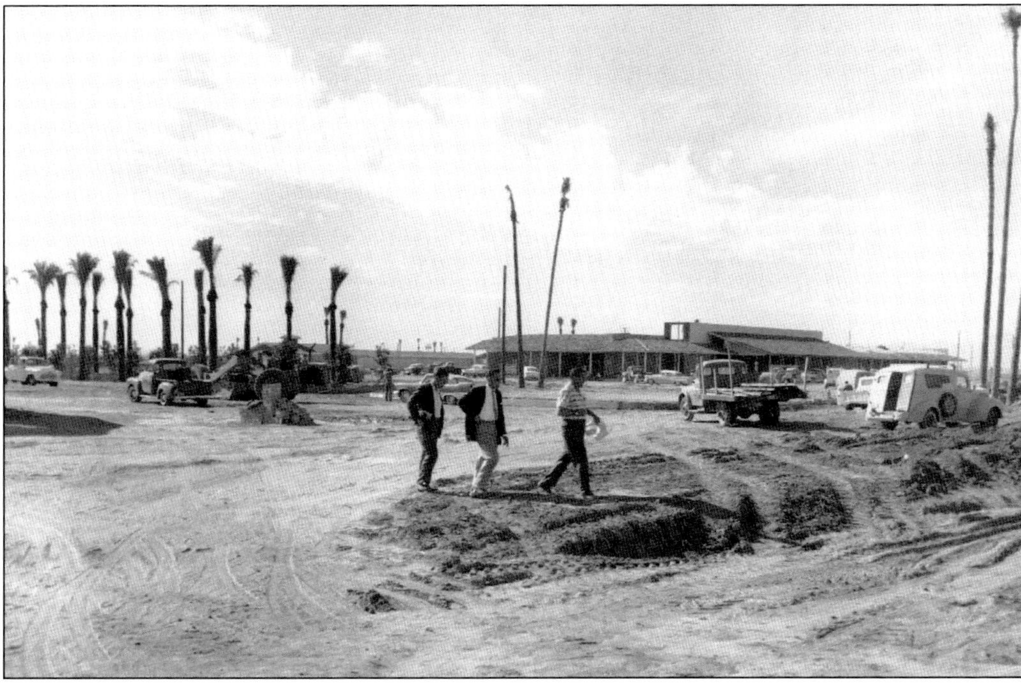

Workers inspect what will be the entrance to Sun City at 107th and Grand Avenues. In the background is the Sun City Shopping Center (today Grand Center). Company officials convinced the Safeway grocery chain to anchor the shopping center and serve as the community's first grocery store.

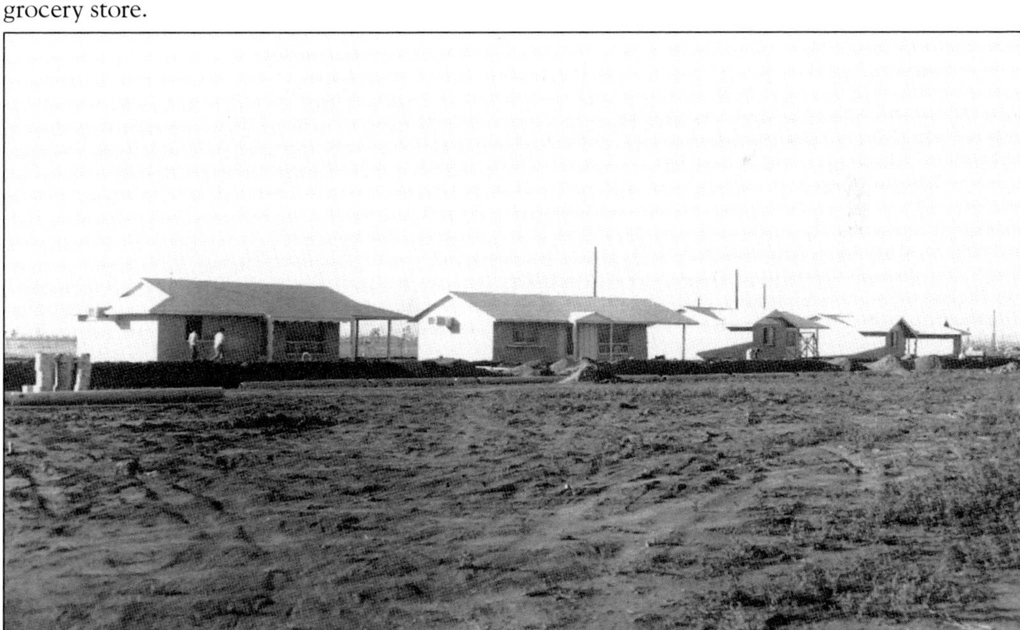

Work began on the first homes on the unpaved Oakmont Drive. The company would have five model homes ready for prospective buyers to preview when the community opened on January 1, 1960. The very first home, shown on the left in this photograph, serves today as the headquarters of the Sun Cities Area Historical Society and home to the Del Webb Sun Cities Museum.

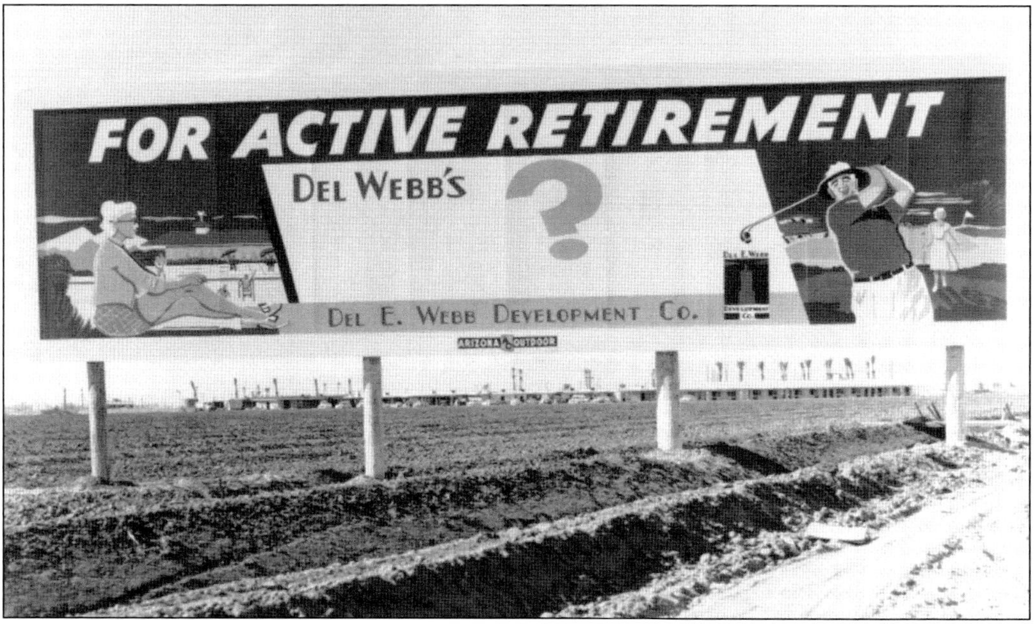


DEVCO began marketing the new community long before a final name was chosen. In fact, the community did not earn its famous name until December, one month prior to opening. A nationwide "Name This Active Retirement Community" contest was conducted, and legend has it that Del Webb himself chose "Sun City" as the winning entry. This billboard promoting the yet-to-be-named community was located on Grand Avenue heading toward Sun City.

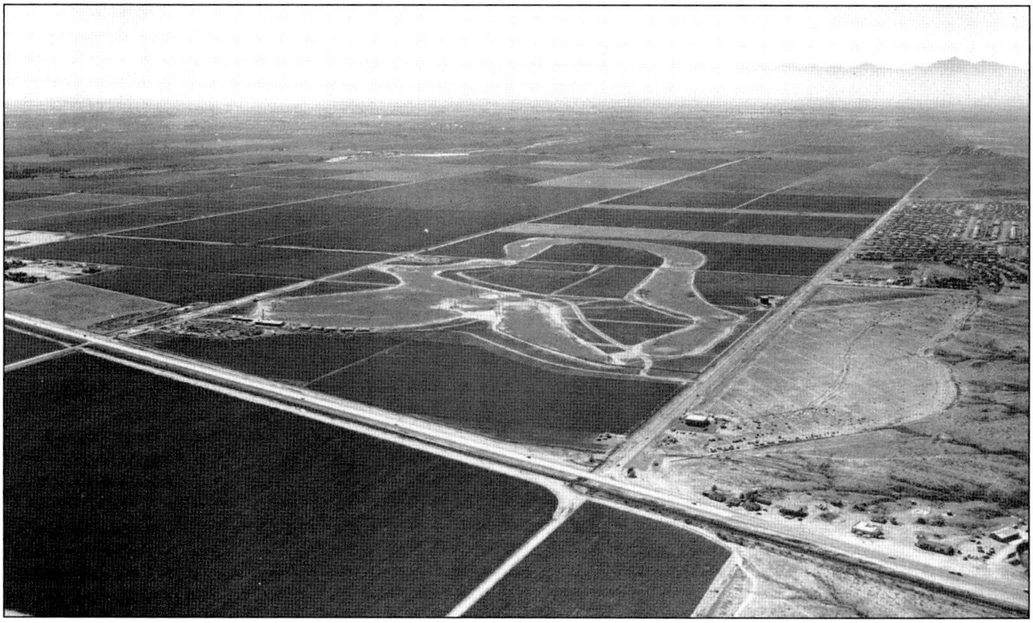

Here is an aerial shot of Sun City just two months before it opened in 1960. Grand Avenue can be seen running right to left, with Sun City's shopping center, recreation center, and model homes located off 107th Avenue (near the left in the photograph). The north-south road to the right is 111th Avenue, which would serve as the western boundary to Sun City. Youngtown can be seen in the upper right.

# *Four*

# Opening Year

On January 1, 1960, the public got its first glimpse of Sun City, the nation's first active-adult resort retirement community.

Despite a nationwide advertising blitz prior to opening, company officials still had their doubts about the eventual success of their newest project. Would anyone show up on opening day?

Their fears were quickly calmed. By early morning, thousands of cars were backed up 2 miles east along Grand Avenue to view the new creation. According to Webb records, over 100,000 visitors toured the new model homes during the first three days of the grand opening. Incredibly, 237 homes or apartments were sold during that first three-day weekend.

Sun City was an immediate and overwhelming success! On that opening weekend, prospective buyers were able to tour five model homes and 14 apartments and preview one recreation center, a professional golf course, shopping center, and hotel/restaurant. It was more than enough to impress many of those who turned out, and homes were snatched up at a record pace.

According to the Sun Cities Area Historical Society, Wendell and Emilie Draser were the first to move into their new Sun City home. Records also reveal many of the first weekend's buyers purchased more than one home at the same time. Others who bought homes that first weekend went on to buy several more homes in Sun City—changing homes as model styles changed.

The community grew quickly. By the end of the first month, the company had sold all 400 homes scheduled to be built the first year. A second phase, consisting of 675 homes, was quickly put on the drawing board.

By April, when the first residents moved in, 700 homes had already been sold. The company had projected to sell 1,700 homes in its first three years of marketing Sun City. By the end of 1960, a total of 1,300 homes had already been purchased.

According to the book *Jubilee: The 25th Anniversary of Sun City*, 59 days after it first opened, Sun City was Arizona's "fastest growing city."

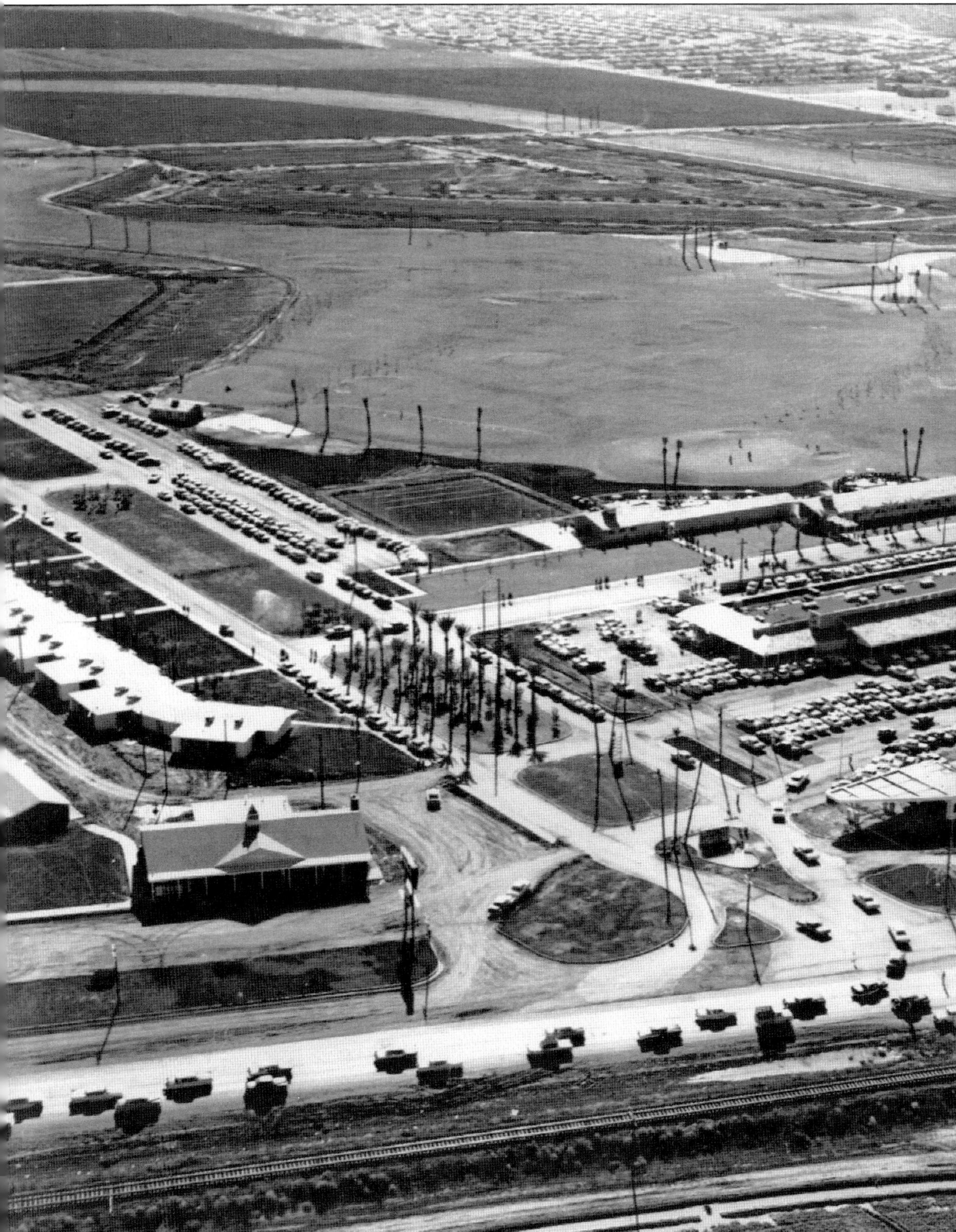

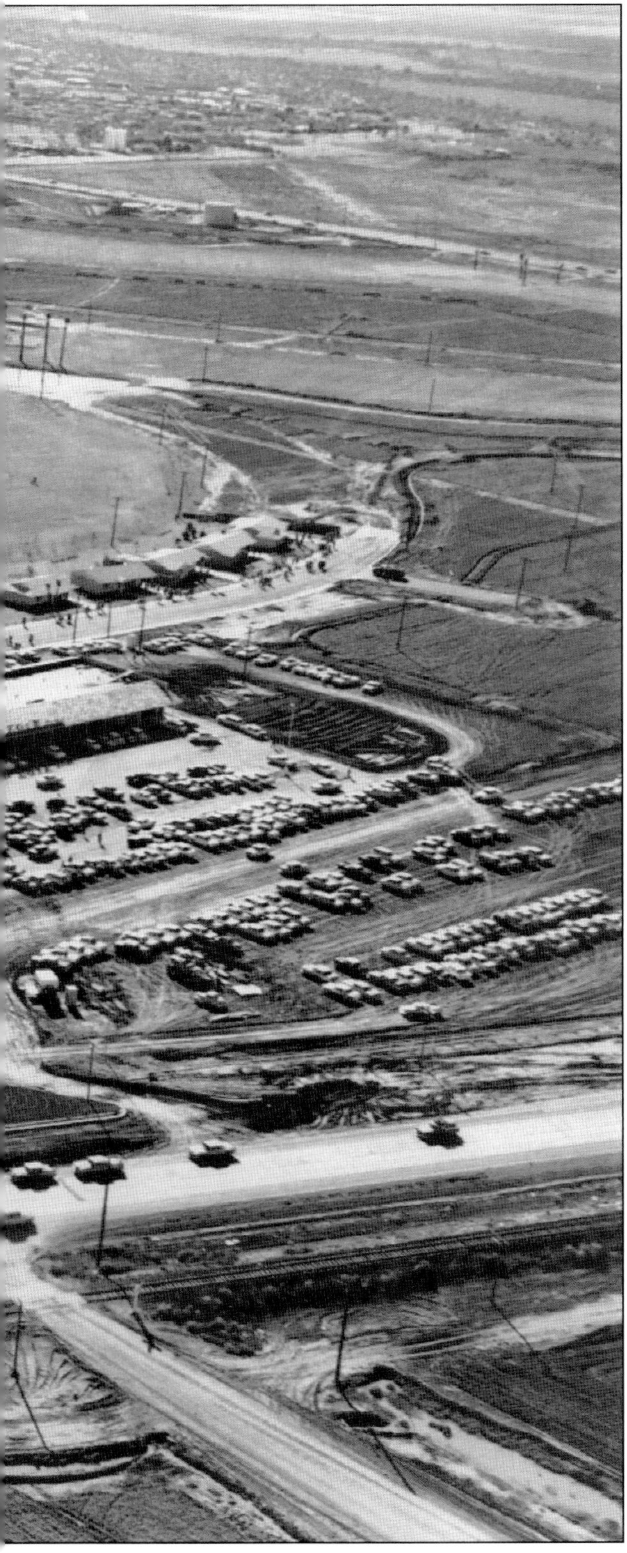

Sun City officially opened January 1, 1960. Despite concerns no one would show up, more than 100,000 visitors toured the community the first three days. The tremendous response can be seen here just after dawn on January 1, as cars are backed up 2 miles east along Grand Avenue trying to turn left into the new community at the intersection of 107th and Grand Avenues. The Hiway House Motor Hotel and apartments are on the lower left, Sun City Shopping Center (now Grand Center) is on the right, and the Community Center (now Oakmont Recreation Center) is behind the shopping center. West of the recreation center on Oakmont Drive are the first five model homes. North Golf Course is under construction.

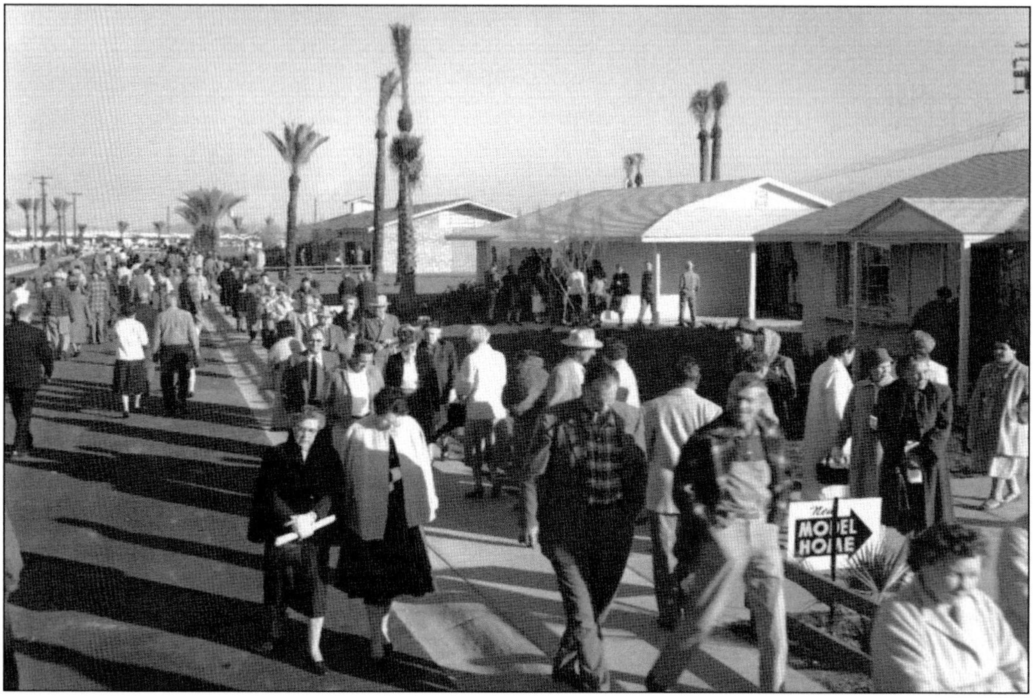


Sun City, by anyone's standard, was an immediate success. In all, 237 homes with a value of more than $2.5 million were sold during that first three-day weekend. This photograph looks east along Oakmont Drive. The first building on the right is the Community Center, and the first model home is now the Del Webb Sun Cities Museum.

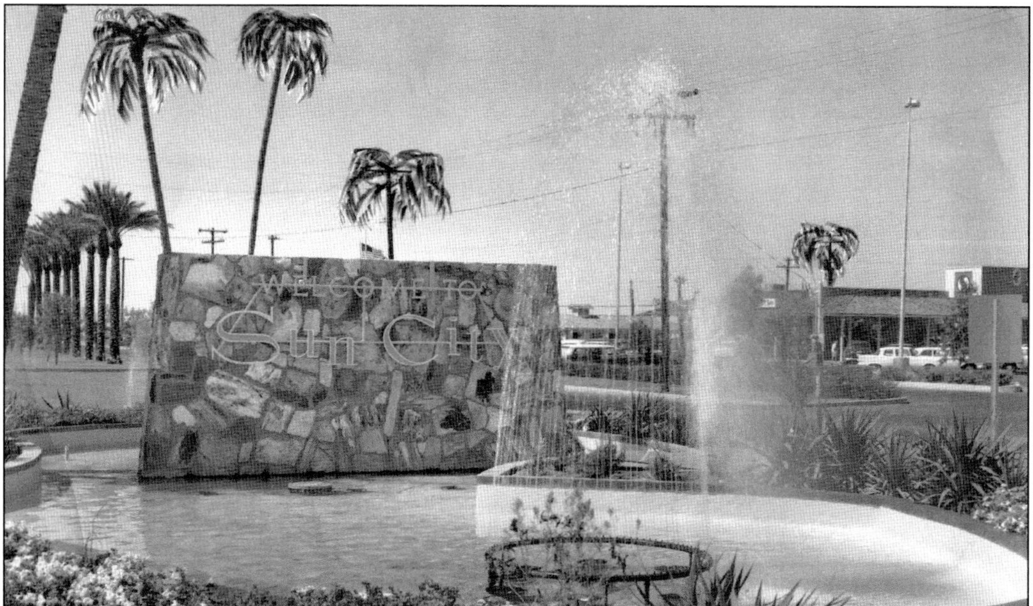


Sun City's original welcome sign was located at 107th and Grand Avenues. The fountain froze solid on New Year's Eve 1959, and the community's opening-day ceremonies scheduled for the next day had to be delayed one hour until the water began flowing again.

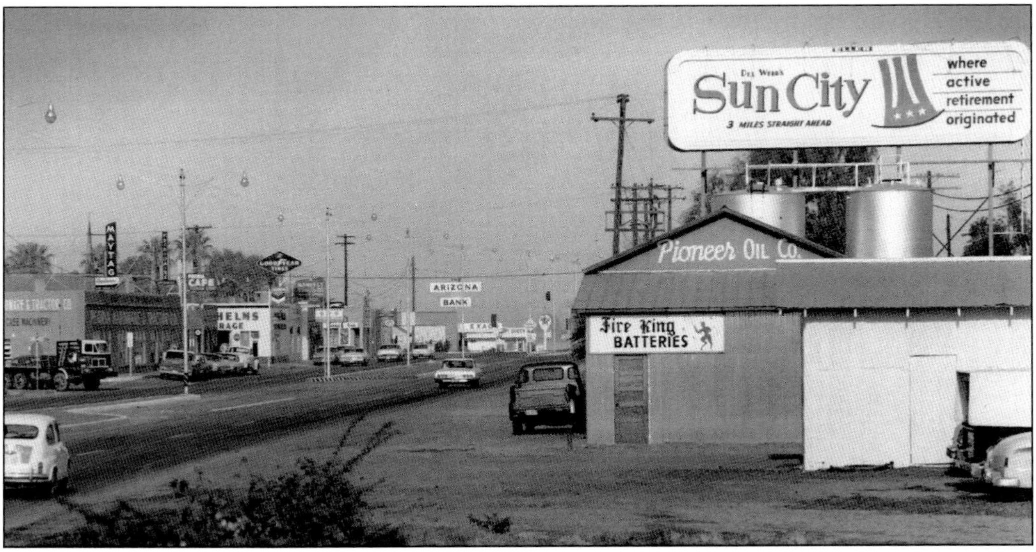


A nationwide contest was held to select a new name for the community. Of the thousands of entries received, the name "Sun City" was submitted by four different people. Del Webb made the final decision himself and is responsible for selecting the name that has become synonymous with active-adult living. Drivers passing through downtown Peoria, Arizona, on Grand Avenue in 1960 would have seen this billboard.

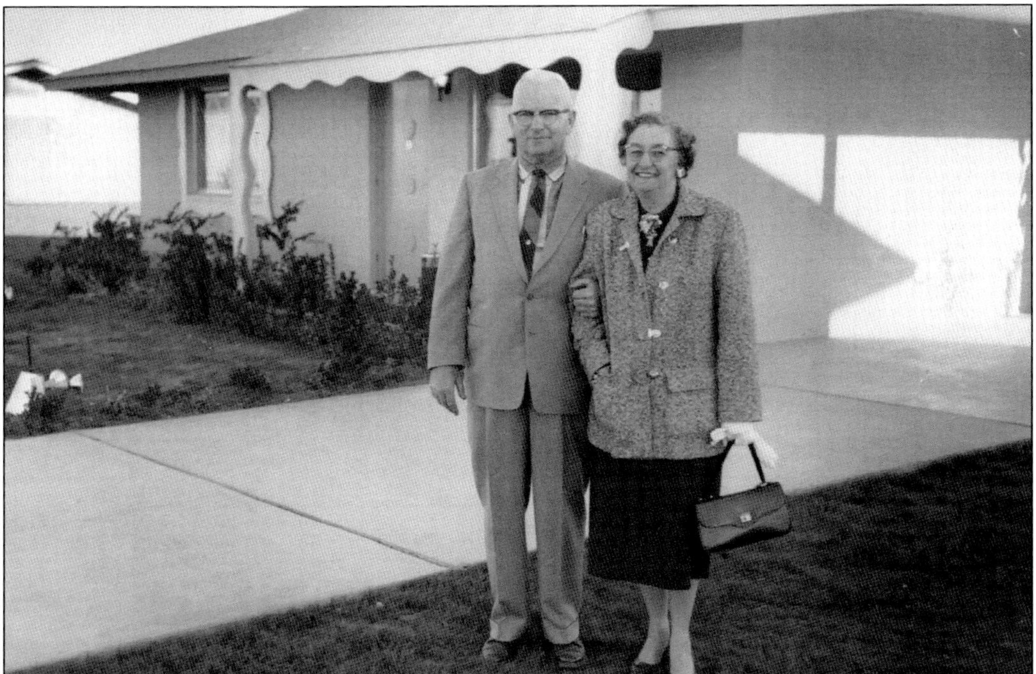

Mr. and Mrs. E. A. Britton of Eugene, Oregon, received this home at 12801 Augusta Drive for being the winners of the "Name This Active Retirement Community" contest held in 1959. The Brittons were one of four entrants who submitted the name "Sun City," and a drawing was held to determine a winner. The two-bedroom home sold for $8,500. The Brittons moved into their new home in October 1960 but sold it the following March.

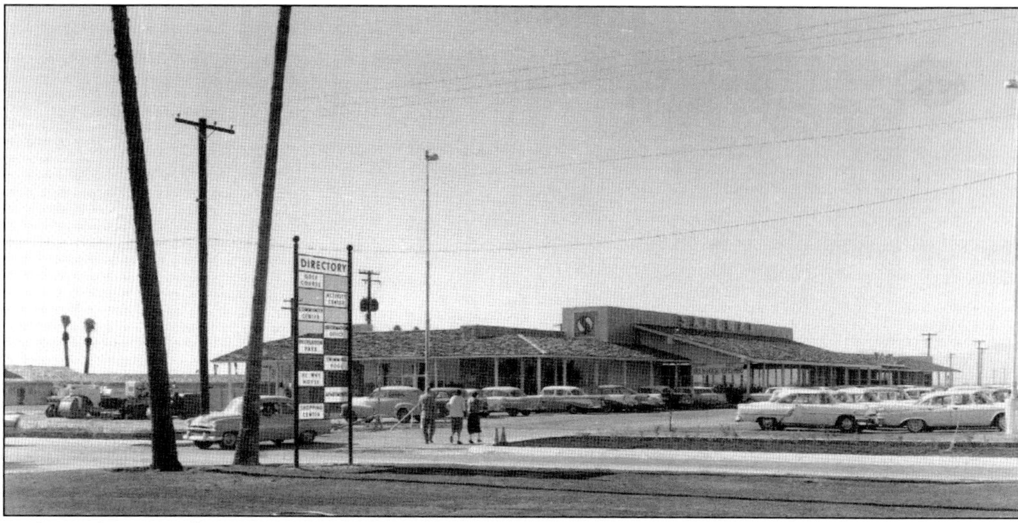


Safeway became the community's first grocery store and was located on the west side of the Sun City Shopping Center (today Grand Center). By the middle of the first year, the shopping center included the supermarket, a T. G. and Y. variety store, drugstore, barbershop, laundromat, drapery shop, and a service station.

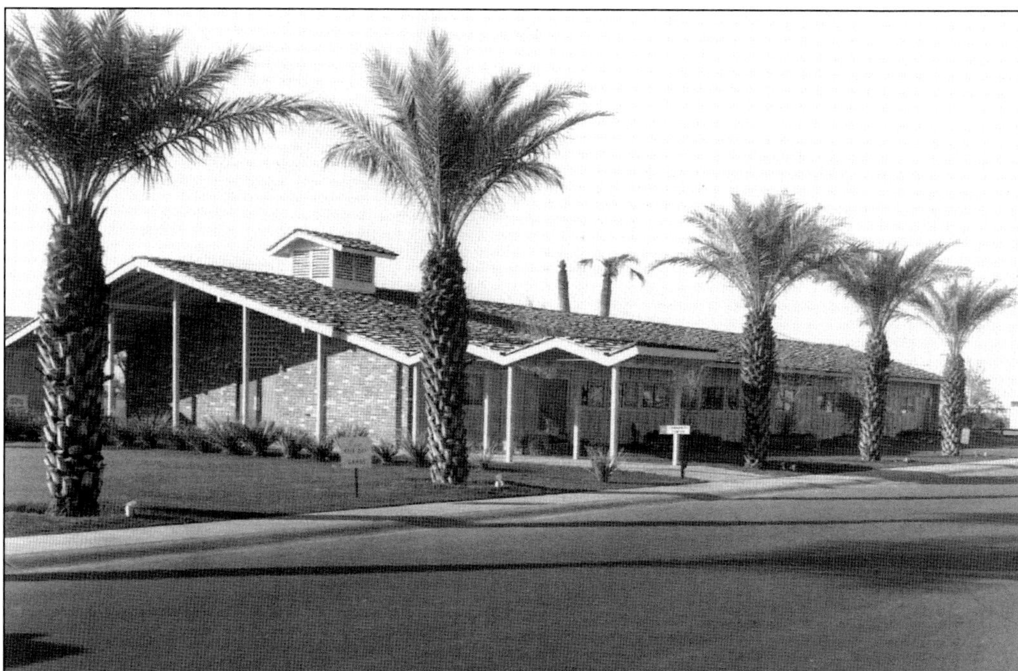

A full range of recreational amenities is what separated Sun City from any other master-planned community available in the country at that time. DEVCO spent more than $1.5 million in building recreational amenities prior to the opening of Sun City. The Community Center (now Oakmont Recreation Center) was Sun City's first recreation center. It included a crafts building, swimming pool, shuffleboard, lawn bowling, croquet courts, and horseshoe pit.

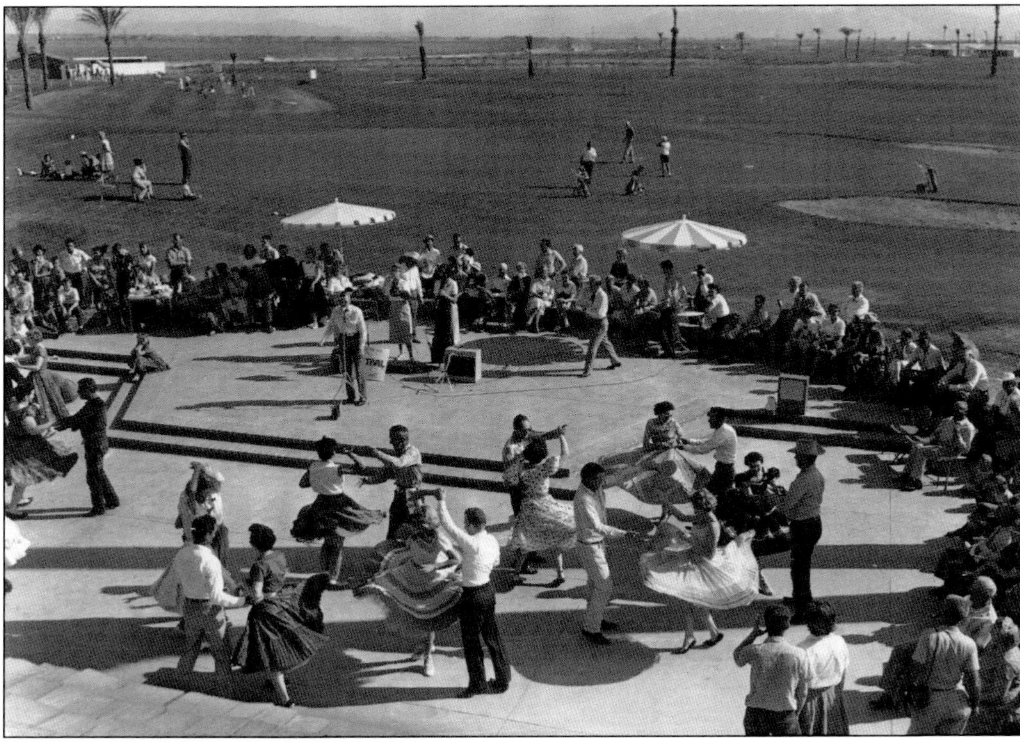

A Webb corporation promotional photograph and description published in March 1960 perfectly summarizes the "fun-in-the-sun" attraction of Sun City. The description read, "Sunday afternoon glimpses of what's to come in the way of relaxed living: Square dancers create a whirl of color on the spacious (Community Center) patio, while in the background golfers putt on the ninth green during a sunny afternoon of golf."

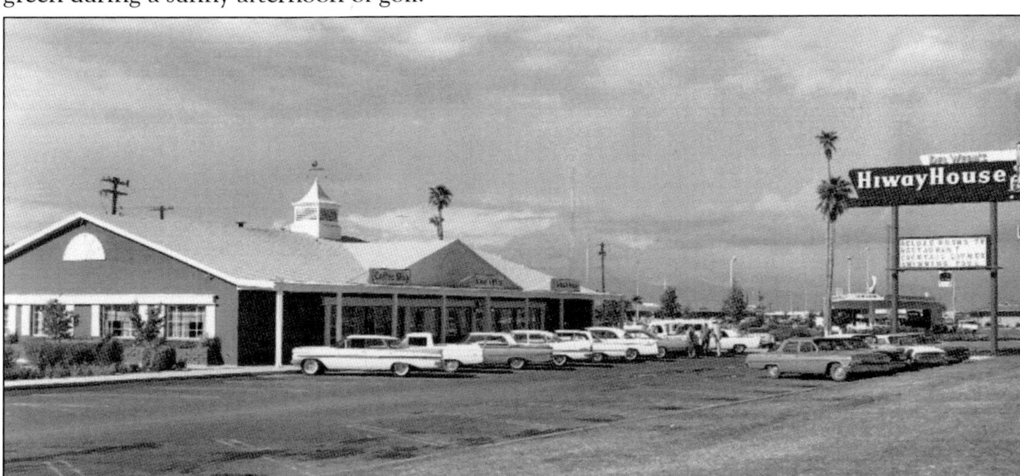


Del Webb's Hiway House Motor Hotel was popular in the early 1960s. Located on the southeast corner of 107th and Grand Avenues, the Hiway House featured a restaurant, cocktail lounge, 12 hotel rooms, and 14 one-bedroom apartments. The name was changed in 1963 to the King's Inn and sold by Webb in the 1970s. It was torn down in 1989 to make way for a shopping center, appropriately named King's Inn Center.

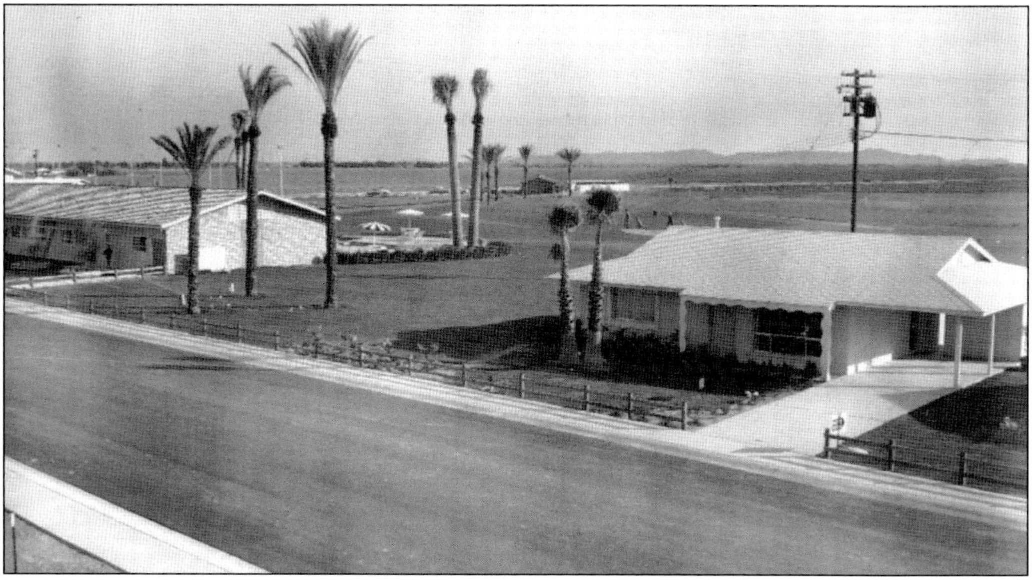

The first model home—the Kentwood—was located at 10801 Oakmont Drive in January 1960. The home today is the headquarters for the Sun Cities Historical Society and the Del Webb Sun Cities Museum. The first homes sold for $8,500 to $11,750, allowing the Webb company to tout their residences as the nation's first and only houses available on a golf-course lot for less than $10,000.

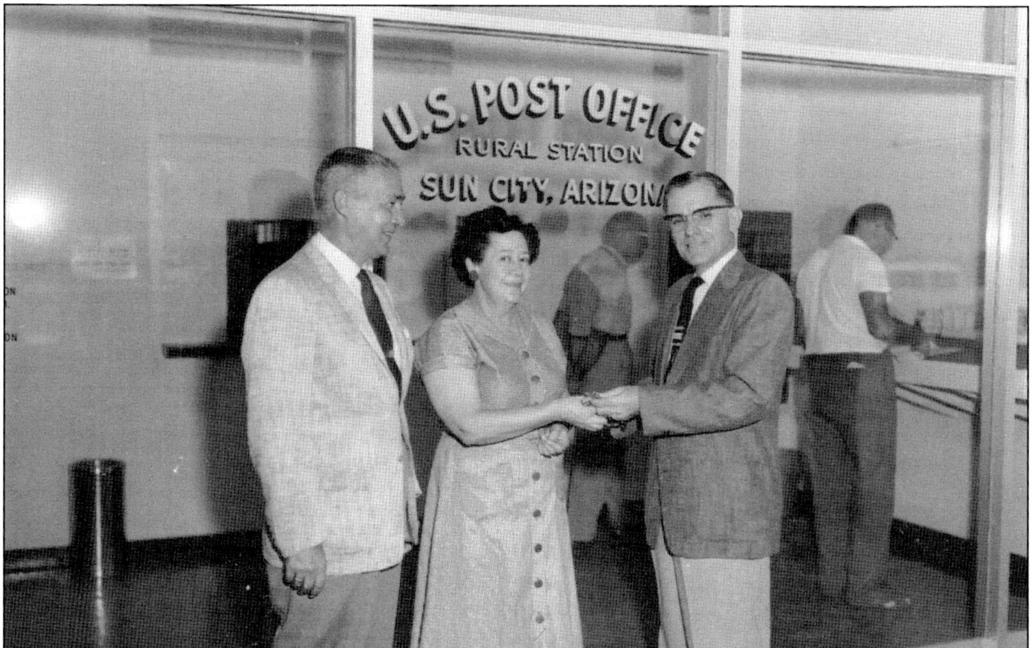


Sun City's first post office opened April 4, 1960. A special "first-day cover" promoting the community was created and mailed to 3,000 persons throughout the nation, including Pres. Dwight D. Eisenhower. On October 28, postal clerk Mary Garretson received her keys to the office from Phoenix postmaster William Mason, right, and DEVCO activities coordinator Tom Austin, left.

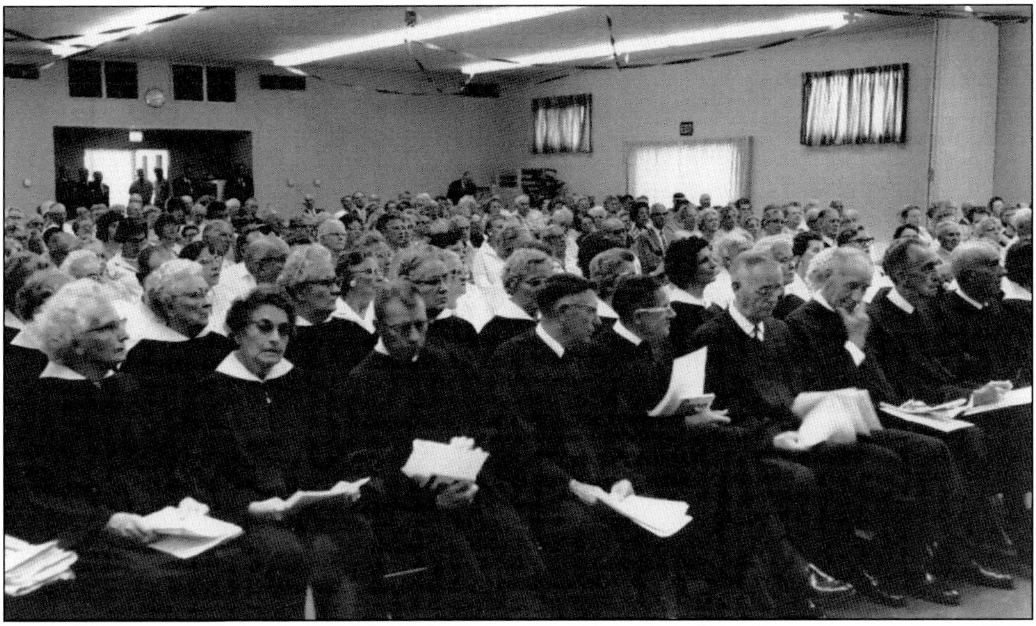

Faith and religion were always integral to the Sun City lifestyle. When the community first opened, religious services were held at the Community Center. One of the first residents of the community, Dr. Walter Witt, organized the first church in Sun City. His "Community Church" would become the United Church of Sun City. Located at 11250 North 107th Avenue, the church featured members from 61 different congregations.

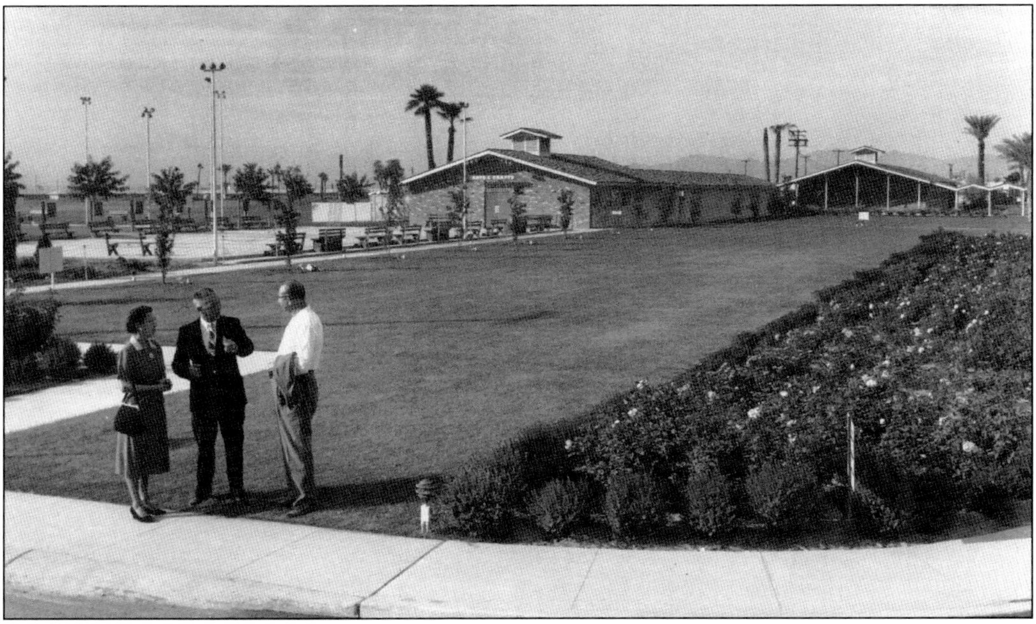

The Community Center, at the corner of 107th and Oakmont Avenues, was the site of a community rose garden in 1960. DEVCO provided the amenities and planned the activities in the early days, but it was always the intention to have the residents assume control. Activities available the first year included lapidary, ceramics, sewing, swimming, woodworking, lawn bowling, shuffleboard, and croquet.

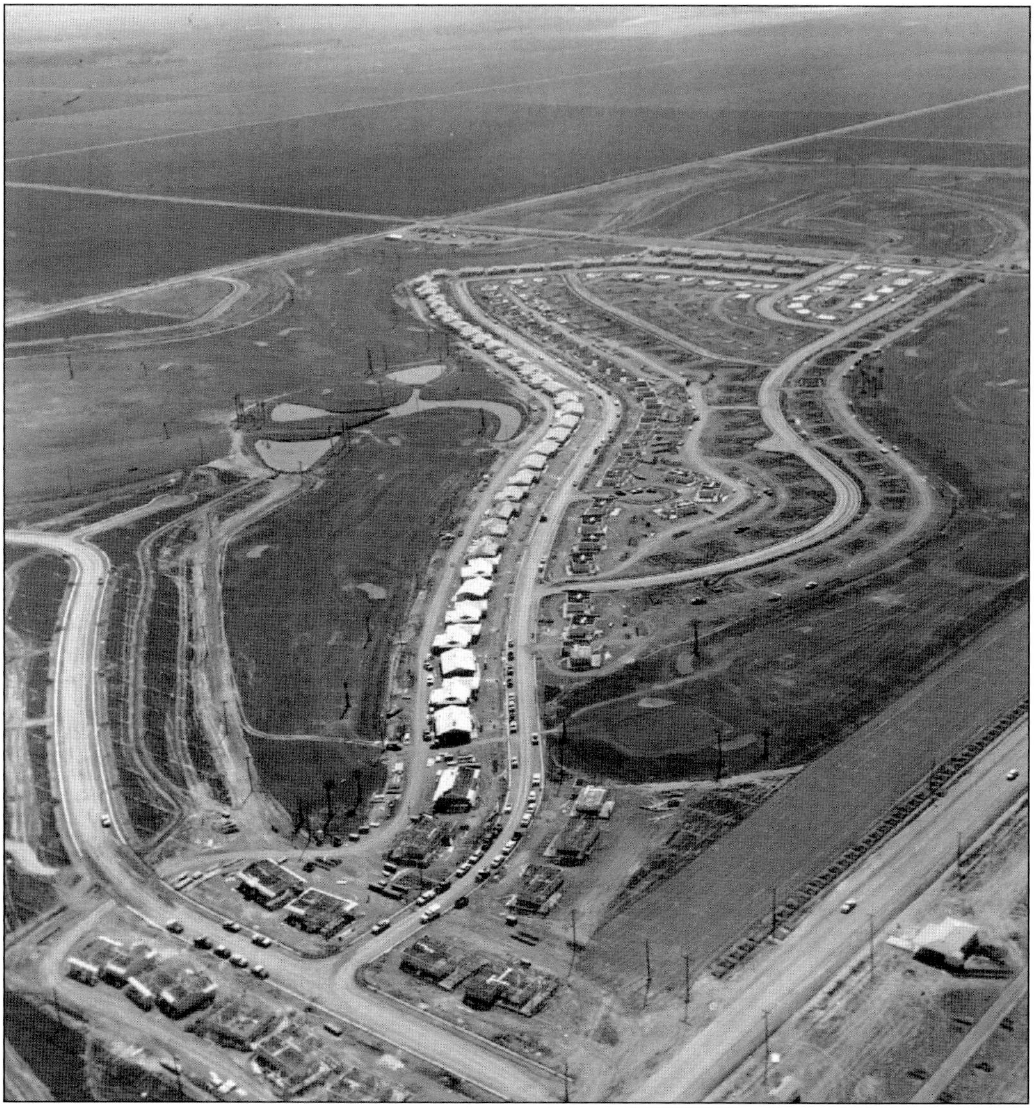

The first year was a phenomenal success by anyone's definition. The first homes were ready for occupancy by April, and by the end of the year, 1,300 homes had been sold, making Sun City Arizona's "fastest growing city." The second nine holes of the community's first golf course opened in December, and it was reported that Hole 18—a 596-yard, par 5 shot—was the longest hole in the Phoenix metropolitan area. Thirty-two clubs organized the first year, and the first church opened the next. Residents formed the Sun City Civic Association and in January 1961 voted to assume ownership of the first recreation center. DEVCO would celebrate the second anniversary by opening its second set of model homes and the second recreation center. Sun City was off and running.

# *Five*

# The Early Years

Sun City introduced the world to "resort retirement," and its initial success earned international fame and attention. The community was highlighted in newspaper and magazine articles throughout the country, was featured on the national news, and was profiled on numerous television shows.

Del Webb made the cover of *Time* magazine in 1962 when the publication hailed Sun City as "a new way of life for the old."

Sun City's first decade saw continued growth and expansion. To keep pace with the exploding population, the Del E. Webb Development Company (DEVCO) added two more recreation centers in the 1960s, along with several golf courses, an outdoor amphitheater, and additional shopping centers.

But success did not come without growing pains. Home sales actually started to slow by mid-decade, prompting a change in the local management team and a move toward more contemporary (and more expensive) home styles.

DEVCO was quick to turn over ownership of its recreation centers to residents. The three original recreation centers were at first assigned to specific units or neighborhoods. Residents living in one Sun City neighborhood were restricted to using one specific recreation center and prohibited from using another.

All that changed in 1968 when the community voted to bring all three existing recreational centers under one umbrella. That organization would later become the Recreation Centers of Sun City, Inc., and from that point on all residents not only shared the facilities, but shared in the cost to operate and maintain those amenities.

In 10 short years, Sun City had become the most famous retirement community in the nation. In 1969 alone, the company set a new record by selling 2,038 homes and apartments; the 10,000th home was sold in 1970.

Over the next 10 years, expansion would push the border 4 miles further north and provide room for more than 15,000 additional homes, four new recreation centers, five golf courses, and, most importantly, a major hospital.

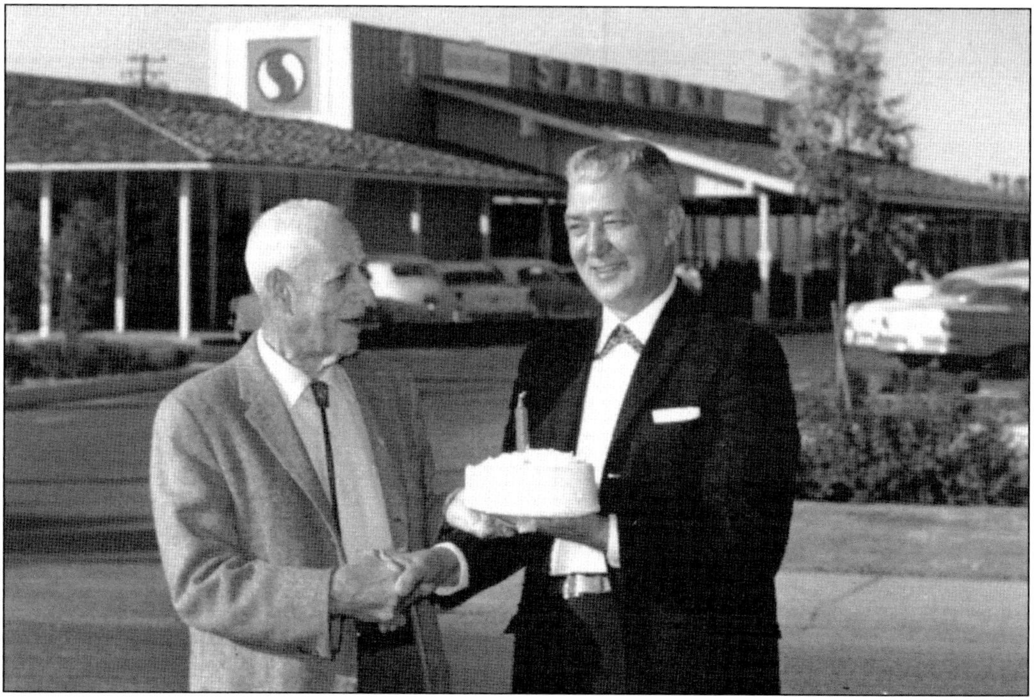

Ralph Hawley, left, president of the Sun City Civic Association, and Tom Austin, DEVCO coordinator, share a first anniversary birthday cake in January 1961. As a birthday gift, DEVCO turned over ownership of the Community Center to residents of the community via the Civic Association, while the company turned its attention to a new series of model homes and a new recreation center.

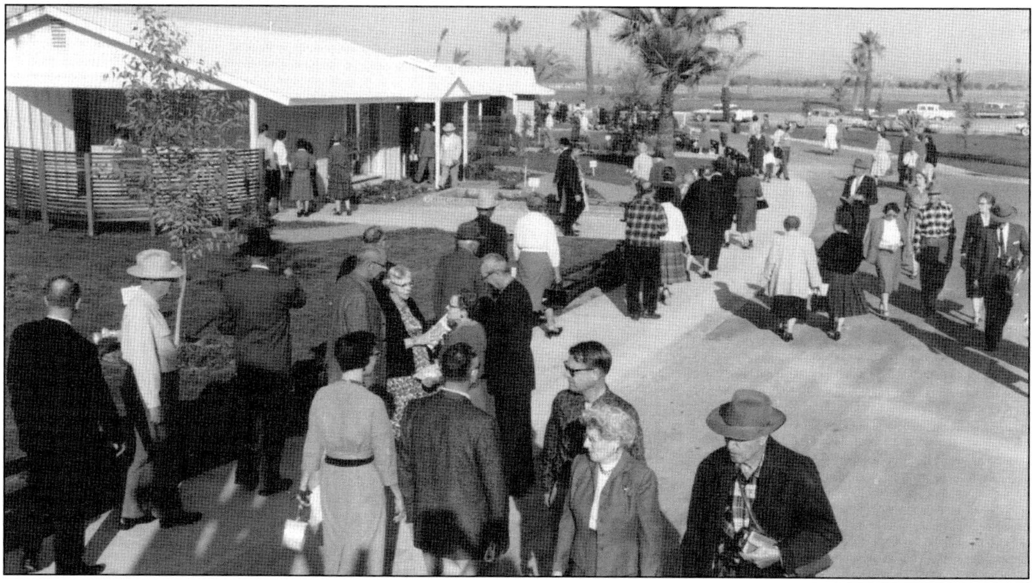

Visitors previewed the second set of model homes and the second recreation center, Town Hall Recreation Center (now Fairway Recreation Center), at the corner of 107th and Peoria Avenues. The new series of model homes was unveiled January 29, 1961, and 40,000 attended the opening. The second section of Sun City to be constructed featured 1,975 homes and 400 apartments.

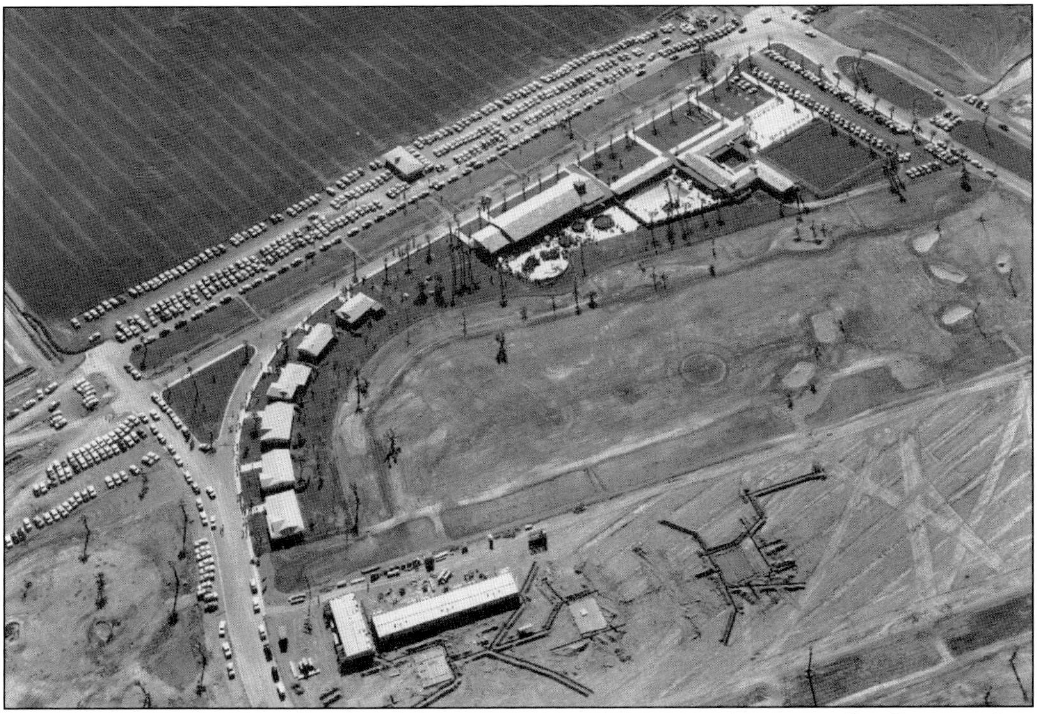

A second series of six model homes, a new recreation center, and a golf course officially opened on January 29, 1961. Peoria Avenue runs left to right in this photograph with Town Hall Recreation Center to the right. The new model homes are to the left. Sun City would soon jump south of Peoria Avenue, and the community's third recreation center would be built on the visible farmland.

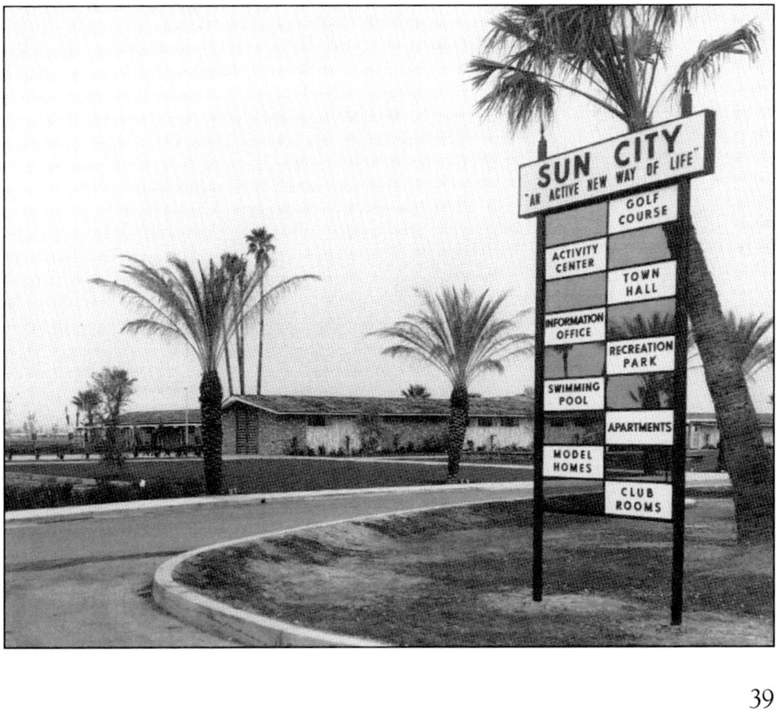


Visitors to Sun City's newest model homes and northernmost entry at Peoria and 107th Avenues were greeted in 1961 by this welcome sign. The sign stood for more than four decades. Visible is the Town Hall Recreation Center (now Fairway Recreation Center). Fairway Recreation Center was completely demolished in 2009–2010 and rebuilt from the ground up.

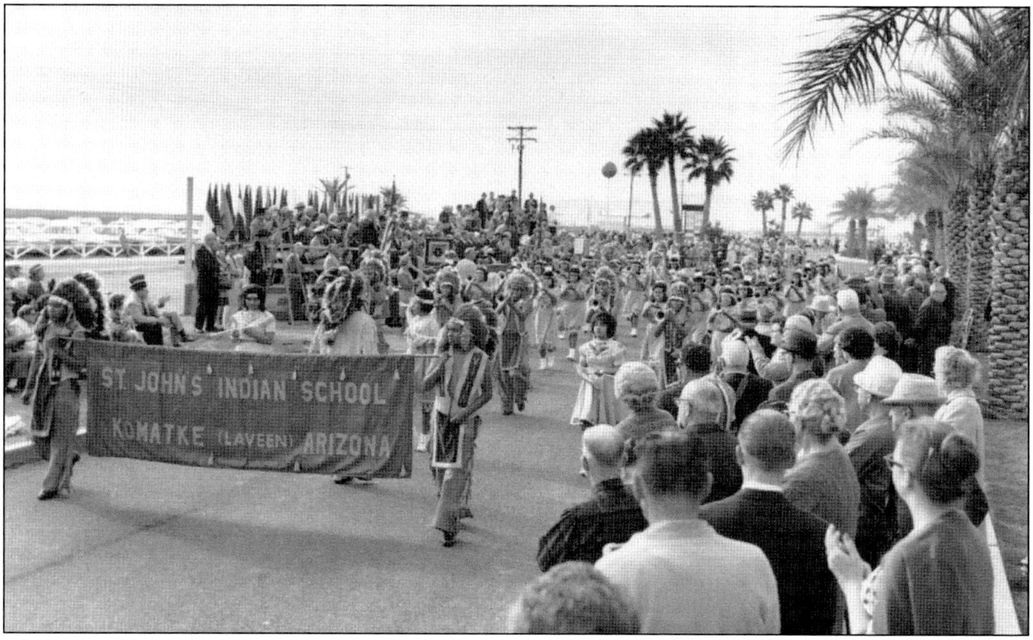


To celebrate the community's first anniversary, as well as the opening of its second series of model homes, DEVCO staged a parade along Peoria Avenue. This photograph is of Peoria Avenue looking west toward 107th Avenue. If looking closely, Del E. Webb can be identified sitting in the first row of the reviewing stand.

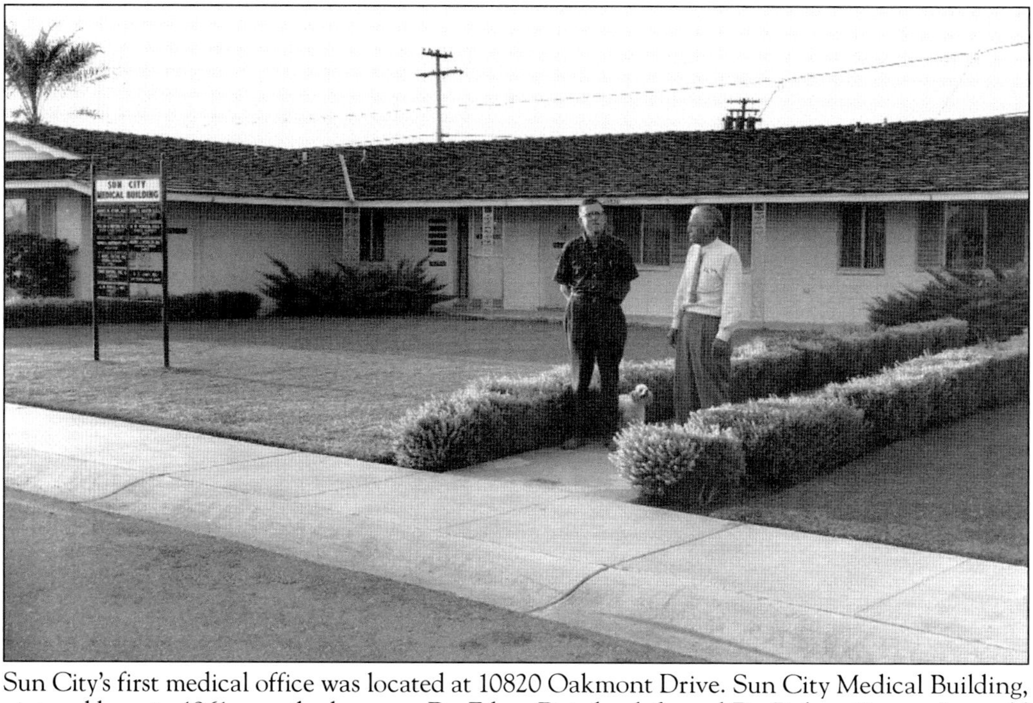


Sun City's first medical office was located at 10820 Oakmont Drive. Sun City Medical Building, pictured here in 1961, was the home to Dr. Edgar Deissler, left, and Dr. Robert Stump. It would be several years before the nearest hospital would open in Youngtown, and nearly 10 years before Sun City would have its own hospital.

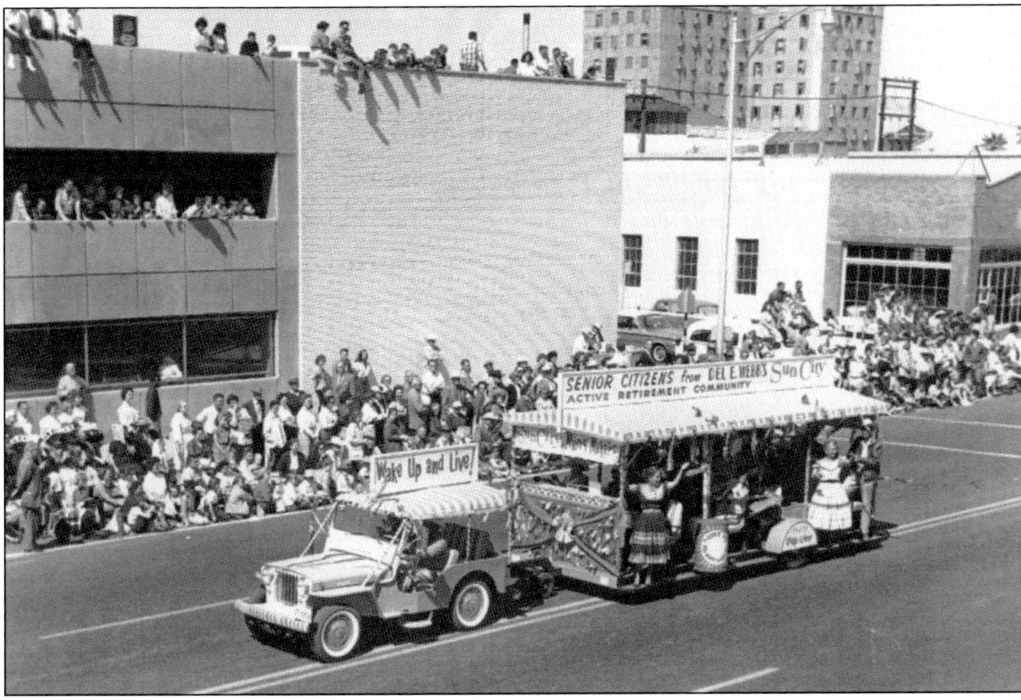


The Del E. Webb Corporation took advantage of the 1961 Phoenix Chamber of Commerce parade in Phoenix to debut its "Wake Up and Live Senior Citizens" float. More than 300,000 people watched the giant Phoenix Jaycees Rodeo parade and saw a pink and white Sun City float with its lively Merry Makers band offering a variety of music, including the song, "Wake Up and Live in Sun City."

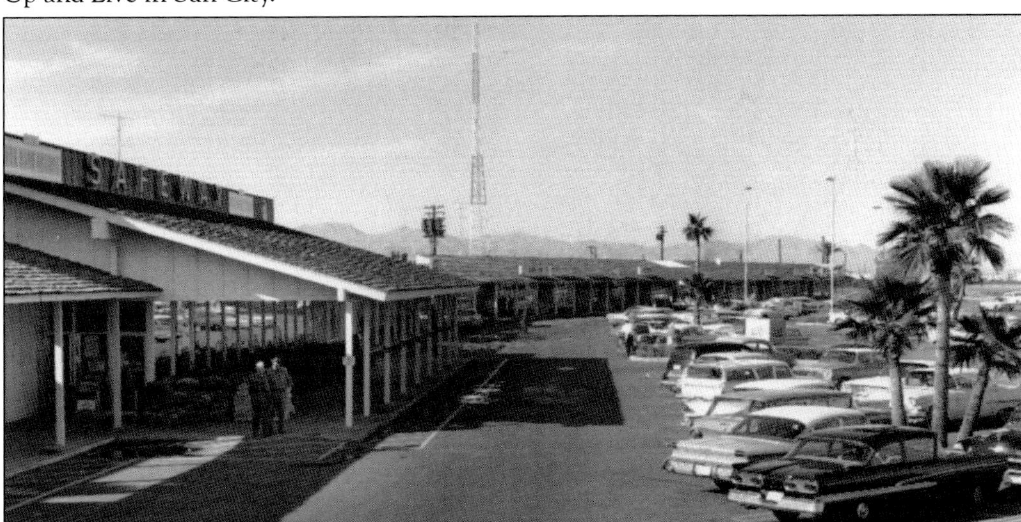

A large celebration was held in April 1961 to mark the expansion of the Sun City Shopping Center (now known as Grand Center). When the community opened, the only occupant was a Safeway grocery store. In 1961, the center's size doubled and 15 new businesses were added. For a number of years, the center would be the site of the community's popular Western Days celebration held in the fall.

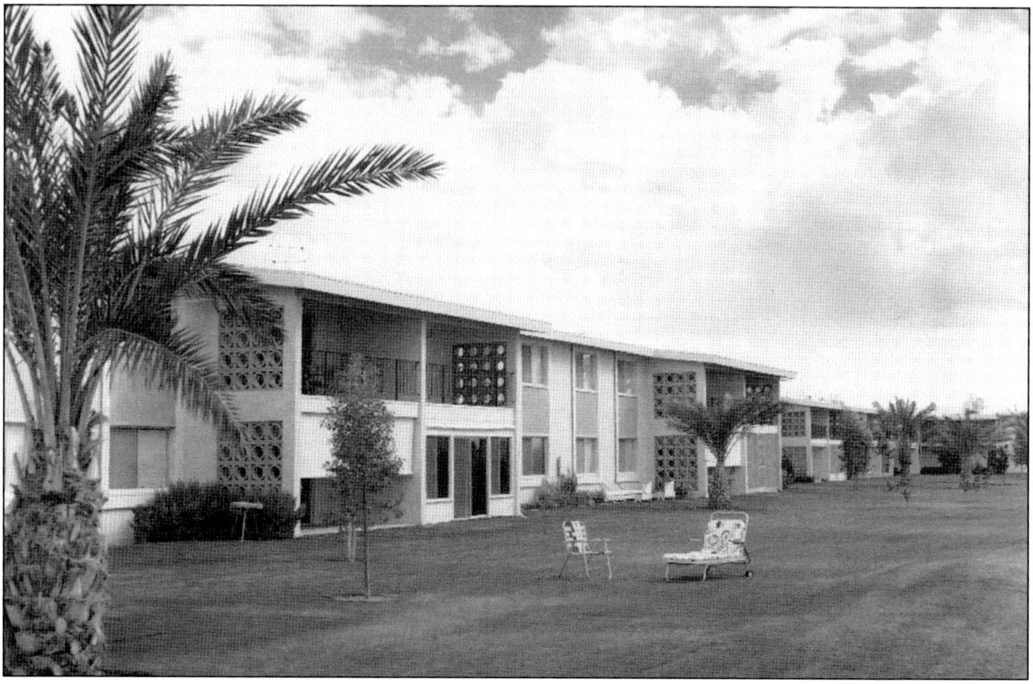

Two-story condominium apartments were constructed overlooking South Golf Course behind Town Hall Recreation Center. Built in 1961, these were the only two-story apartments built in Sun City. More than 4,000 visitors attended an open house unveiling the apartments on April 16, 1961. The apartments sold for $13,200–$15,000, and 27 were sold on opening day.

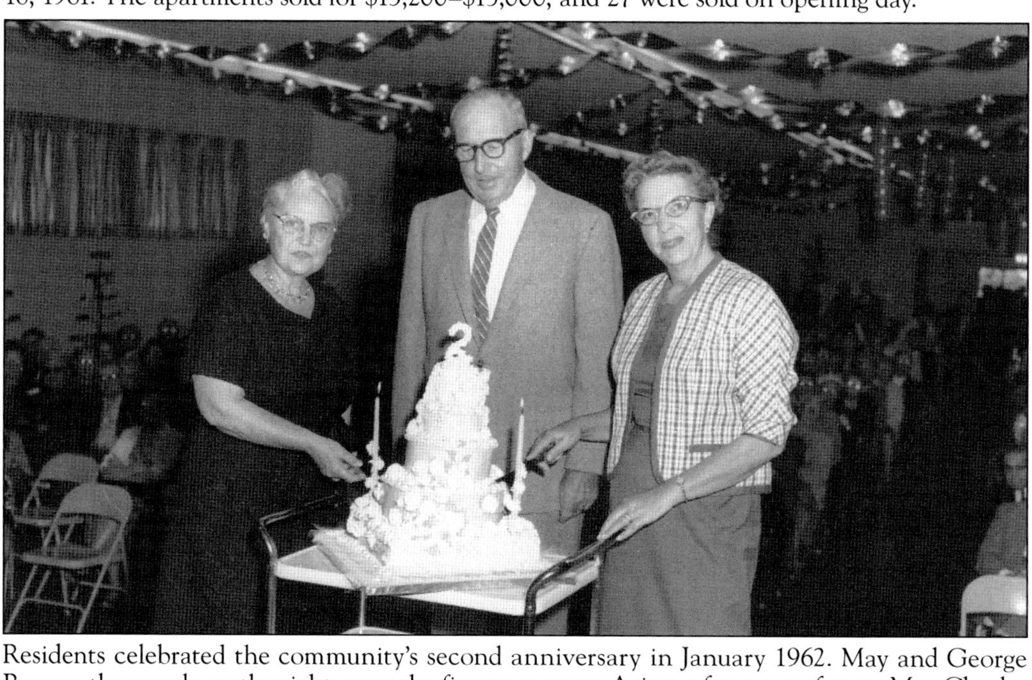

Residents celebrated the community's second anniversary in January 1962. May and George Baynes, the couple on the right, were the first to move to Arizona from out of state. Mrs. Charles Slatten, left, baked the big cake, as well as enough "flat" cakes to feed the 1,200 residents who attended the party. Only one cake remained after the celebration.

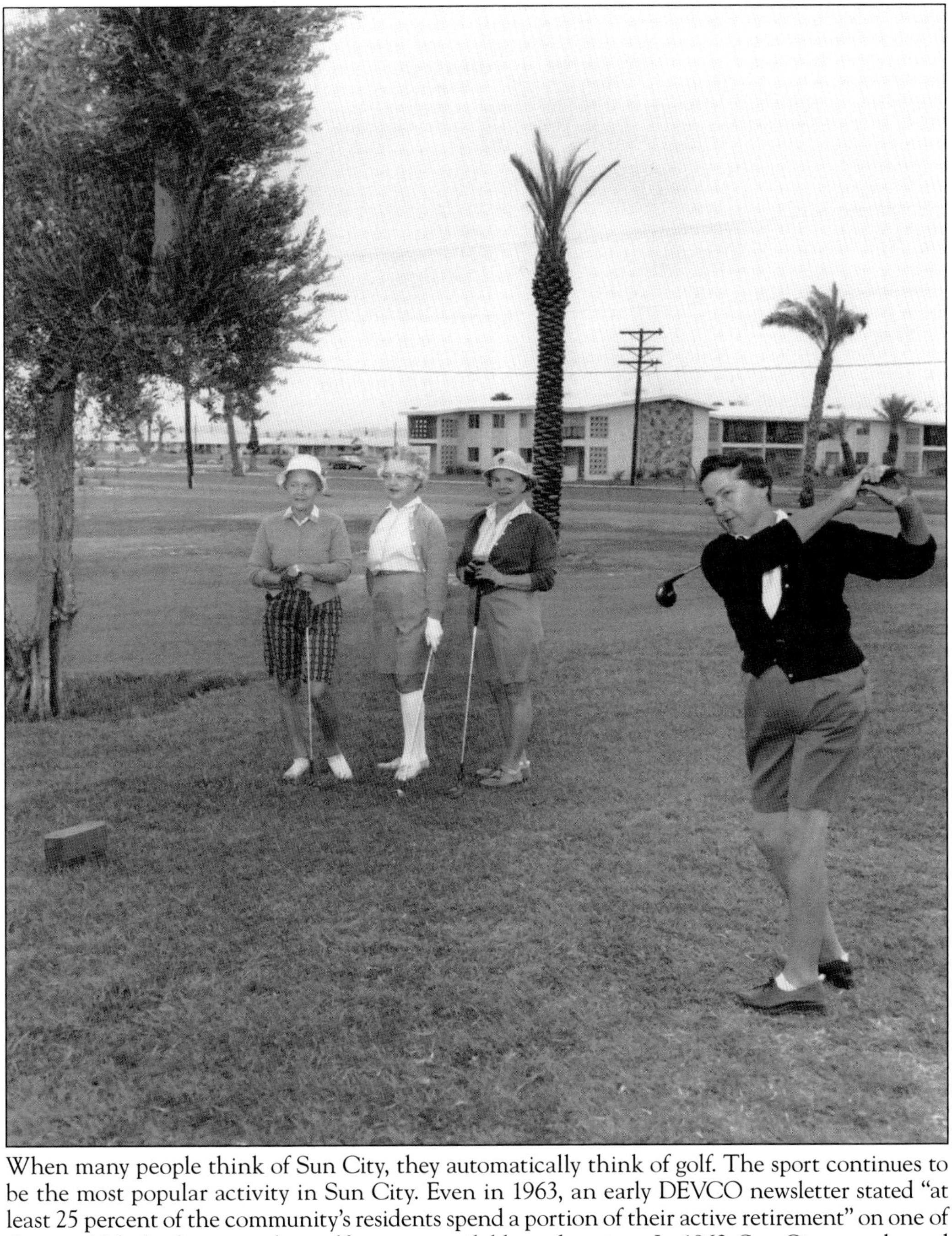

When many people think of Sun City, they automatically think of golf. The sport continues to be the most popular activity in Sun City. Even in 1963, an early DEVCO newsletter stated "at least 25 percent of the community's residents spend a portion of their active retirement" on one of the two 18-hole championship golf courses available at that time. In 1963, Sun City even hosted the U.S. Senior Open Golf Championship Tournament. Shown here driving from the second tee on South Golf Course is Jean Grant. The others are, from left to right, Grace Stotser, Kay Mantor, and Lillian McKinstry.

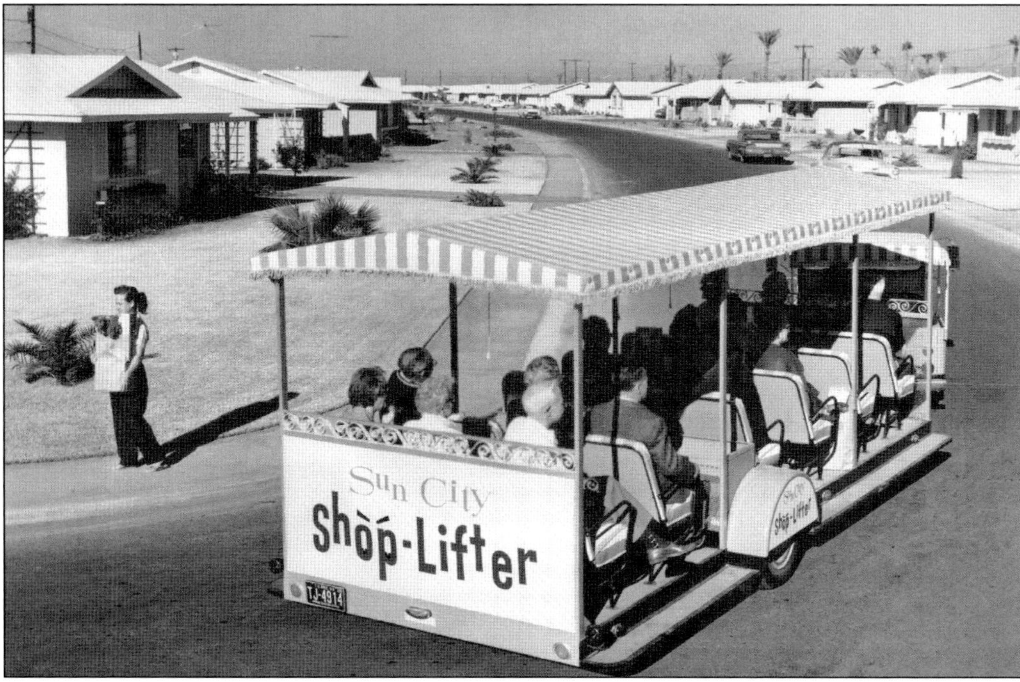


In 1963, DEVCO introduced "The Shop-Lifter," a jeep-pulled trolley that served as Sun City's first public transportation. The trolley would transport residents to the shopping center and other points throughout the community. The Shop-Lifter was replaced a few years later by a minibus sponsored by the Sun City Merchants Association.

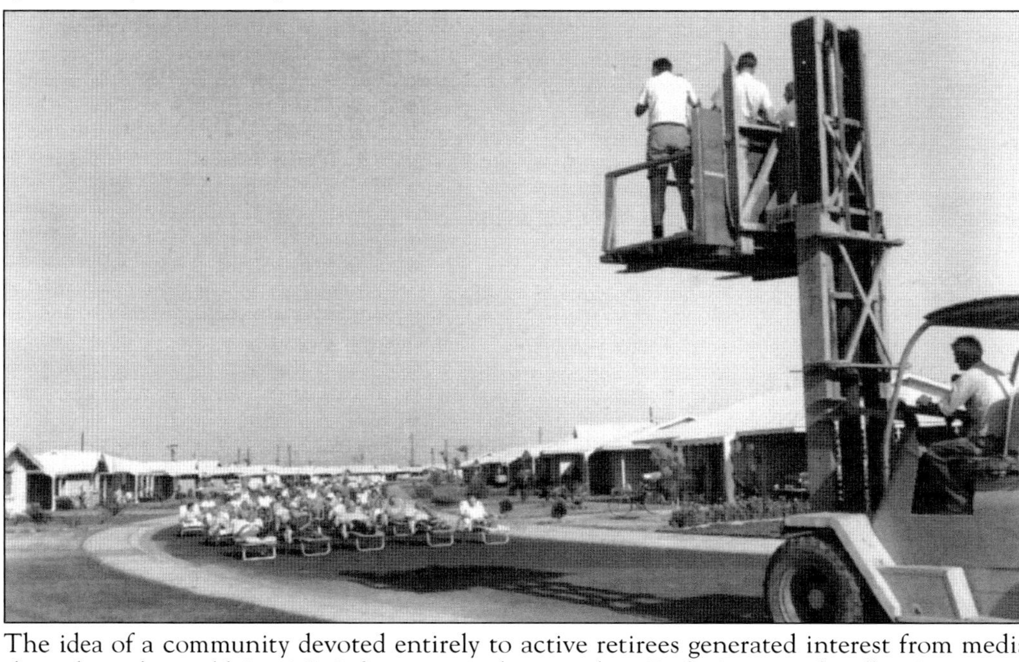

The idea of a community devoted entirely to active retirees generated interest from media throughout the world. In 1961, *Life* magazine photographers Rudy Crane and Wilbur Jarvis used a hydraulic lift to create a photograph featuring more than 100 residents taking part in a "chaise lounge brigade." The photograph was used that fall in a feature article on southwestern living.

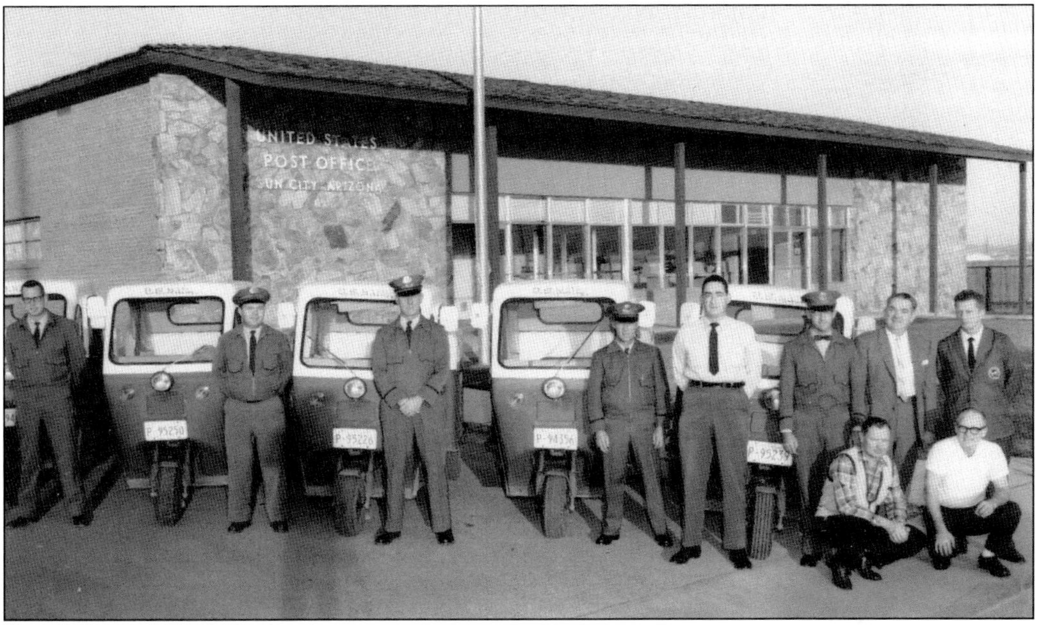


Postmaster Harry Beck and his crew pose for a photograph in 1963 at the opening of Sun City's second post office. It opened July 1, 1962, at 103rd Avenue and Coggins Drive, in the building now occupied by a funeral home. The post office originally wanted residential mailboxes to be at the curb, but protests from residents prompted delivery to the door.

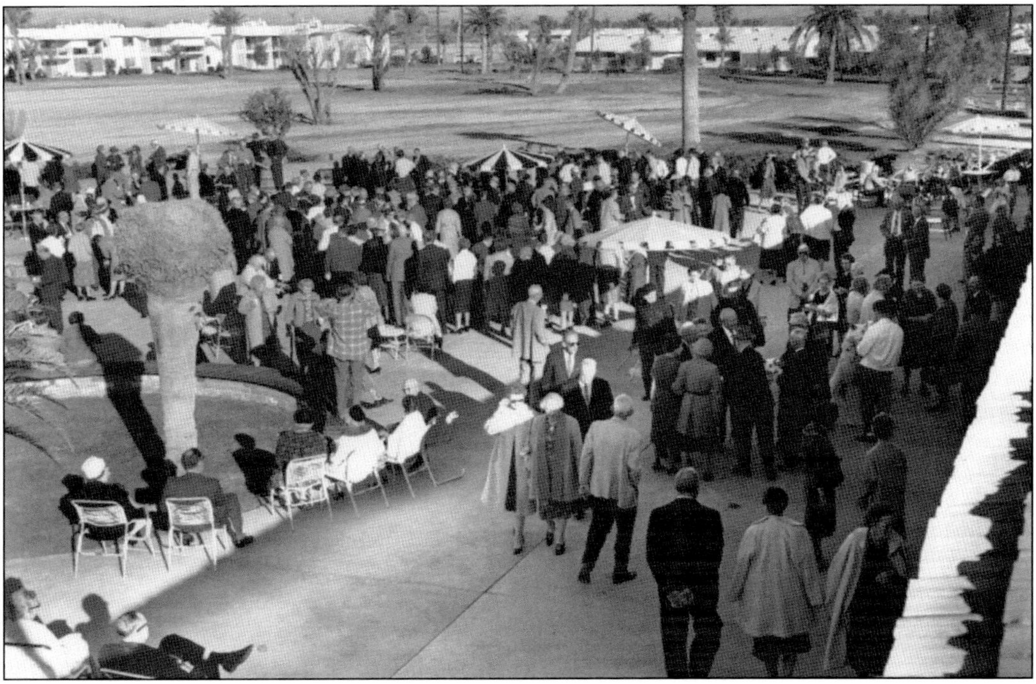

New residents were always officially welcomed to the community during a "Newcomers Coffee" hosted by DEVCO. Shown here is an early-1960s event at Town Hall Recreation Center. The tradition has continued through the years, and Newcomers Coffees today are still conducted on a regular basis in both Sun City and Sun City West.

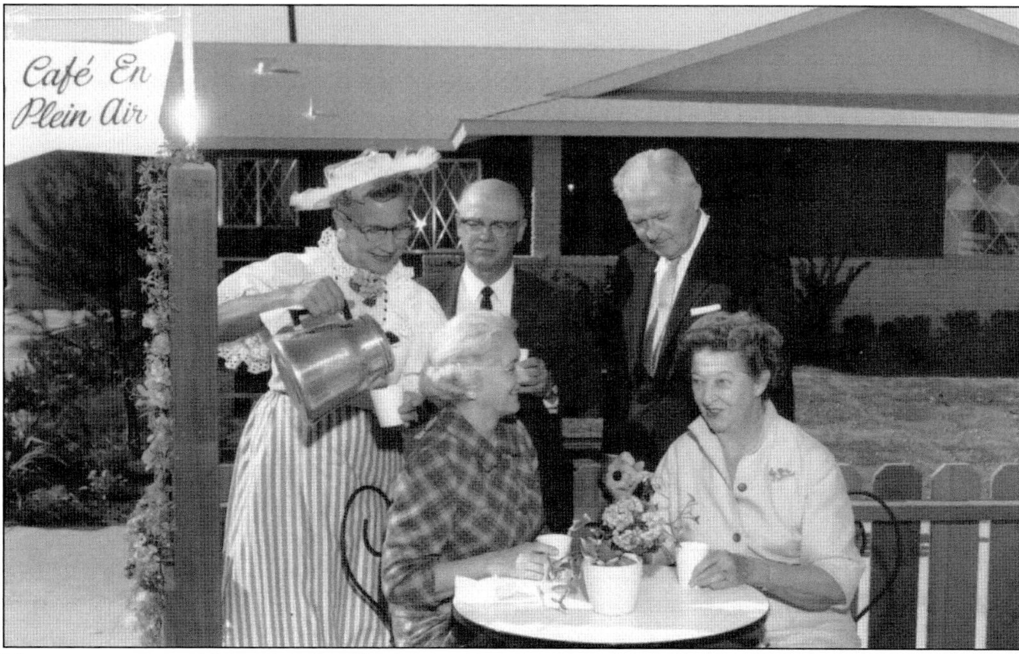


The community celebrated its fourth anniversary in 1964, and Webb employees marked the occasion with the opening of yet another set of new model homes. Unlike previous years, the response was not quite as strong. The company sold 400 fewer homes in 1961 than 1960. Only 395 homes were sold in 1965, prompting a change in management and a move toward larger homes.

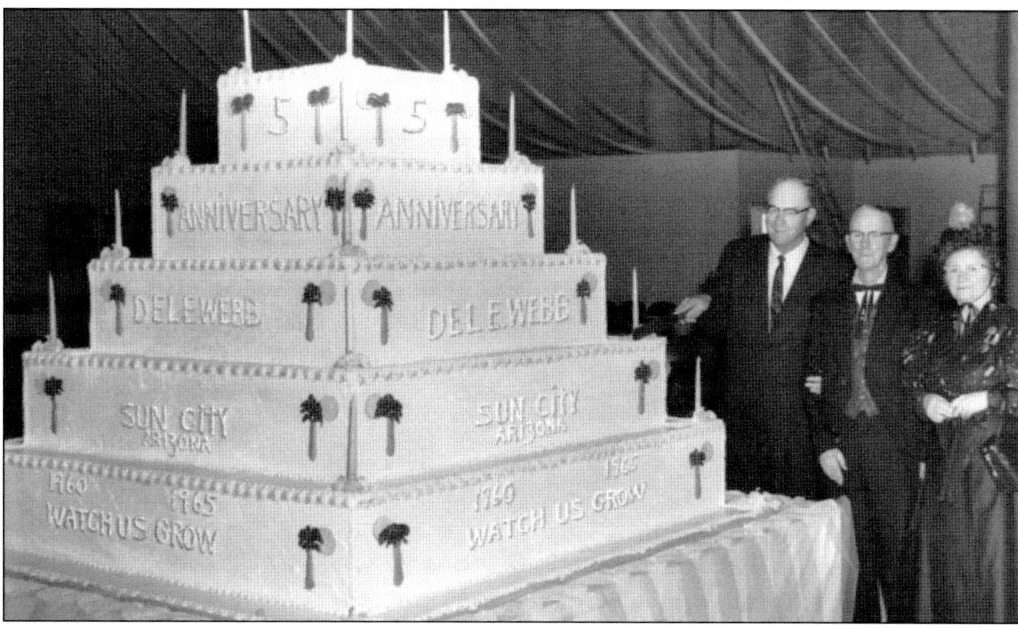


Del E. Webb was on hand to participate in Sun City's fifth anniversary celebration held January 9–10, 1965. In this photograph, Webb prepared to cut the five-tier birthday cake with assistance from Mel and Etta Phelps. An estimated crowd of 3,000 attended the Anniversary Ball held January 9 in Snyder's Van and Storage warehouse. The 7-square-foot, 5-foot-tall cake was created by Betty's Bakery. Mel Phelps died in 1987 at age 97.

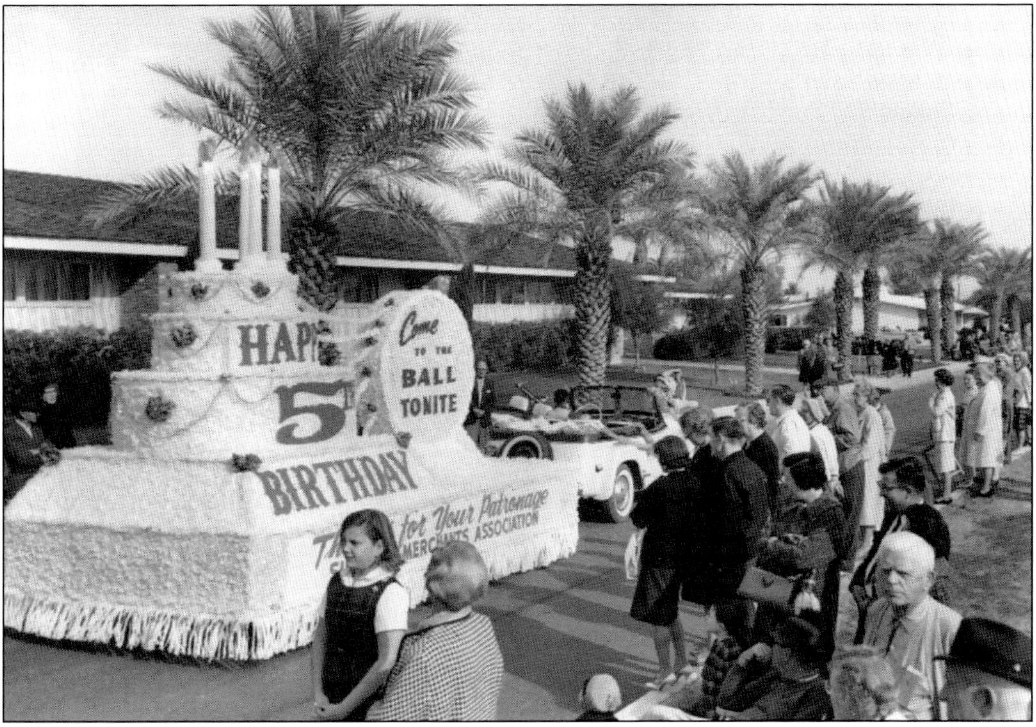


Sun City residents have always enjoyed celebrating their community's birthday. For the fifth anniversary, a parade was held January 9, 1965, along Peoria Avenue. The merchants association's float encouraged residents to "Come to the Ball" later that evening. According to a story that week in the *Sun City Citizen* (later the *Sun City Independent*), a crowd of 3,000 turned out to view the parade.

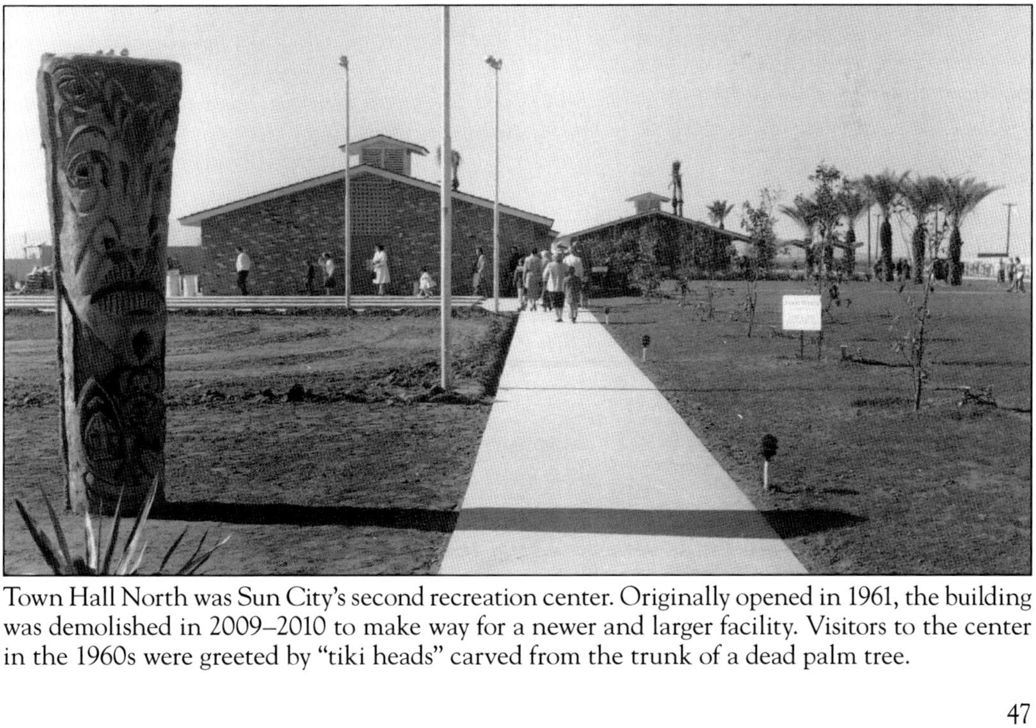

Town Hall North was Sun City's second recreation center. Originally opened in 1961, the building was demolished in 2009–2010 to make way for a newer and larger facility. Visitors to the center in the 1960s were greeted by "tiki heads" carved from the trunk of a dead palm tree.

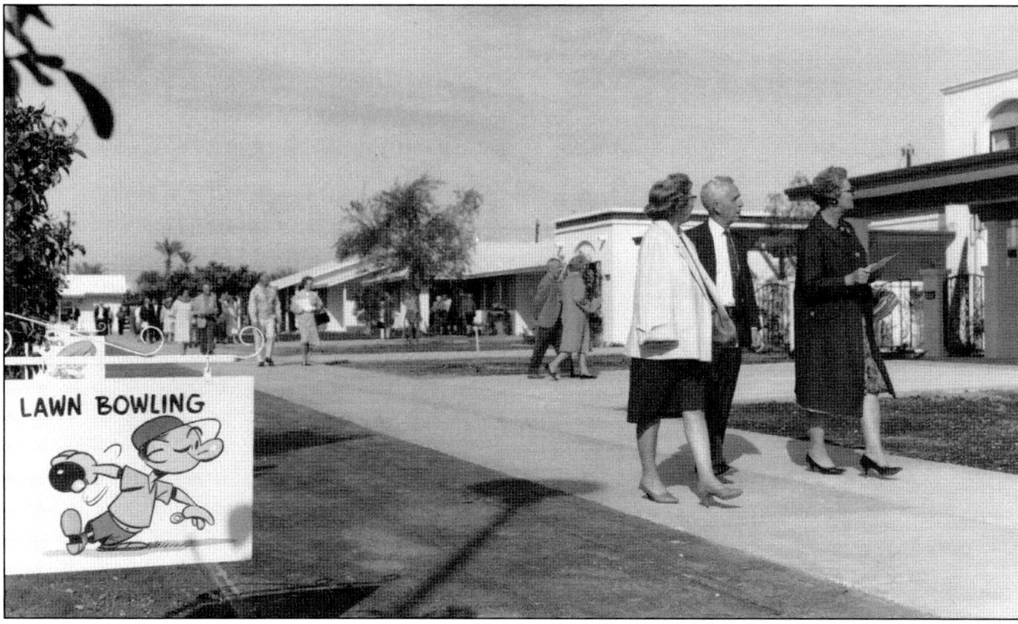


DEVCO's third set of model homes was unveiled in 1965 on Deanne Drive. The first no-frills models in the early 1960s catered to "middle-of-the-road" retirees. By the mid-1960s, designers were offering larger and more contemporary homes that reflected the upscale tastes and desires of new retirees. All those who bought a home from DEVCO in the 1960s also received a complimentary American flag, a practice that continued through the 1970s.

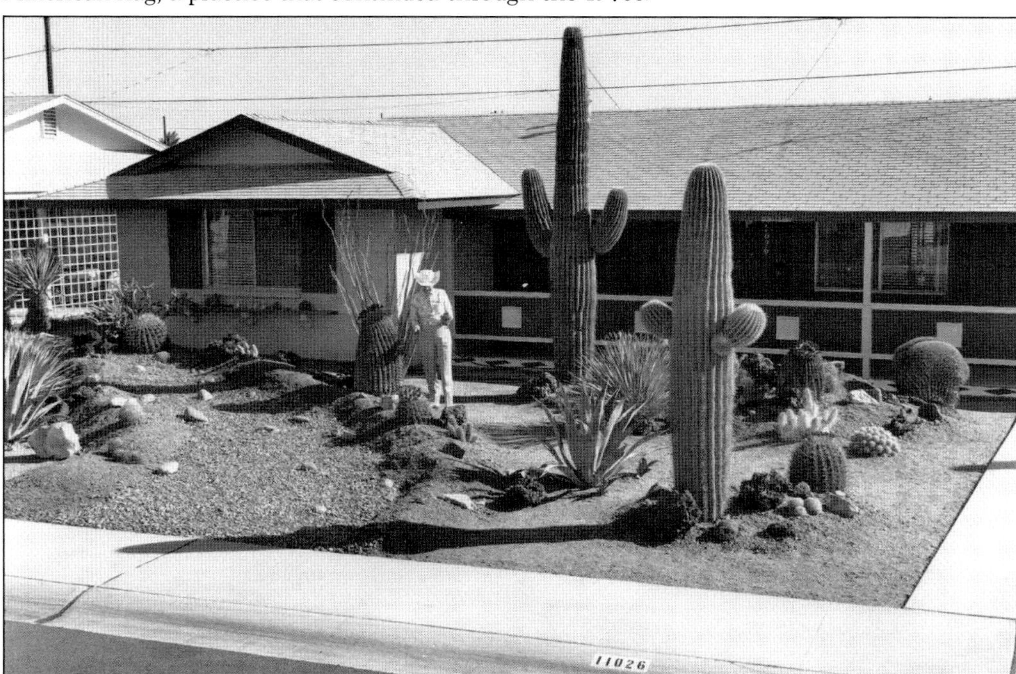


The Mountjoy series was a popular 1960s model home. The basic price for the two-bedroom, two-bathroom home was $12,750. Installing rock lawns or adorning the lawns with cacti were popular trends for those relocating to the desert from the East or Midwest.

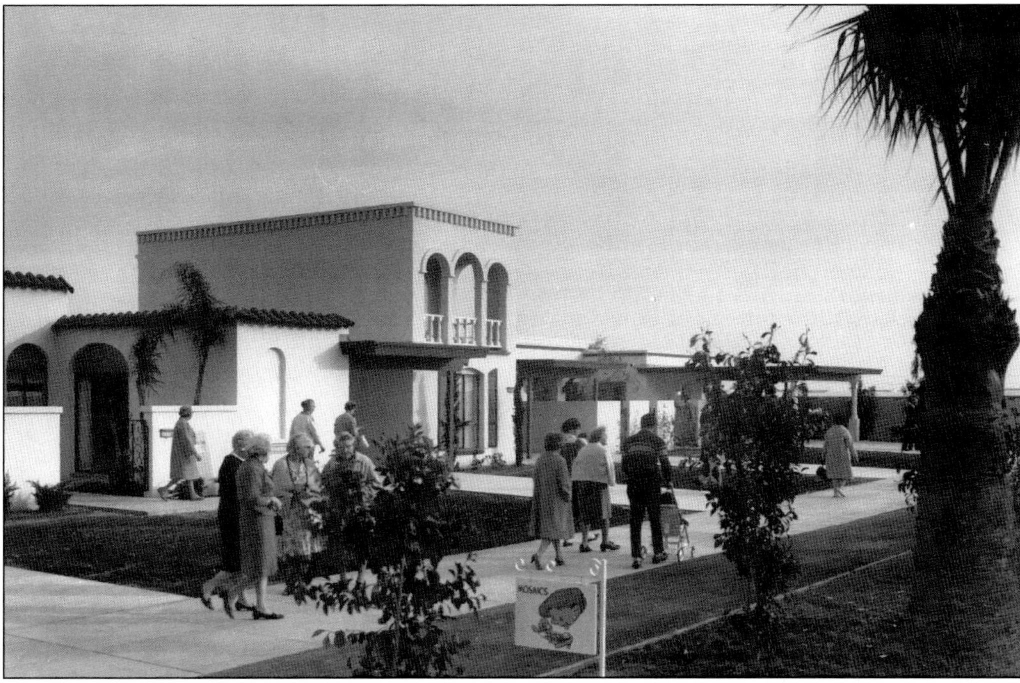

The Mediterranean Villas Series 40 models, introduced in 1966, were dramatically different from the homes first introduced in 1960. The homes were located off 106th Avenue south of Peoria Avenue and sold for a base price of $19,900. Most of the early models were designed by architect Wesley Matthews. By now, buyers had a variety of styles and options to choose from, ranging from duplexes and patio homes to garden apartments.

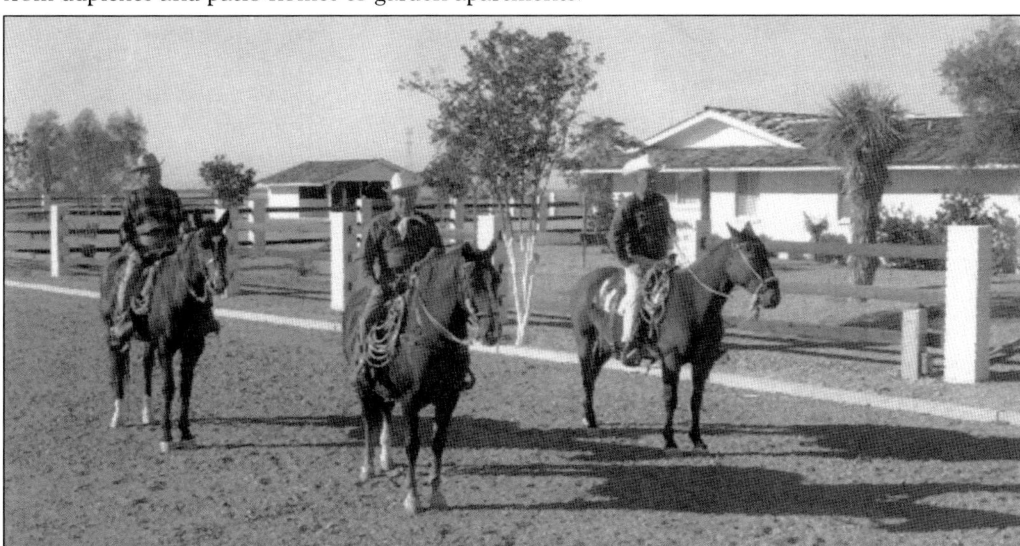

DEVCO opened its most unique model homes in 1967: Rancho Estates. The neighborhood, located south of Youngtown along 111th Avenue, offered 1-acre lots with horse privileges and special fencing. DEVCO president John Meeker figured the larger lots would appeal to retired ranchers and farmers. Shown in November 1967 are, from left to right, Jim Garnett, Walter Young, and Bud Wilson.

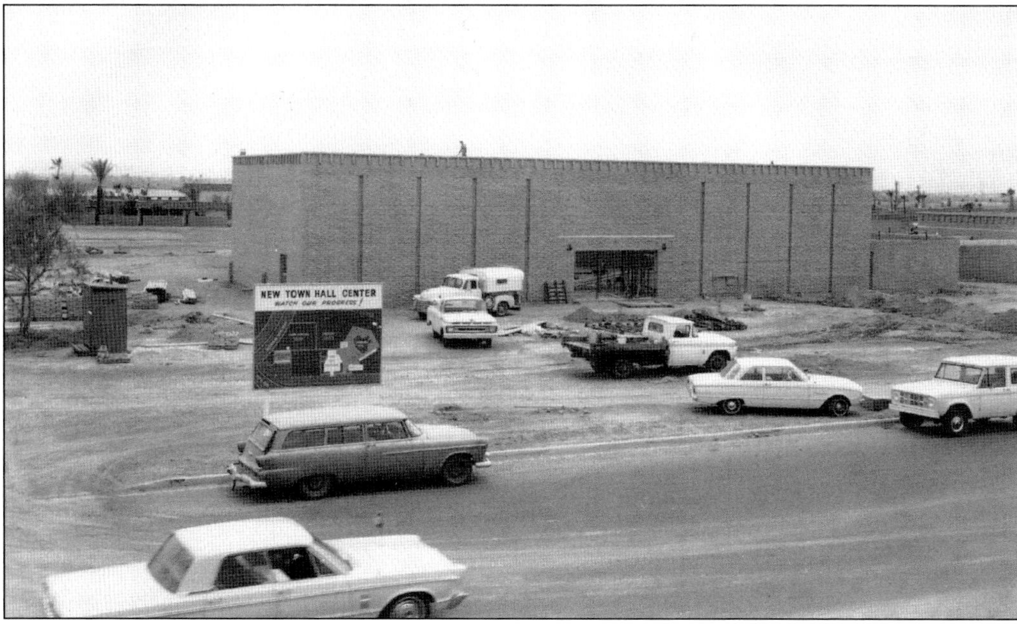


Sun City's third recreation center, Town Hall South, opened in June 1967. Much larger than the previous two centers, the new facility offered tennis courts and an auditorium more than three times larger than the one built in Sun City's first recreation center. The building is today known as Mountain View Recreation Center.

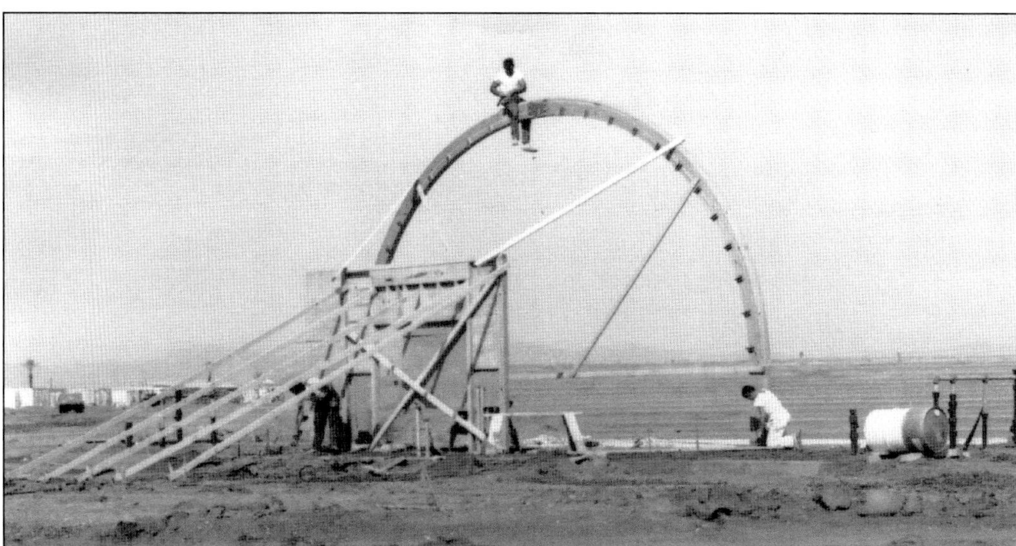

One of DEVCO's most ambitious projects was construction of an outdoor amphitheater, which began in 1965. The Sun Bowl, located at 107th Avenue and Clair Drive, attracted some of the biggest names in show business over the years and served as the site of the community's annual Easter Sunrise Service. The new 7,500-seat amphitheater replaced a smaller outdoor "Greek Theatre" originally located at Fairway Recreation Center.

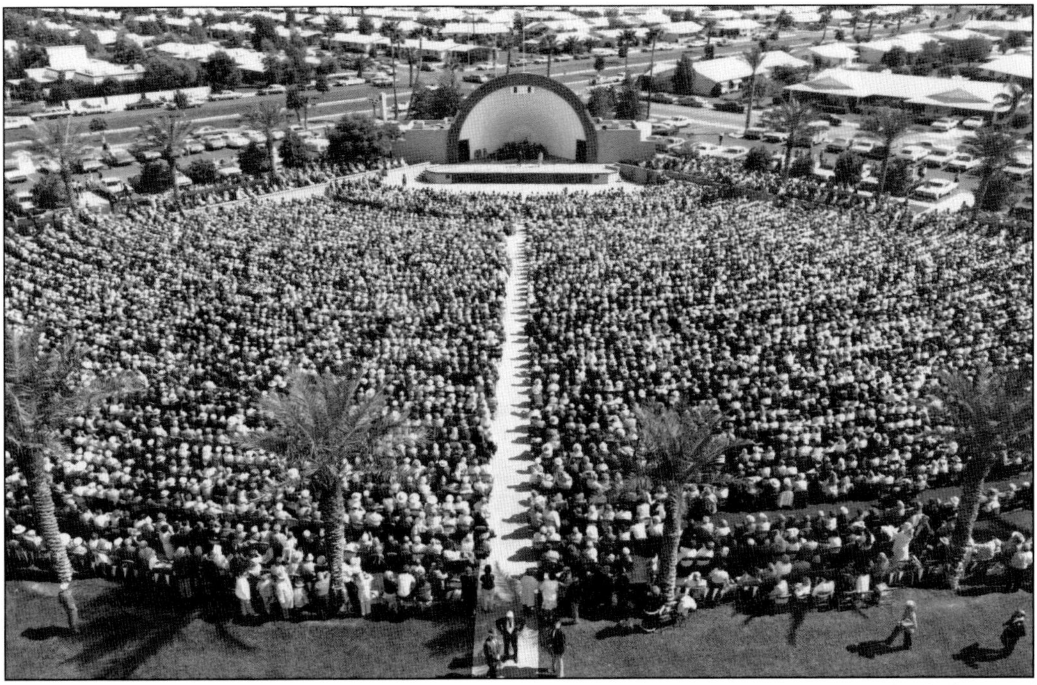

A sell-out crowd attended the official opening of the Sun Bowl in January 1967, which featured entertainment by Liberace. Over the years it has hosted concerts, community celebrations, and club activities. The list of performers who have graced the Sun Bowl's stage include Guy Lombardo, Jimmy Durante, Lawrence Welk, Fred Waring and the Pennsylvanians, Roger Williams, Rich Little, and more.

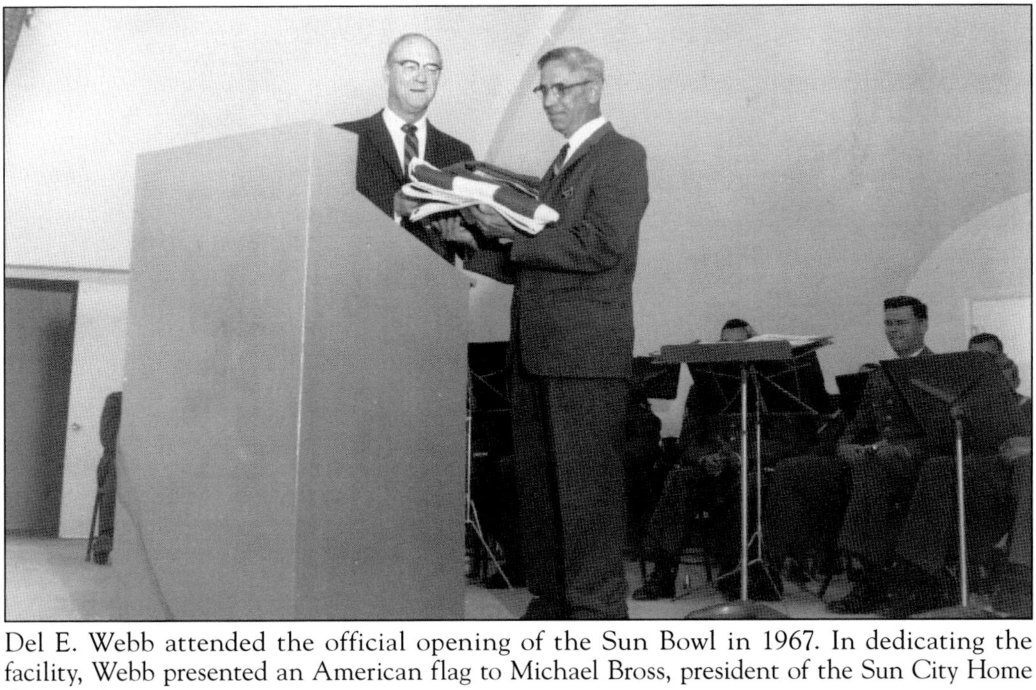

Del E. Webb attended the official opening of the Sun Bowl in 1967. In dedicating the facility, Webb presented an American flag to Michael Bross, president of the Sun City Home Owners Association.

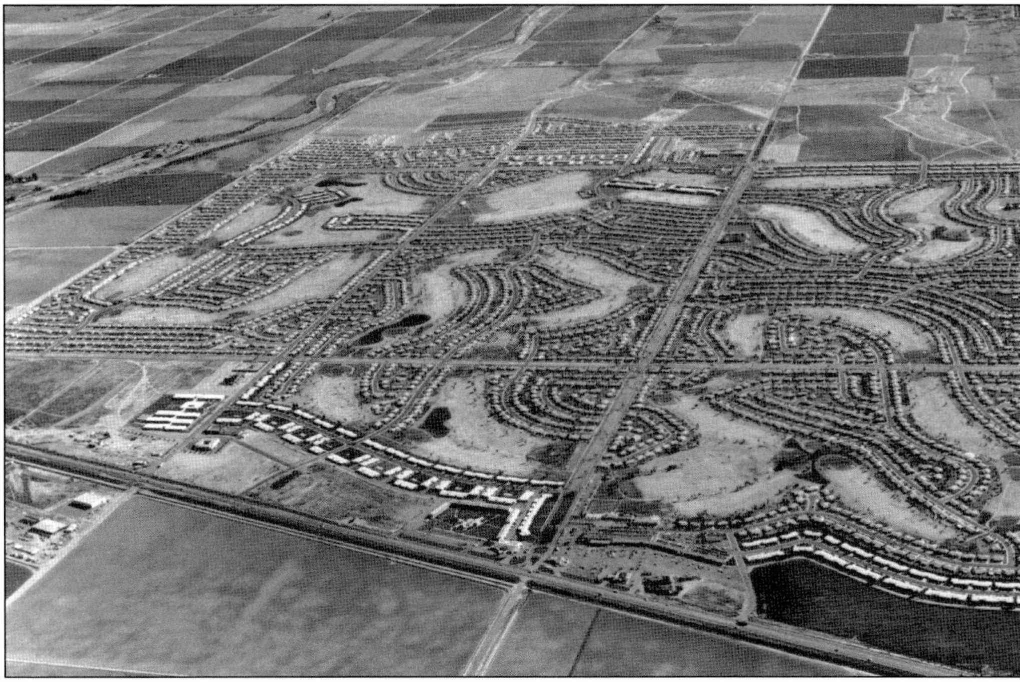

Pictured here is phase one of Sun City, south of Grand Avenue, as it appeared toward the end of the 1960s. DEVCO had used up all its land south of Grand Avenue and in 1968 had been given approval by Maricopa County to begin phase two, which would expand the community north of Grand Avenue. Grand Avenue is the major highway running left to right in this photograph.

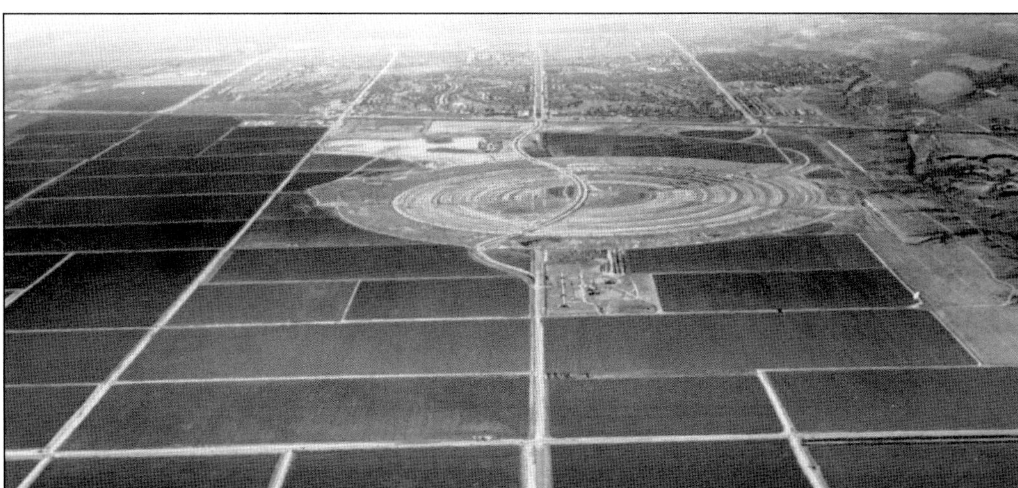

DEVCO began work on phase two in 1969. The new homes were designed to be bigger and more elaborate than those built in Sun City's first phase and were constructed in unique "circular" neighborhoods. Phase two would also include three more recreation centers, two man-made lakes, and a major state-of-the-art hospital and medical complex. The original Sun City can be seen in the distance.

# *Six*

# The Second Decade

As Sun City's first decade came to a close, the Del E. Webb Development Corporation had already begun plans to extend the community north of Grand Avenue. The company had used up all its original land south of Grand Avenue; demand remained strong and there was no reason not to forge ahead with expansion.

Phase one—the original development south of Grand Avenue—included three recreation centers, a hotel, several shopping centers, an outdoor amphitheater, 13 congregations, and the community's first retirement home.

At the start of the second decade, Boswell Memorial Hospital was nearly complete, as was the fourth recreation center and the community's first man-made lake. Phase two extended the community's boundaries 2 miles north to Bell Road.

Original homes in 1960 sold for less than $9,000. New homes in 1970 sold for $30,000. By the end of the decade, new homes were selling well above $60,000. Phase three—the final homes built in Sun City—extended the community's boundaries another 2 miles farther north to Beardsley Road. The community's final recreation center was built in 1979 and turned over to residents in 1980.

By 1978, DEVCO had shifted its focus to a new retirement community just down the road from Sun City. Sun City West would open in December of that year and eventually become the company's second largest retirement community (second, of course, to Sun City). To prepare for its exodus, DEVCO began selling to private companies most of its Sun City holdings—shopping centers, buildings, and remaining vacant land.

During the first two decades, the developer was always there to fix this problem or that, to work closely with government officials to protect Sun City's well-being, and to make sure everything looked perfect to the outside world.

DEVCO had worked with residents to help them learn how to manage the recreation facilities. A home owners association emerged to help maintain community standards established by DEVCO. Most important, volunteers stepped forward to help and continue to do so 50 years later.

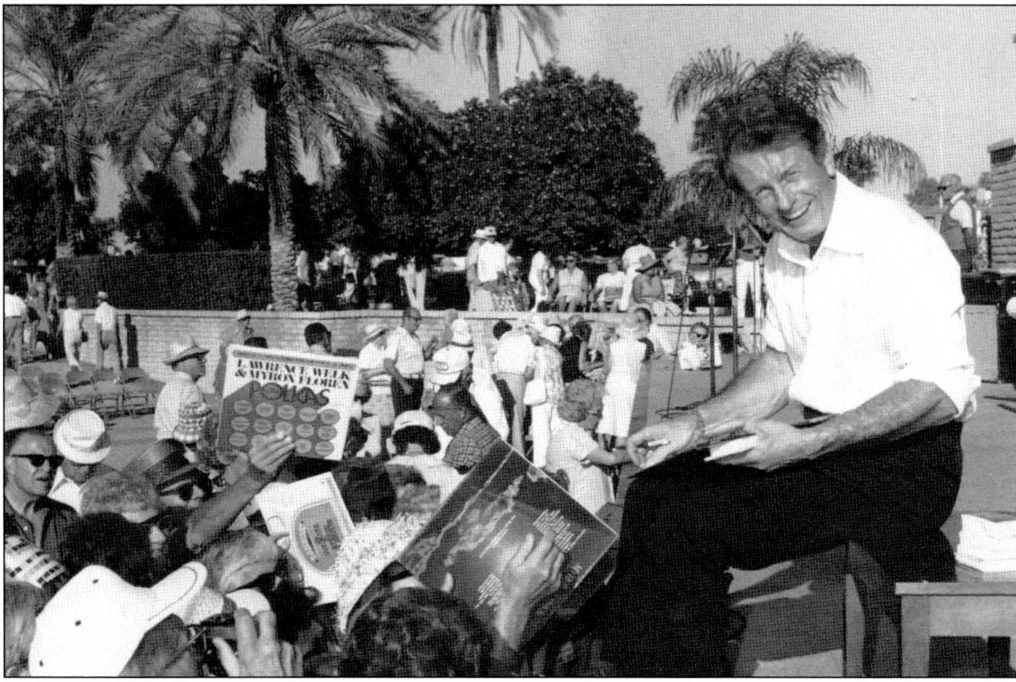


Residents celebrated the community's 10th anniversary in 1970 with a special outdoor concert at the Sun Bowl featuring Myron Floren, a popular accordionist and regular performer on the *Lawrence Welk Show*. By 1970, Sun City had become Arizona's 12th largest city.

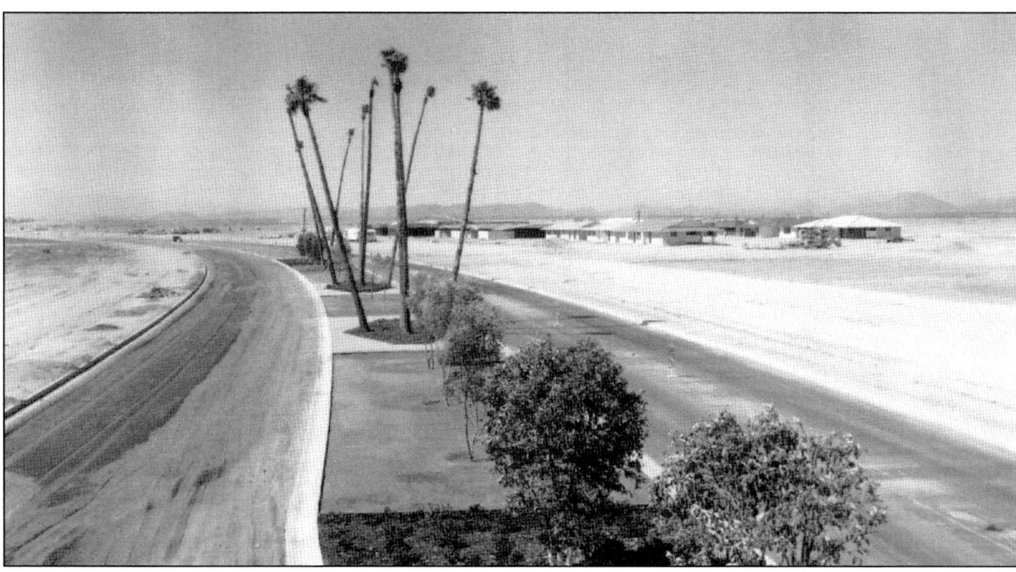

Work begins on Del Webb Boulevard, and new model homes are under construction. As DEVCO expanded Sun City, the company was quick to turn over amenities to residents. The Sun City Community Association, which managed the recreation centers, became the Recreation Centers of Sun City, Inc. In 1972, the first three recreation centers in phase one were renamed Oakmont (Community Center), Fairway (Town Hall North), and Mountain View (Town Hall South).

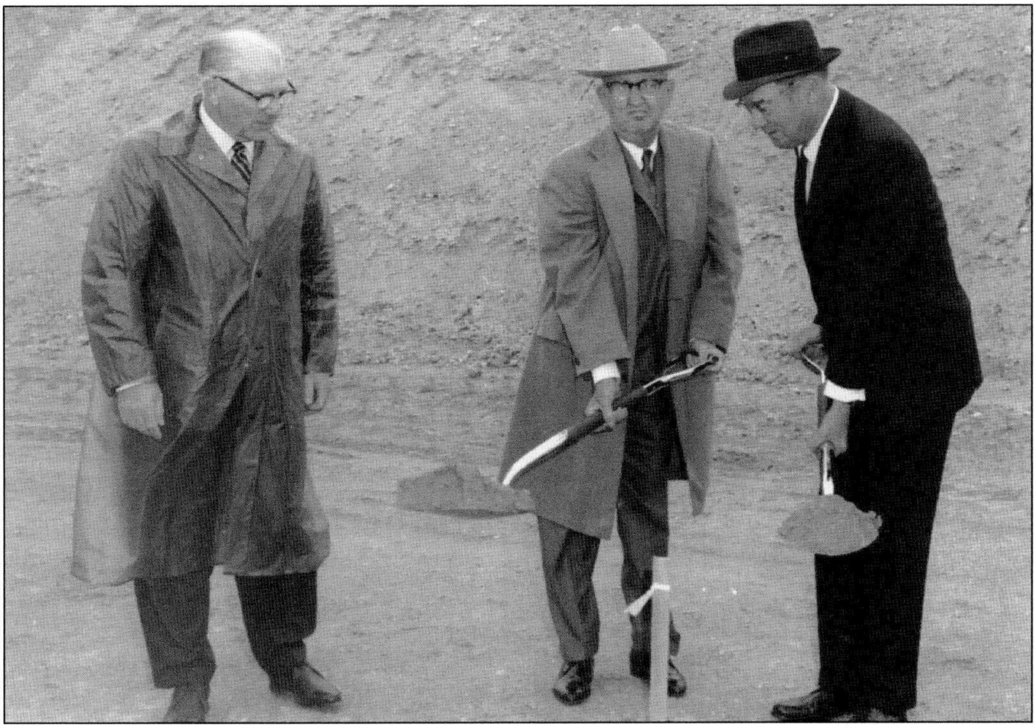

Groundbreaking ceremonies were held January 24, 1969, for the Walter O. Boswell Memorial Hospital. Pictured from left to right, William Chapman of DEVCO, William Boswell, and Del E. Webb take part in the festivities. The hospital was built with funds that included $1 million in private donations from residents, a $1.2 million grant from the Boswell family, and $500,000 from the Del E. Webb Corporation.

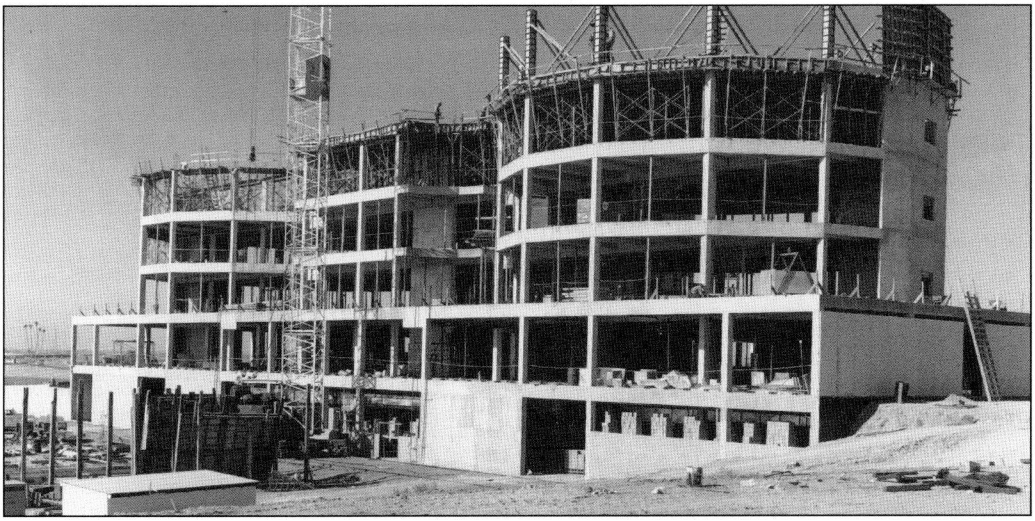

Boswell Memorial Hospital is under construction in December 1969. The first two towers of the four-tower, 120-bed hospital would be dedicated November 6, 1970. The architect had been sent to leading hospitals across the nation in order to design a state-of-the-art facility. The use of circular floors with patient rooms along the outside and the nurse stations in the center was a new concept at the time.

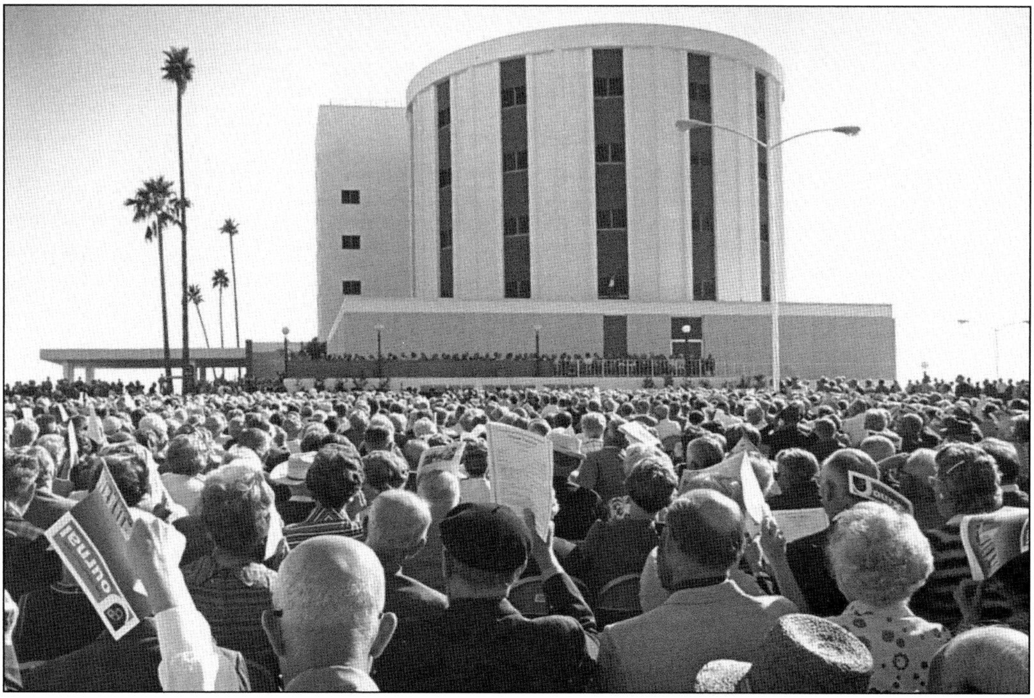

More than 5,000 residents attended the official grand opening of the hospital's first two towers on November 6, 1970. Ten days later, Sun City resident Stuart Beecher became Boswell Memorial Hospital's first patient. A third tower opened in 1979 and the fourth in 1982. (Banner Boswell Medical Center.)

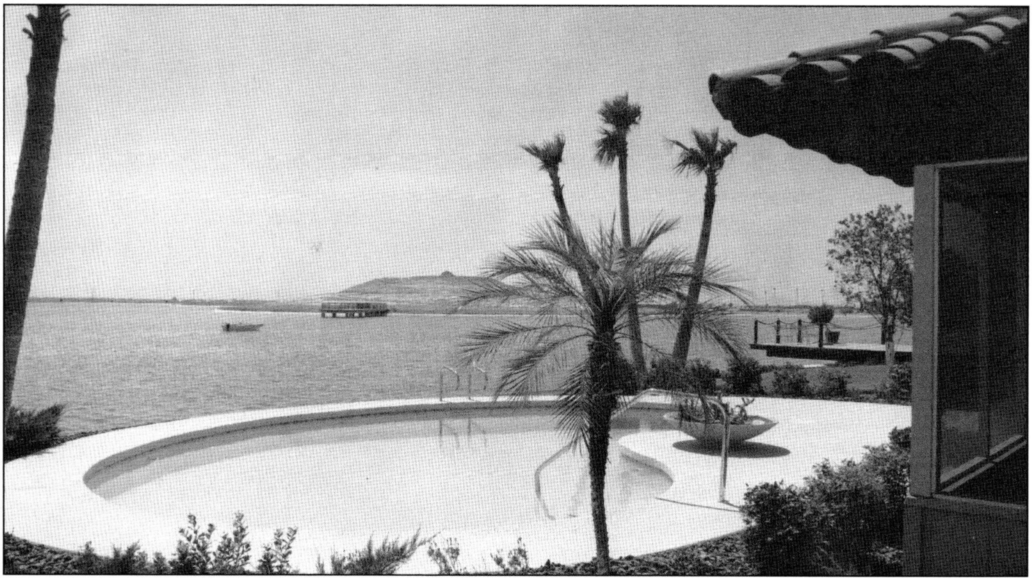

Viewpoint Lake was created next to Lakeview Recreation Center and across the street from Boswell Hospital to offer residents fishing and boating opportunities. The brainchild of DEVCO president John Meeker, it was often referred to as Meeker's Lake, and the mini-mountain as Meeker's Mountain. The mountain was created from dirt removed to create the lake. The mountain offers picnic areas, a picturesque park and waterfall, and mountain-top gazebo.

Visitors to Sun City in the 1970s were welcomed by an elaborate sign at the corner of Del Webb Boulevard and Grand Avenue. The electric sign replaced the simple fountain that greeted residents 10 years earlier. It is rumored that the huge sign was used in a previous life at one of Webb's Las Vegas casinos. It was eventually dismantled in the early 1980s.

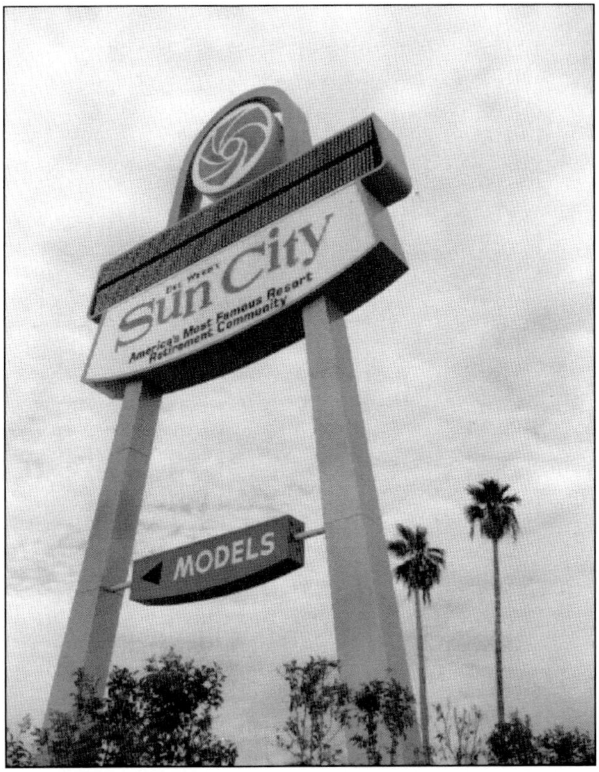


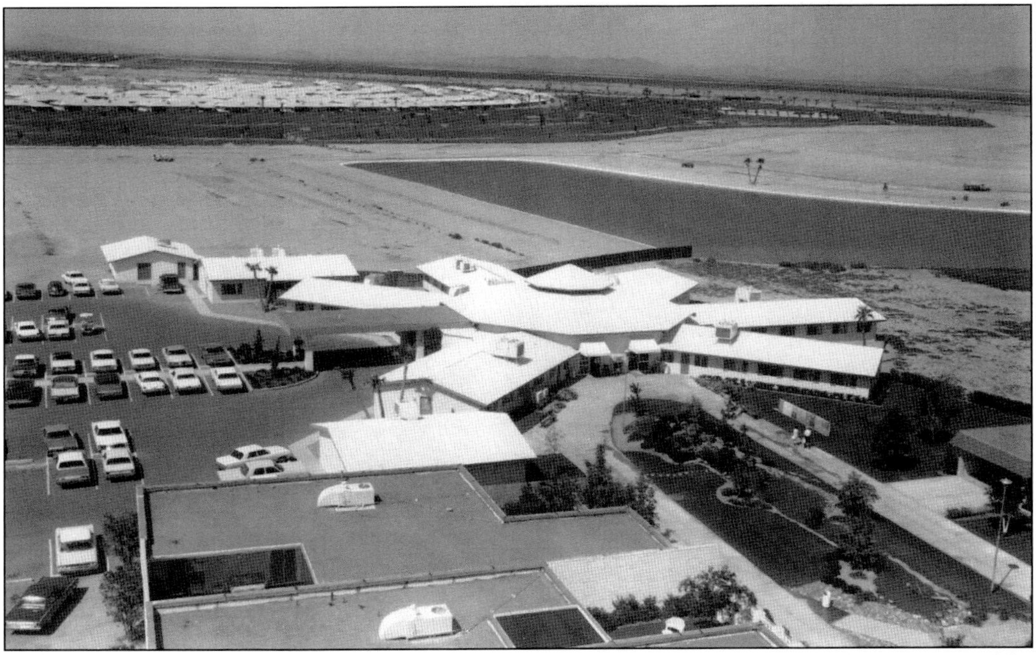

DEVCO's newest sales pavilion to sell homes in phase two was constructed in 1969. Unlike the first five model homes available in 1960, this sleek, ultra-modern sales pavilion displayed the company's newest offerings. It was located on the shores of Viewpoint Lake, just north of Lakeview Recreation Center.

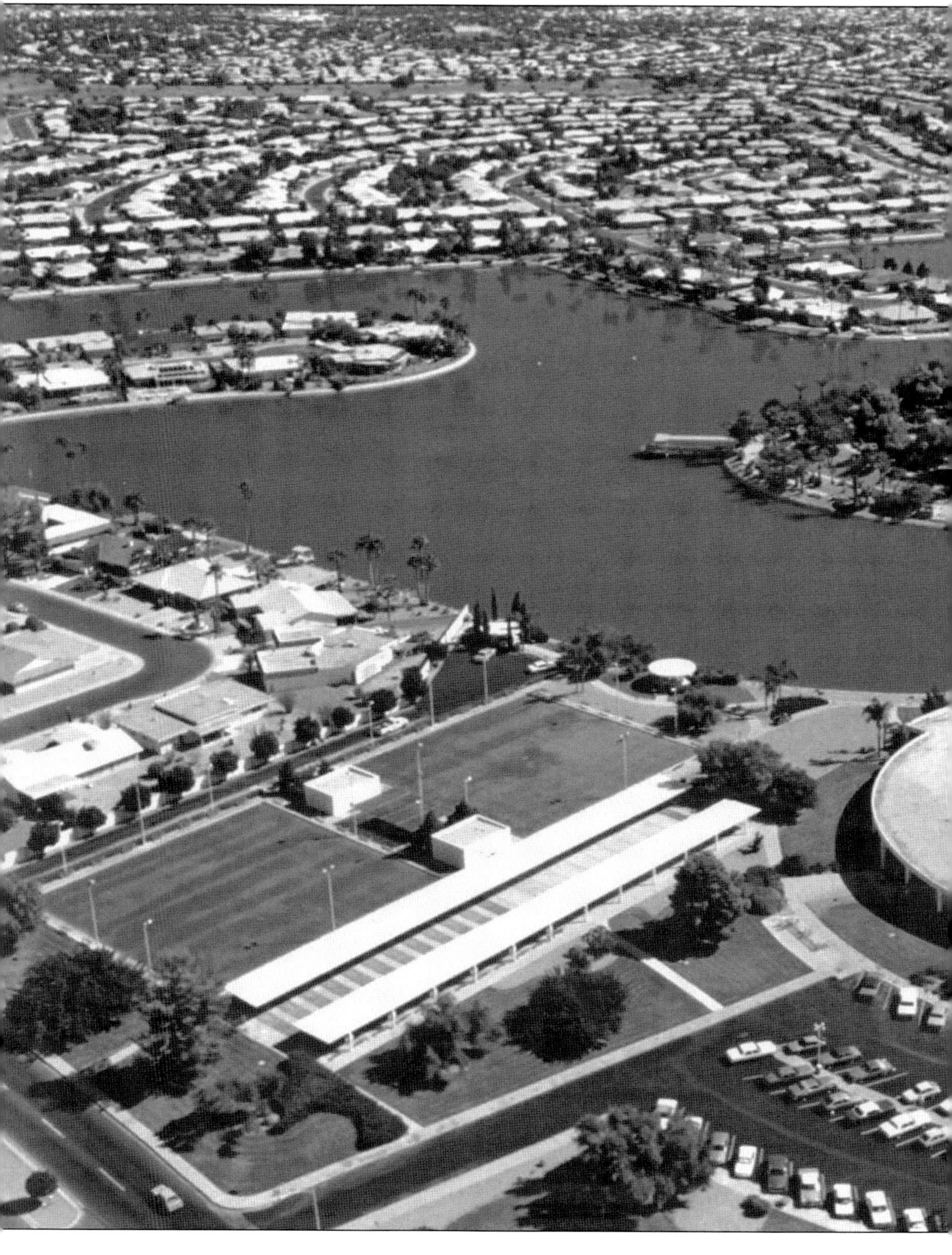

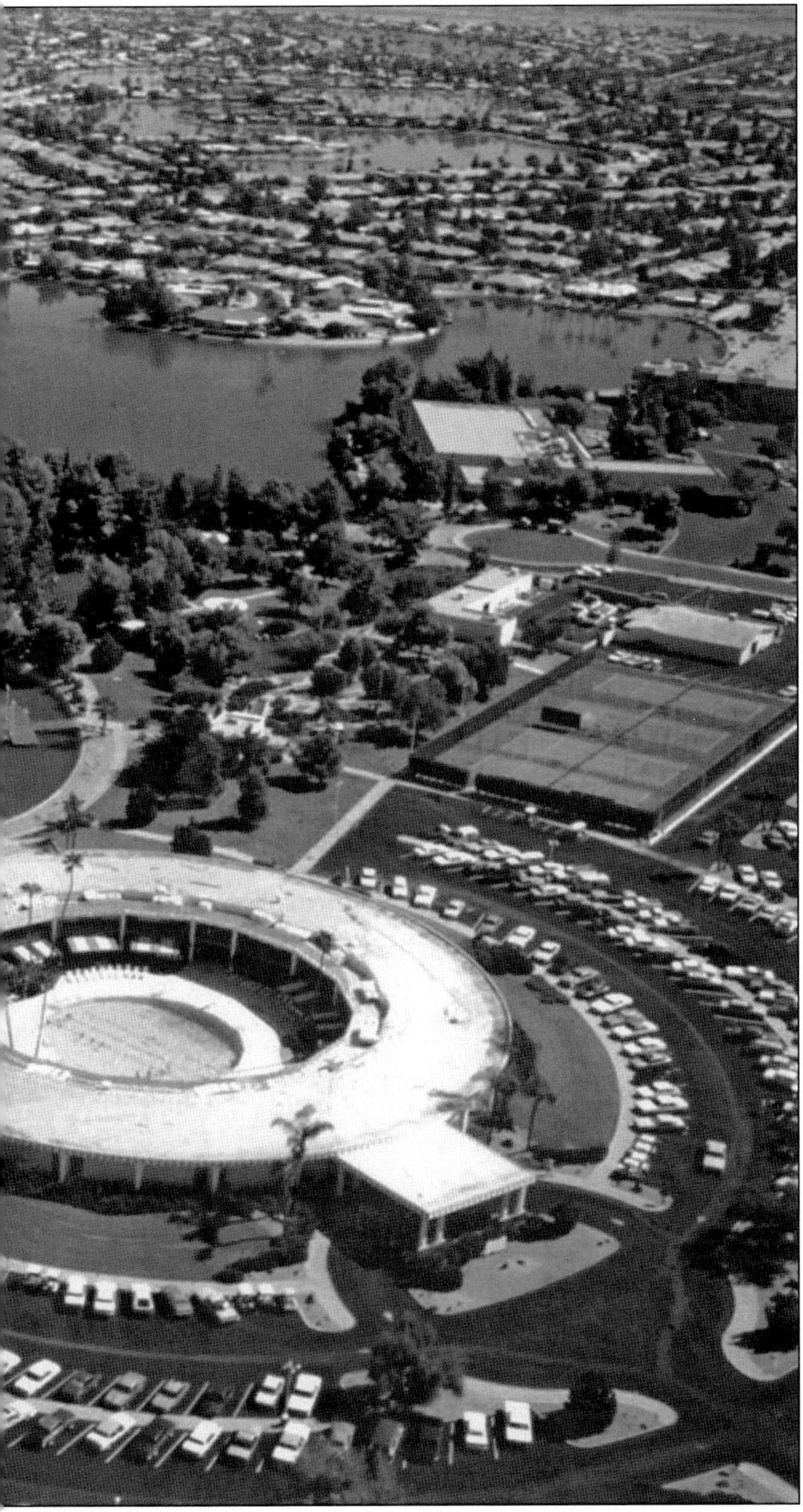

Lakeview Recreation Center opened in January 1970. Sitting adjacent to Viewpoint Lake, Sun City's fourth recreation center was even more elaborate than the first three. The 15.6-acre facility would include a swimming pool, mini-golf course, tennis courts, bocce, lawn bowling, and shuffleboard and would serve as a home to dozens of clubs and other activities. Sun City's first bowling alley was located next to the center, as well as a large picnic area and a mini-mountain overlooking Viewpoint Lake that offered a picturesque view of Sun City. The center today serves as the corporate headquarters for the Recreation Centers of Sun City, Inc. Even as residents were celebrating the opening of their newest recreation center, plans were already under way to build the next facility, Sundial Recreation Center.

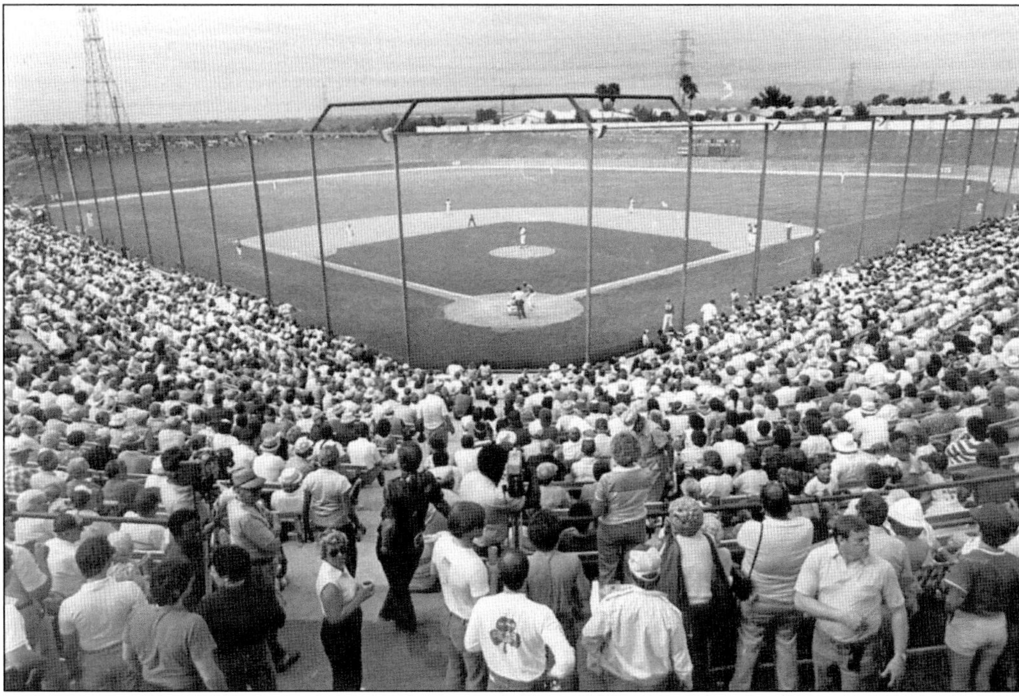

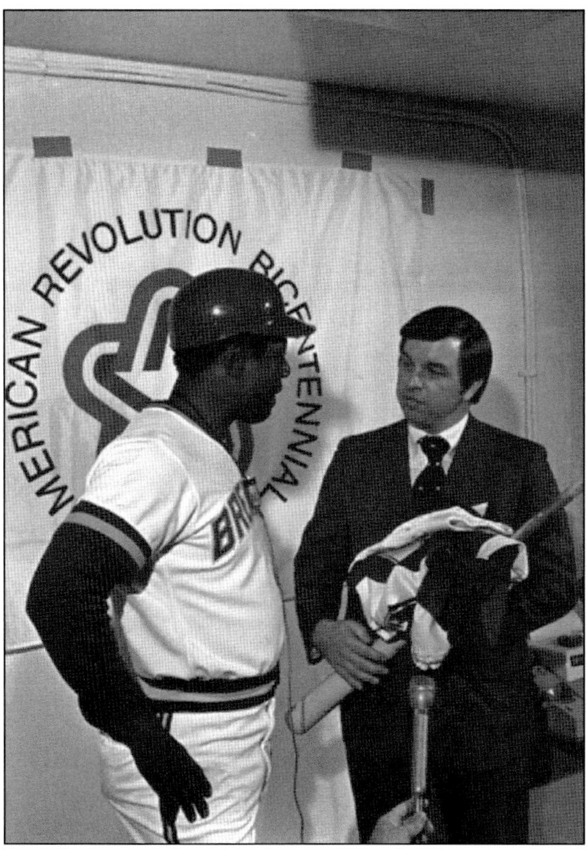


Professional baseball came to Sun City in 1971 with the opening of Sun City Stadium on the corner of 111th and Grand Avenues. The stadium was initially used by the San Francisco Giants, but eventually became the spring training home of the Milwaukee Brewers. The Sun City Saints, a nationally ranked women's fast-pitch softball team, also played at the stadium and was enormously popular with local fans. (Independent Newspapers, Inc.)

Some of baseball's biggest names played at Sun City Stadium. Hank Aaron returned to Milwaukee as the game's reigning home run king and played the last few years of his career with the Milwaukee Brewers. In 1976, "Hammerin' Hank" was welcomed to Sun City when the Brewers arrived for spring training. The Brewers played in Sun City from 1973 to 1985. (Independent Newspapers, Inc.)

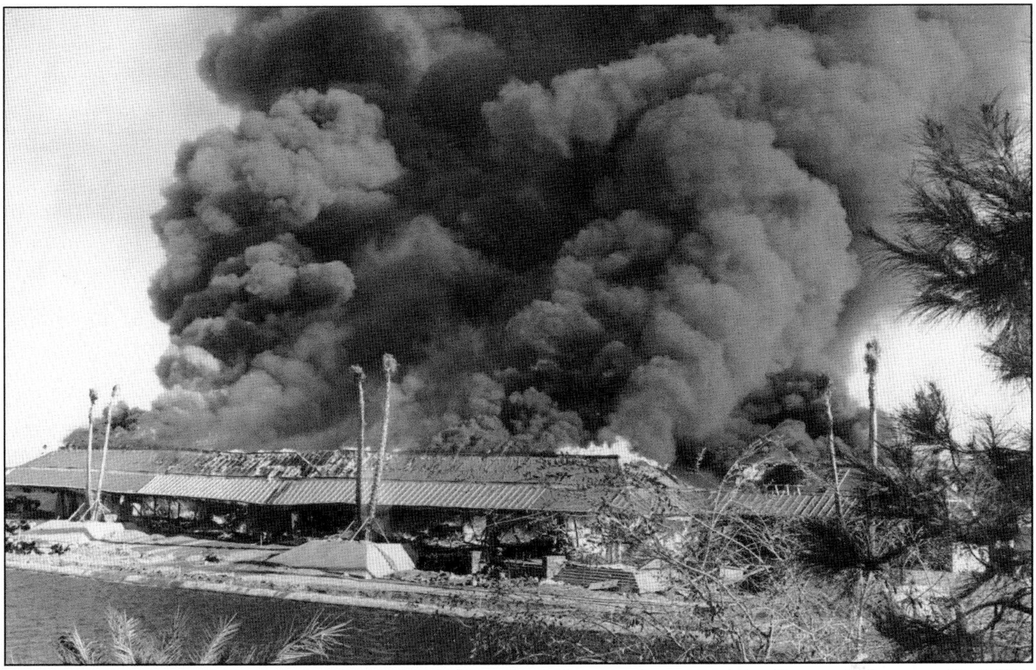

The Lakes Club, a private social club built by DEVCO, was destroyed by fire on February 17, 1972, one month prior to its scheduled opening. The fire was started by the flame from a plumber's torch. The facility, located on Viewpoint Lake across the street from Boswell Hospital, was completely rebuilt and officially opened seven months later.

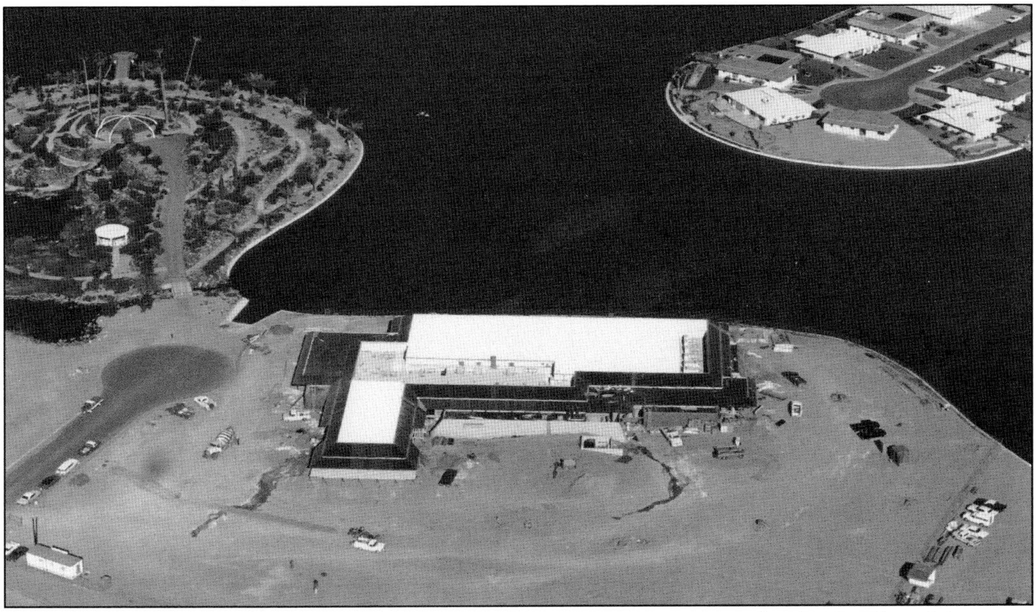

Pictured here is the original Lakes Club under construction just prior to the fire. Lookout Mountain can be seen to the left of the club. The mountain sits between the Lakes Club and Lakeview Recreation Center on Thunderbird Boulevard. Over the years, the Lakes Club hosted some of the community's most important social events. DEVCO sold the club in 1981, and today it serves as a medical office complex.

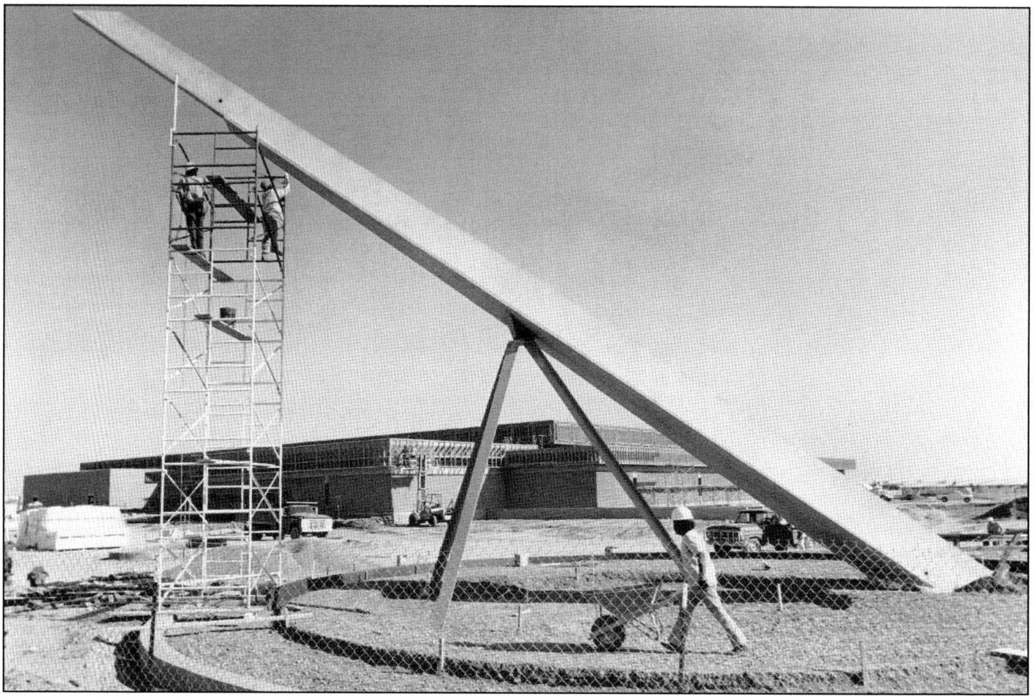

The community's fifth recreation center opened in April 1973. Sundial Recreation Center, located at 103rd Avenue and Boswell Boulevard, featured the community's first indoor swimming pool as well as a giant auditorium that held 1,800 people. Outside the center was a sundial stretching 36 feet tall and 67 feet, 8 inches long.

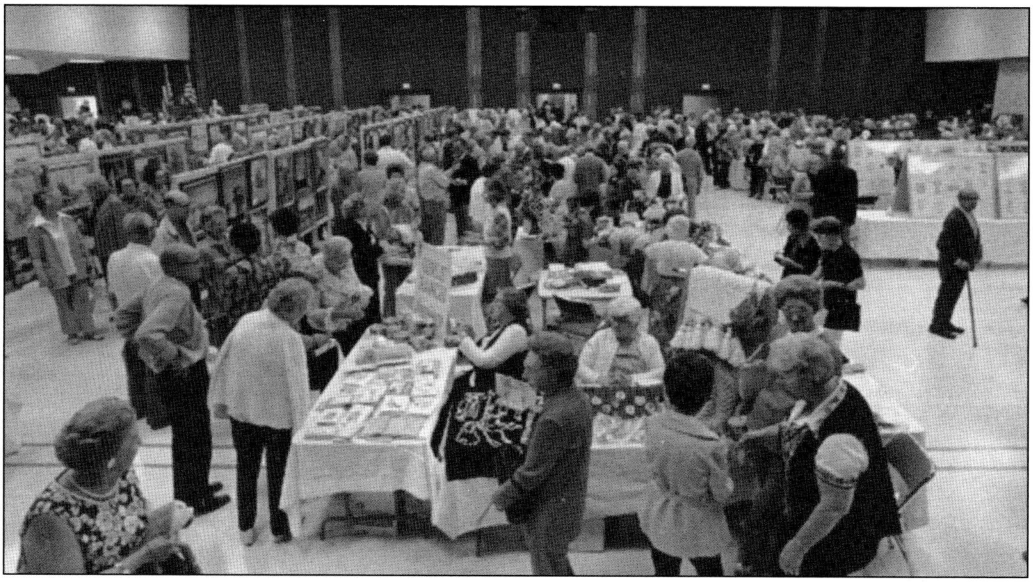

Sundial Recreation Center hosted its first annual Sun City Arts and Crafts Festival in 1974, a tradition that continues to this day. Held the weekend after Thanksgiving, the festival allows Sun City arts and crafts clubs to sell their creations to the general public. The first fall arts and crafts celebrations dated back to 1962 when clubs at the Community Center and Town Hall held fall festivals.

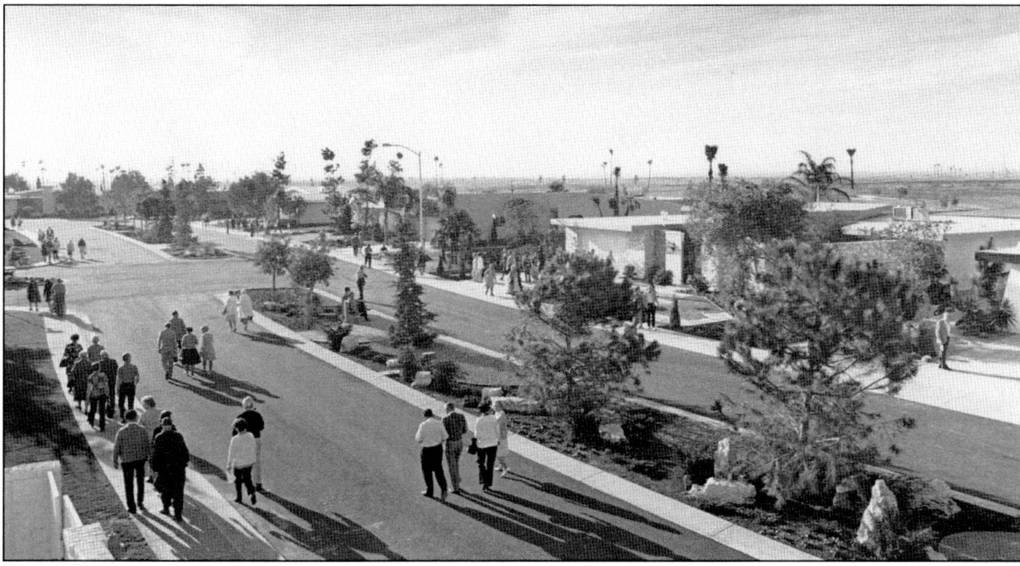

DEVCO moved into phase three, the final phase of Sun City's development, with the opening of its newest model homes series in 1974. The Galleria 100 models were located on Wheatridge Drive and were the first Sun City homes to be constructed north of Bell Road. The last model homes, the Heritage Series, were unveiled in 1976 and ranged in price from $25,990 to $54,990.

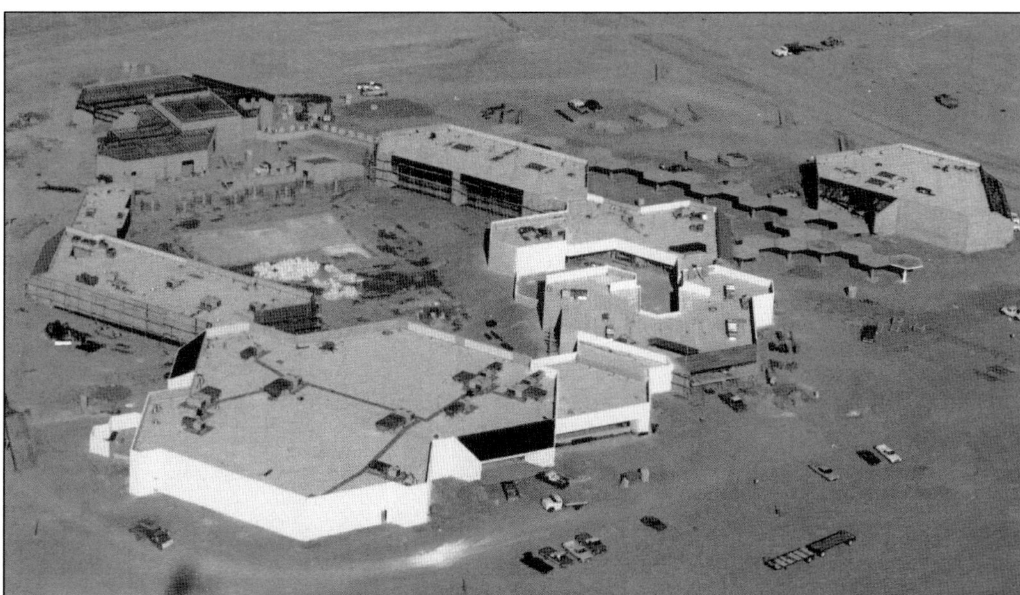

Sun City celebrated the nation's bicentennial by opening its sixth recreation center, aptly named Bell Recreation Center because it was home to a replica of the famous Liberty Bell. Shown here under construction in 1975, the facility was the largest constructed in Sun City. Encompassing more than 27 acres, the center included a bowling alley, library, social halls, and more.

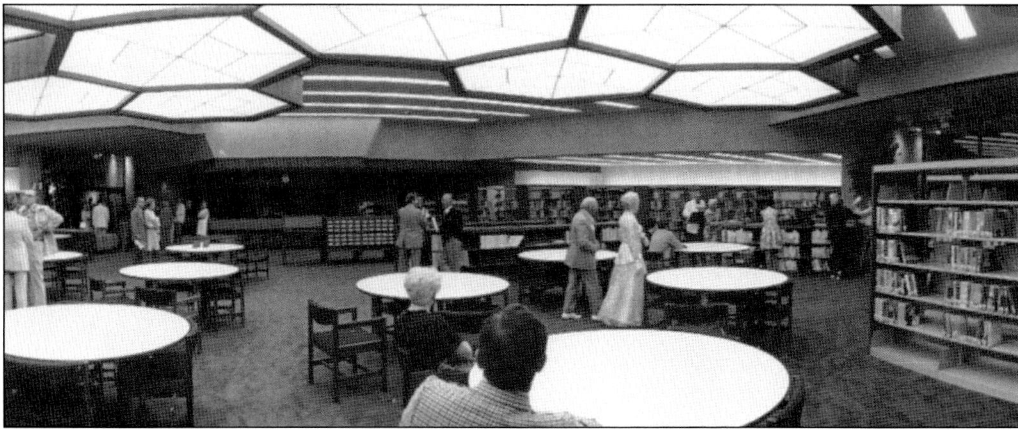

Bell Recreation Center, located at Ninety-ninth Avenue and Bell Road, would house Sun City's second library (the first was located at Fairway Recreation Center). The 10,250-square-foot library has room for 50,000 volumes. Both the library and recreation center opened in April 1976. The recreation center today also serves as home to the Sun City Visitors Center.

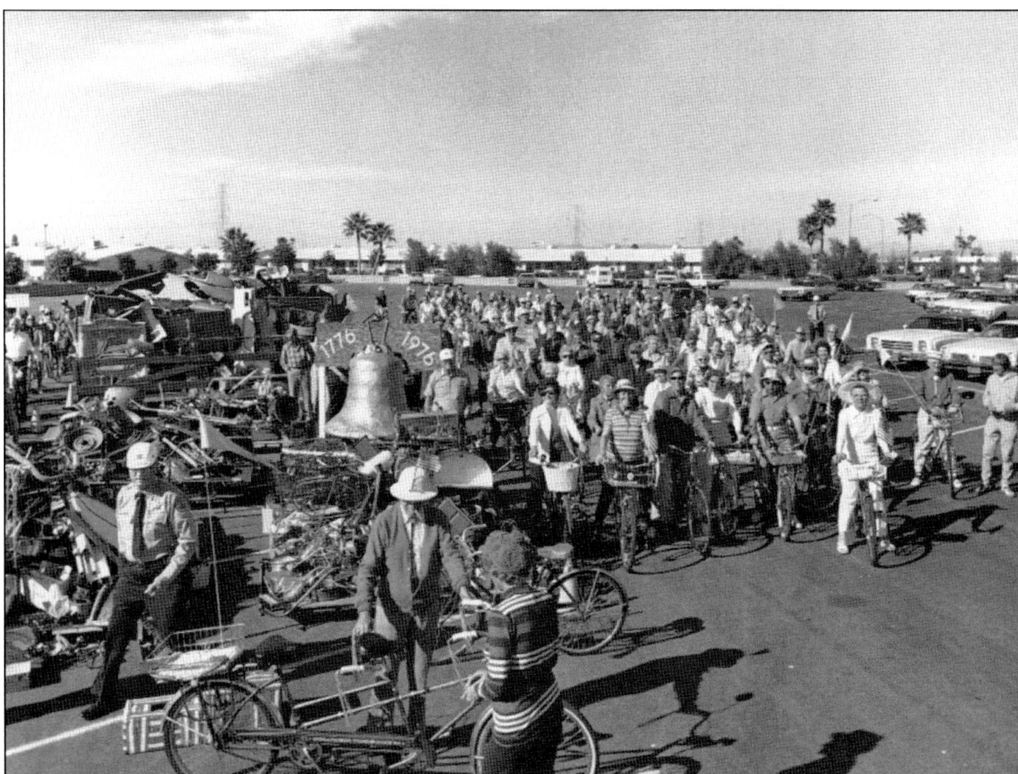


Residents opted to celebrate the nation's bicentennial by creating their own copy of the Liberty Bell. A scrap metal drive was conducted on January 15, 1976, during which more than 1,500 residents delivered over 7,000 pounds of materials to Sun City Stadium. Items were melted down and sent to a foundry in the Netherlands where the replica was cast in the same mold used to create the original bell in 1752.

The Liberty Bell returned to Sun City on July 5, 1976, and was officially dedicated on November 11 in Memorial Garden at Bell Recreation Center. Memorial Garden is home to several other local landmarks, including a statue honoring Sun City's founder, Del E. Webb. The bell's base contains a time capsule set to be opened in 2026. (Independent Newspapers, Inc.)

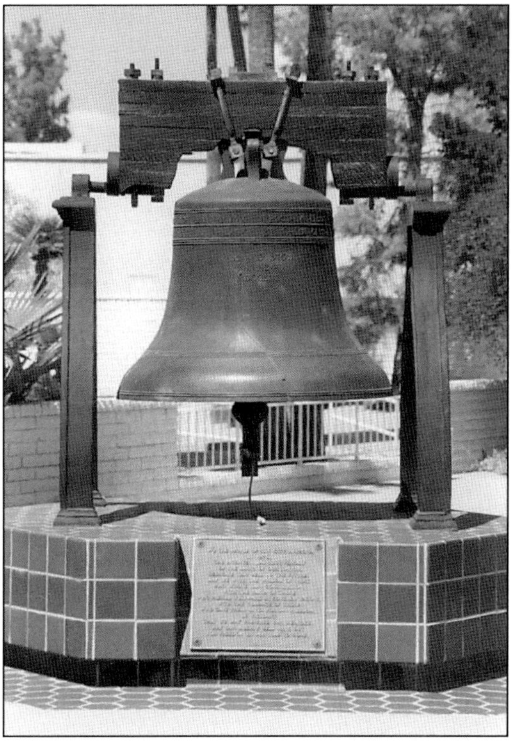

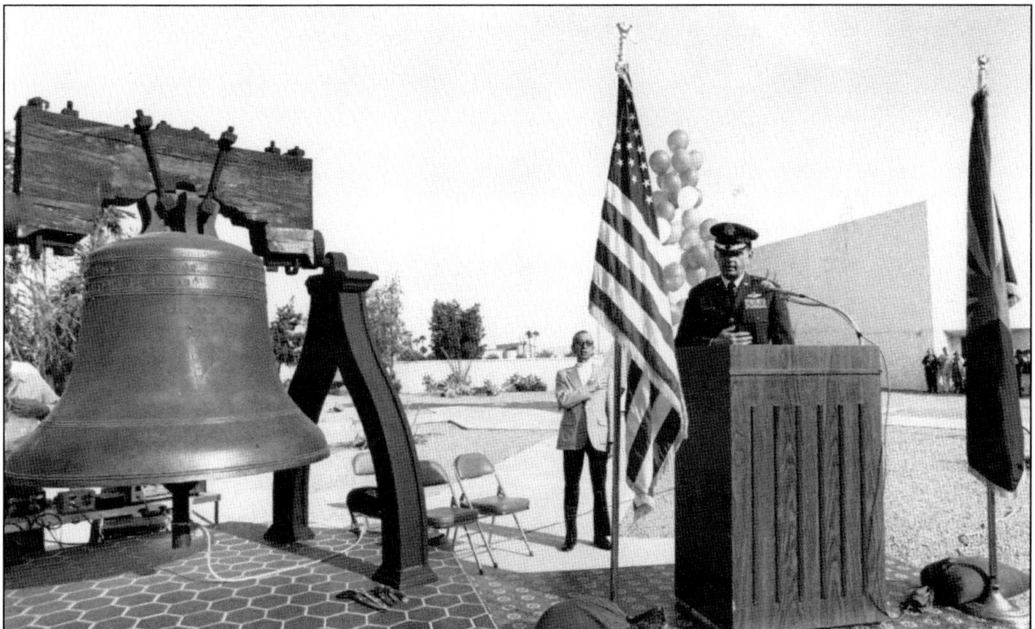

The bell is the centerpiece of the community's annual Ring the Bell ceremony held every Fourth of July since 1983. The ceremony was the brainchild of Doug Morris, editor of the *Sun City Citizen* (now *Independent*), who encouraged readers to "ring the bell" to celebrate freedom. Luke Air Force Base brigadier general Michael Durgan was the guest speaker at the first ceremony. Morris is on the left. (Independent Newspapers, Inc.)

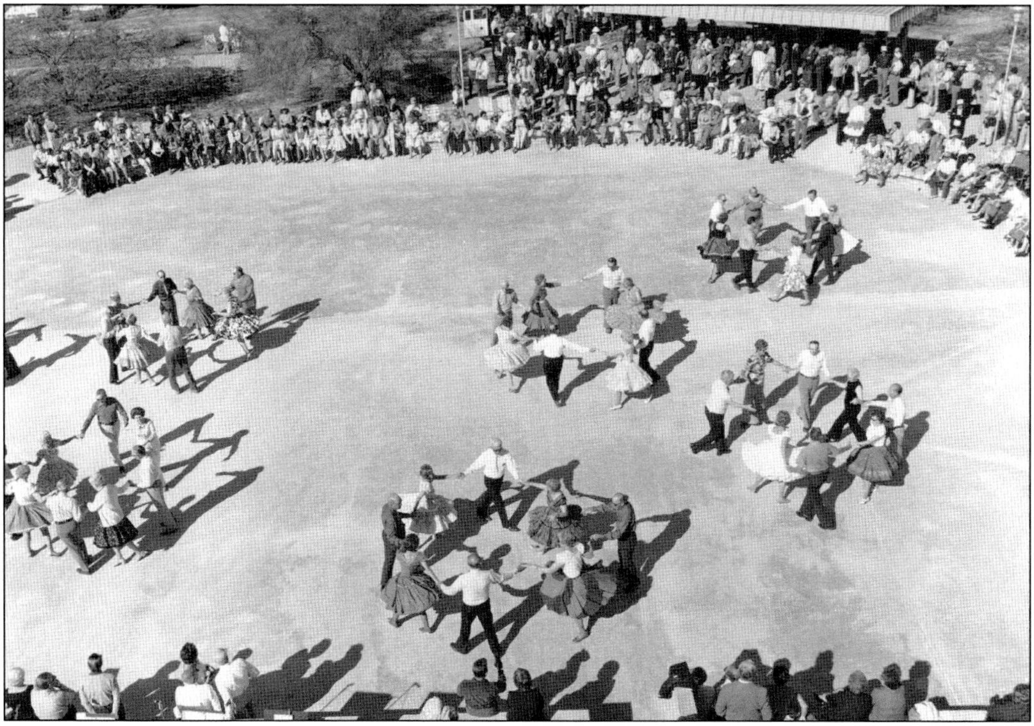

When Del Webb purchased the original land for Sun City from the Boswell Company, an area called Heading Ranch was included in the deal. Located north of Sun City traveling toward Lake Pleasant, DEVCO developed the property into a recreational area for Sun City residents. The area included a shooting range and large picnic area often used for community barbecues and dances. A massive flood destroyed the property in 1980.

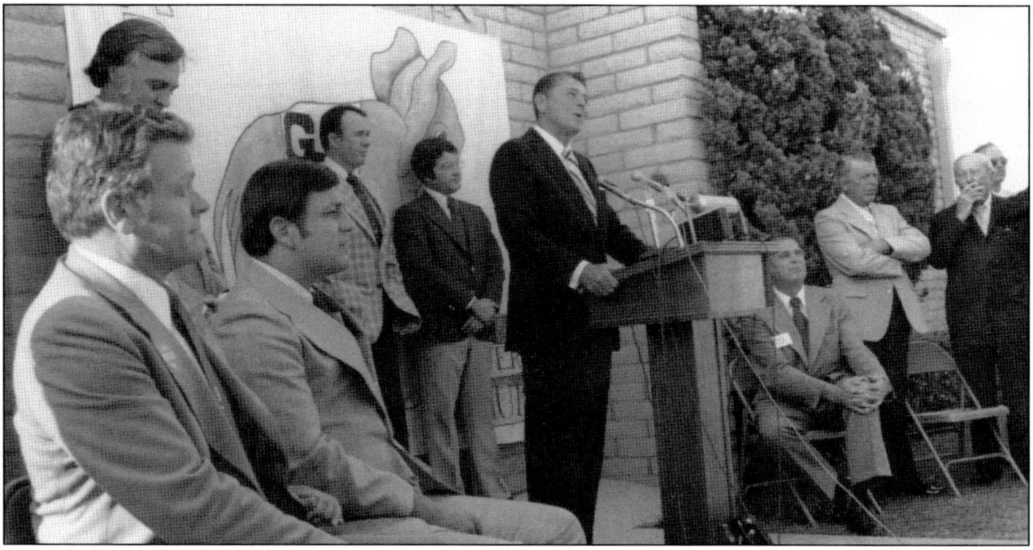

California governor Ronald Reagan visited Sun City in 1976 while campaigning for the Republican nomination for president. Reagan addressed a large crowd at the Sun Bowl. The governor was unsuccessful in his bid that year to gain his party's nomination, losing to Gerald Ford. Reagan returned to Sun City in 1983, this time as president of the United States.

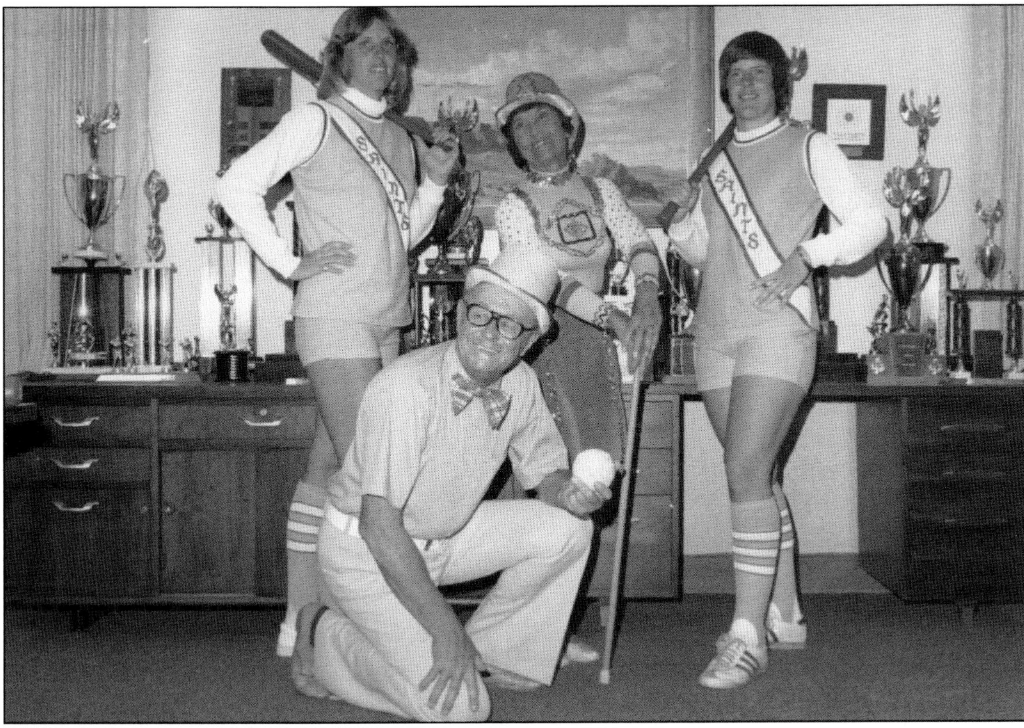


The Sun City Saints, a women's fast-pitch softball team sponsored by local merchants, captured a national championship in 1979. The team was very popular with local fans and consistently attracted home game crowds in excess of 2,000. Joe Davisson, president of the Saints Booster Club, celebrates the team's success with two players and Sun City Poms organizer Corrine Leslie, center.

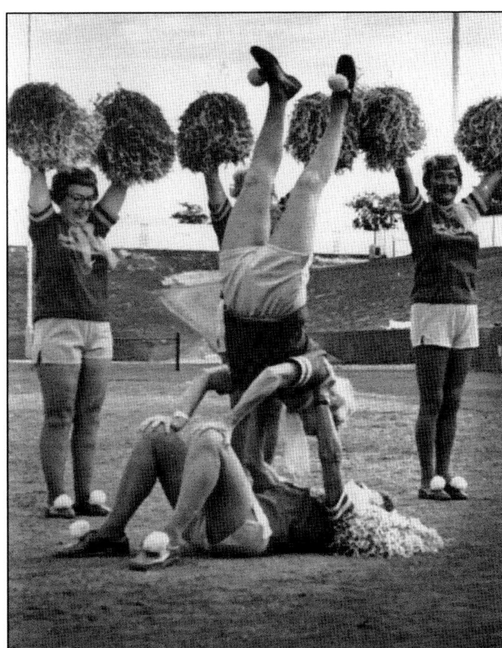

A local "cheerleading" squad was formed in 1979 by Ray and Corrine Leslie to help cheer on the Saints. It marked the first appearance of the now famous Sun City Poms. The Poms ranged in age from 61 to 84 and shattered stereotypes of senior citizens. Over the years, the squad has performed in parades, festivals, and competitions throughout the nation. (Independent Newspapers, Inc.)

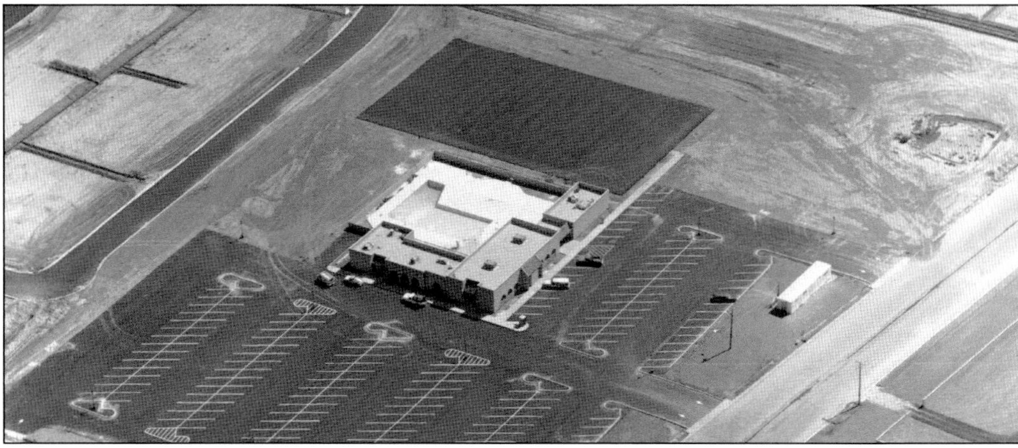

Sun City's final recreation center opened in 1979. A seventh facility, known originally as Union Hills Recreation Center, was meant to provide activities within walking distance of those living in the northern part of the community. Cost overruns at Bell Center forced DEVCO to cancel its plans for the seventh center. An outcry from angry residents who felt they were promised their own facility prompted the company to quickly build the smaller Marinette Center. It was enlarged in 1984.

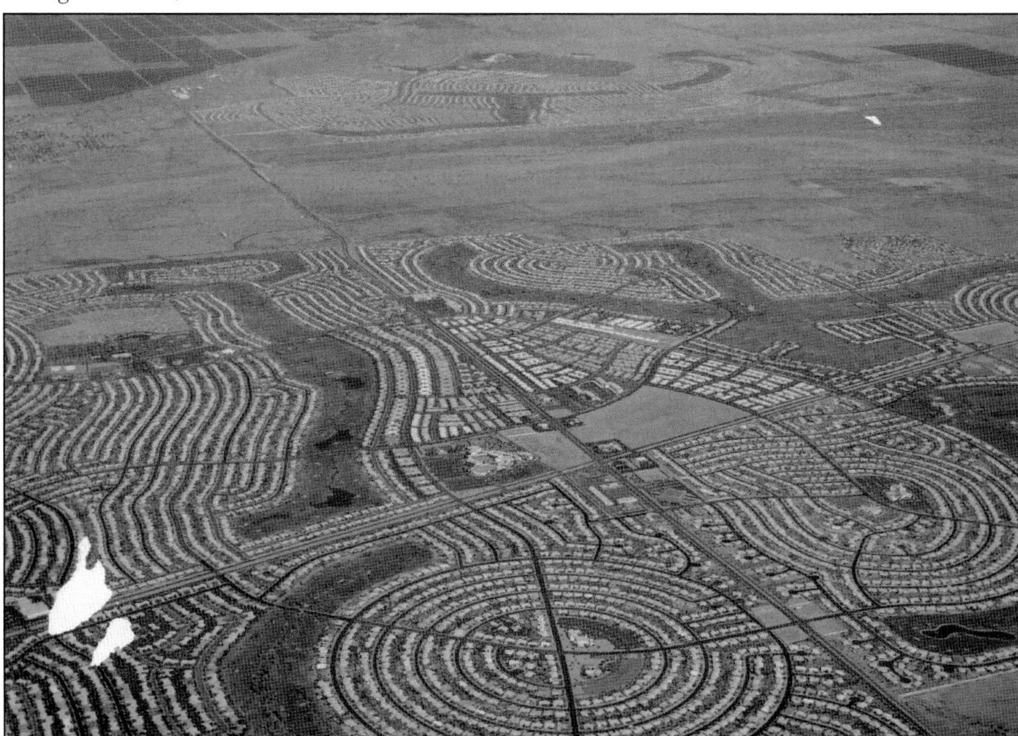

By 1978, Sun City was preparing for life after Del E. Webb. The developer was wrapping up its involvement in Sun City and turning its full attention to building and selling Sun City West, seen here in the upper right corner of the photograph. The view here is looking west with Bell Road running diagonally from the lower right corner out to the new community. The massive Bell Recreation Center is in the middle of the photograph.

# *Seven*

# The Sun City Lifestyle

When Sun City opened in 1960, Del Webb was quoted as saying "his company built the homes, but it was the residents of Sun City who built the community."

Indeed, no one could imagine at the outset what sort of community Sun City would become. After all, Del Webb was a developer. His company specialized in design and construction. Overseeing an entire community—and a new type of community at that—was uncharted territory for the company.

But something unique occurred once people bought their homes. Something no one could have predicted.

They met new friends. They socialized. They volunteered. They played.

The definition of "retirement" was completely rewritten by those who relocated to Sun City. Retirement no longer meant quiet, peaceful hours lounging in a hammock or rocking chair. In Sun City, one grew younger, not older.

Early publicity photographs and advertisements showed residents playing golf, enjoying backyard barbecues with new friends, learning new crafts, and more. Life was good. They had discovered the "Fountain of Youth."

The "Sun City lifestyle" was more than just a promotional gimmick created by the Webb marketing department. It truly did exist and remains as much a lure to new retirees today as it did in 1960.

In the early days, the developer provided the amenities that created the "Sun City lifestyle," an image that has become synonymous with active-adult retirement living. But that lifestyle remains just as positive today, thanks to residents who are proud of their community and devoted to protecting the quality of life perpetuated by those who settled in Sun City before them.

Sun City residents have everything they need right in their own community. The community's boundaries stretch 3 miles wide and 7 miles long, and within those boundaries are 7 recreation centers, 11 golf courses, a hospital, 16 shopping centers, 31 churches, 3 private country clubs, and 2 lakes.

In the early days, the developer provided the amenities that created the "Sun City lifestyle," but it was the residents that turned them into beehives of activity. Today there are hundreds of different clubs and activities available, from competitive sports to service clubs to arts and crafts. Keeping the mind, body, and spirit in top shape continues to be the top priority of residents eager to live long, healthy lives.

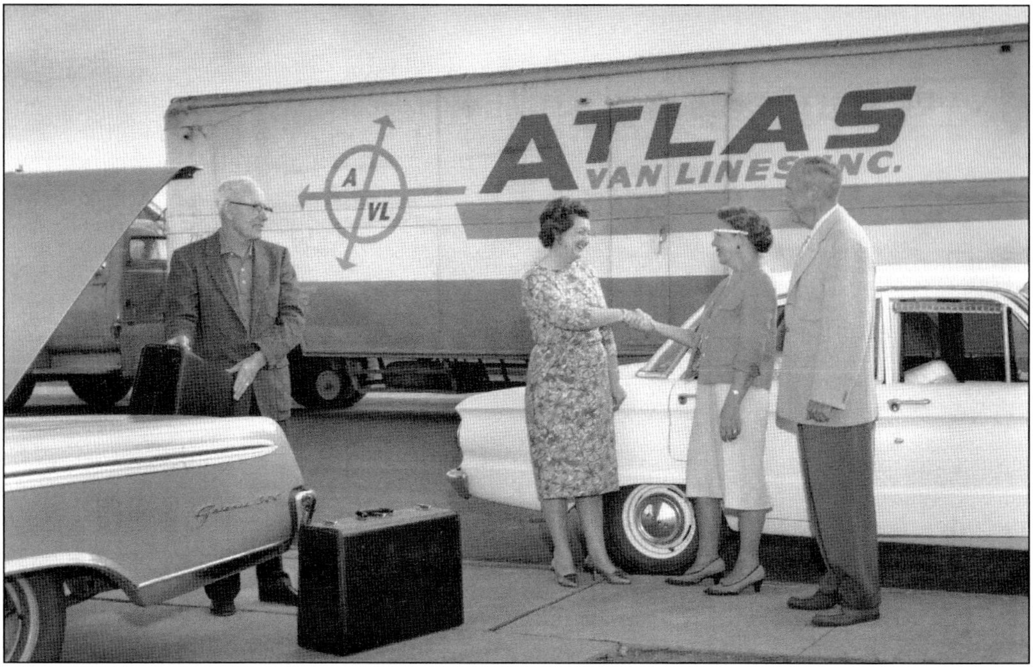


Welcome to Sun City! Most experts predicted Sun City would fail simply because they surmised retirees would be reluctant to pull up stakes, leave their families behind, and move to a new community. An early Webb publicity shot depicted Sun City residents greeted at their doorstep by new neighbors. The photograph was not far off the mark, as most new residents quickly met new friends and found plenty of activities to occupy their time.

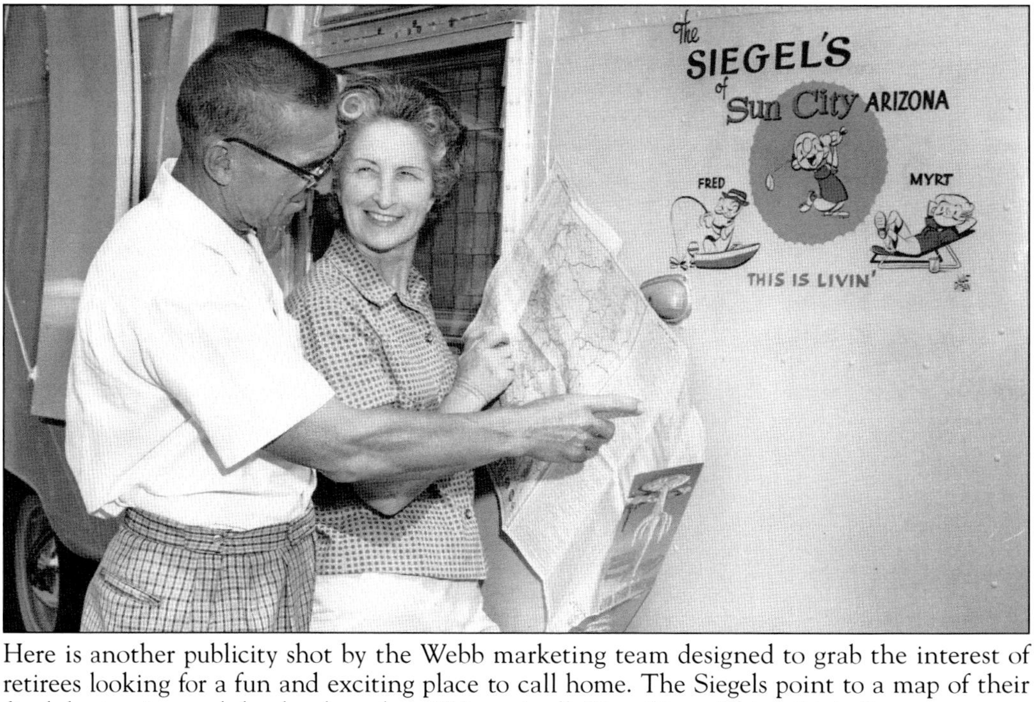


Here is another publicity shot by the Webb marketing team designed to grab the interest of retirees looking for a fun and exciting place to call home. The Siegels point to a map of their final destination and the decal on their RV says it all: "Sun City—This is Livin.'"

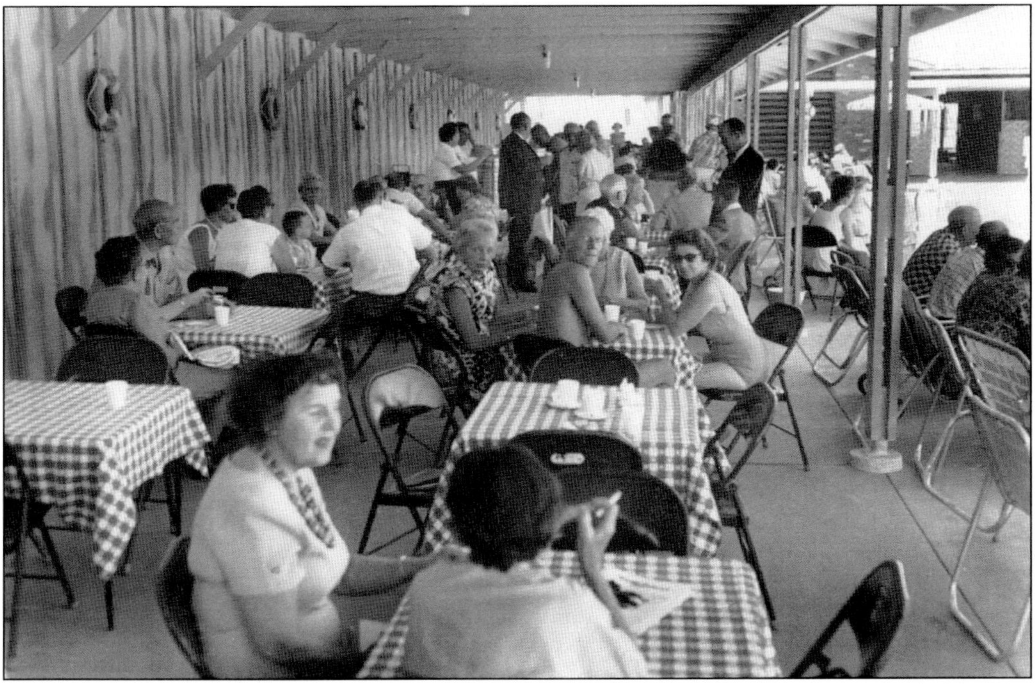

Sun City was a tight-knit community in the early days. Most community events were held at the recreation centers and most social parties were held on the patios or in the backyards of residents. Community barbecues, potlucks, and poolside parties were commonplace in the early 1960s.

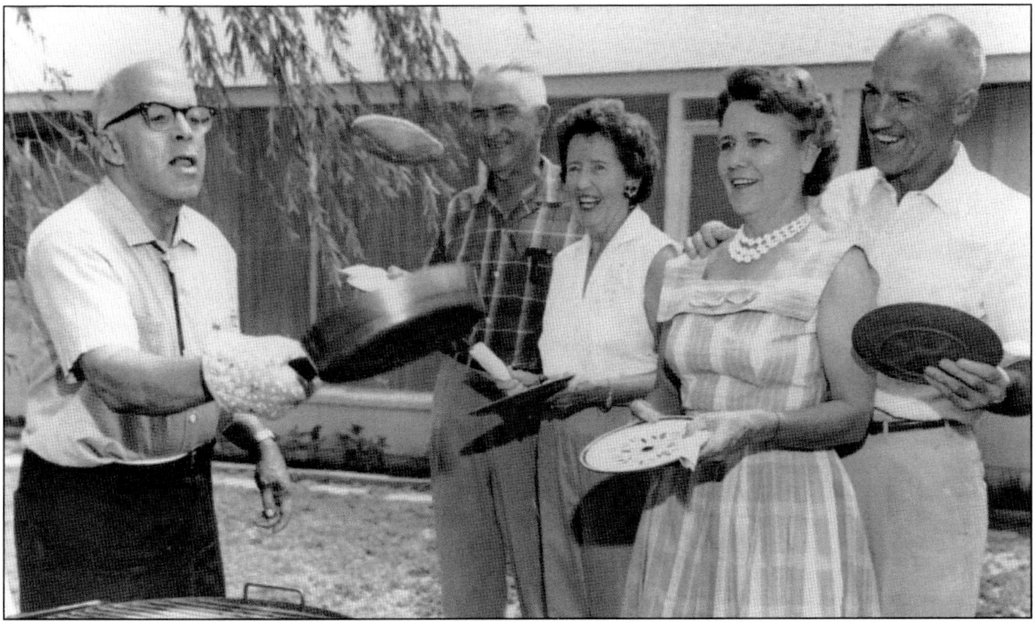

This typical publicity shot is representative of the many photographs taken during the early 1960s by the creative marketing department at the Webb corporation. The photographs nearly always depicted residents socializing and enjoying fun in their new-found retirement haven. The photographs were used in Sun City advertisements and often sent to a new resident's hometown newspaper—just to show the folks back home how fun retirement living could be.

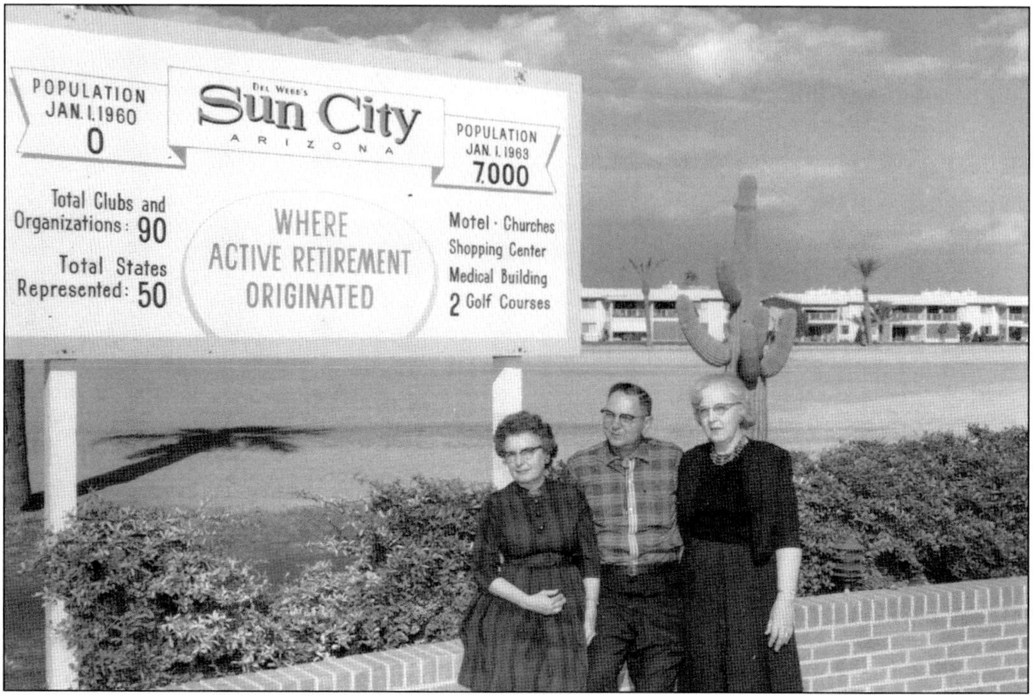


Sun City's population reached the 7,000 mark by 1963, and citizens had their choice of over 90 clubs and organizations. This "growth billboard" was located at Town Hall Recreation Center. The residents in the photograph are identified as Mr. and Mrs. Schilling (left) and Lois Linegar (right).

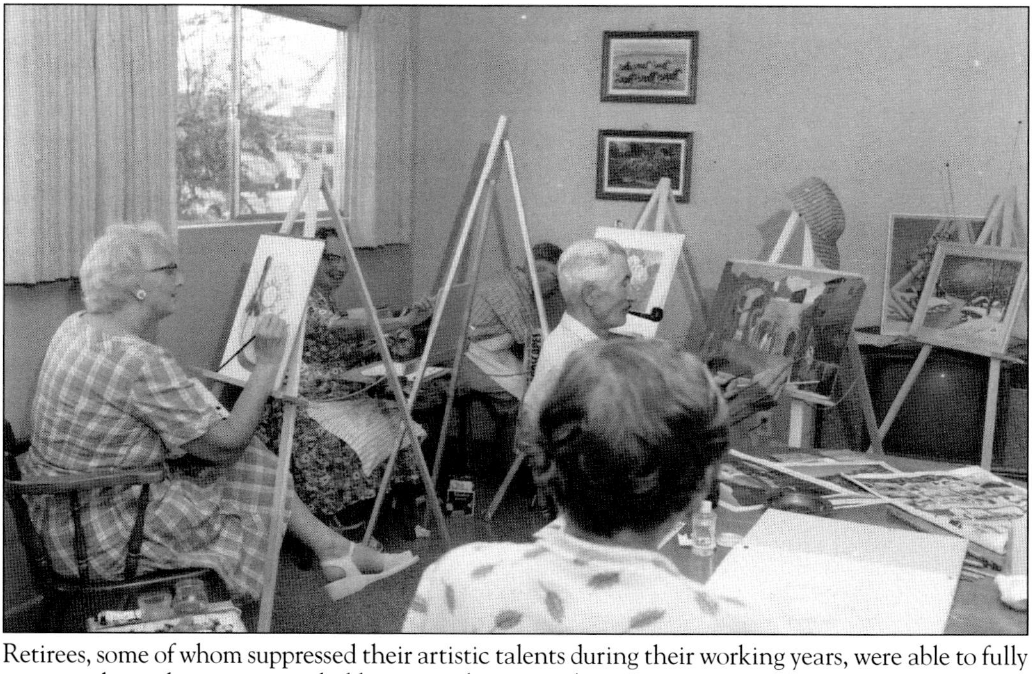

Retirees, some of whom suppressed their artistic talents during their working years, were able to fully immerse themselves in creative hobbies once they arrived in Sun City. Art clubs continued to flourish over the years. Pictured here is an art class in July 1961 at Town Hall Recreation Center.

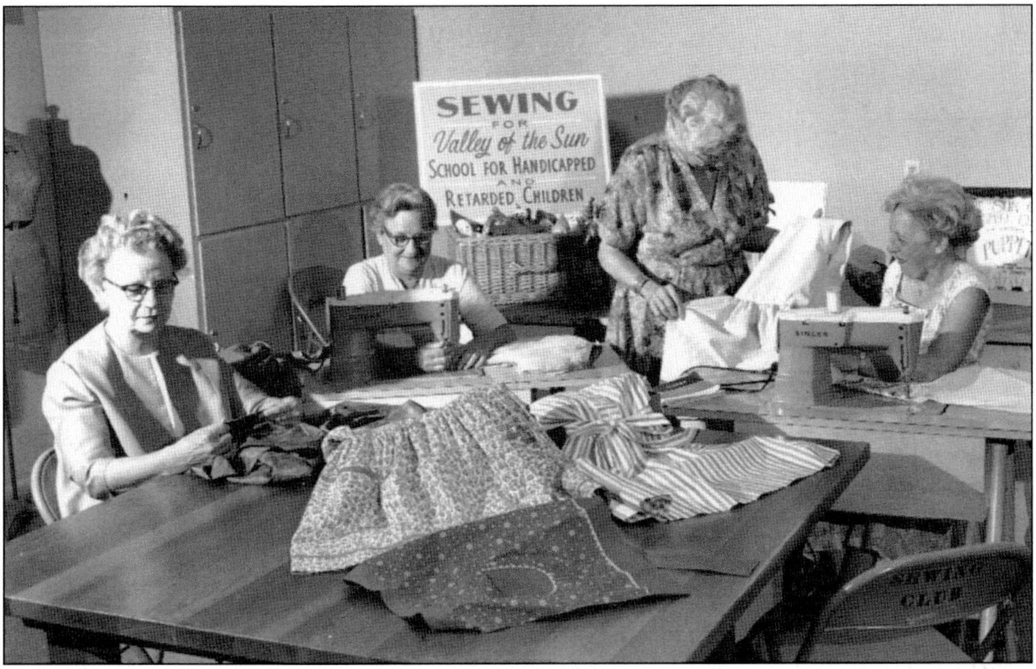


Four members of a sewing club are shown in the early 1960s working on projects for a nearby charity. The club was based at Town Hall Recreation Center. Arts and crafts clubs in Sun City are well known for creating and donating items to charities throughout the valley.

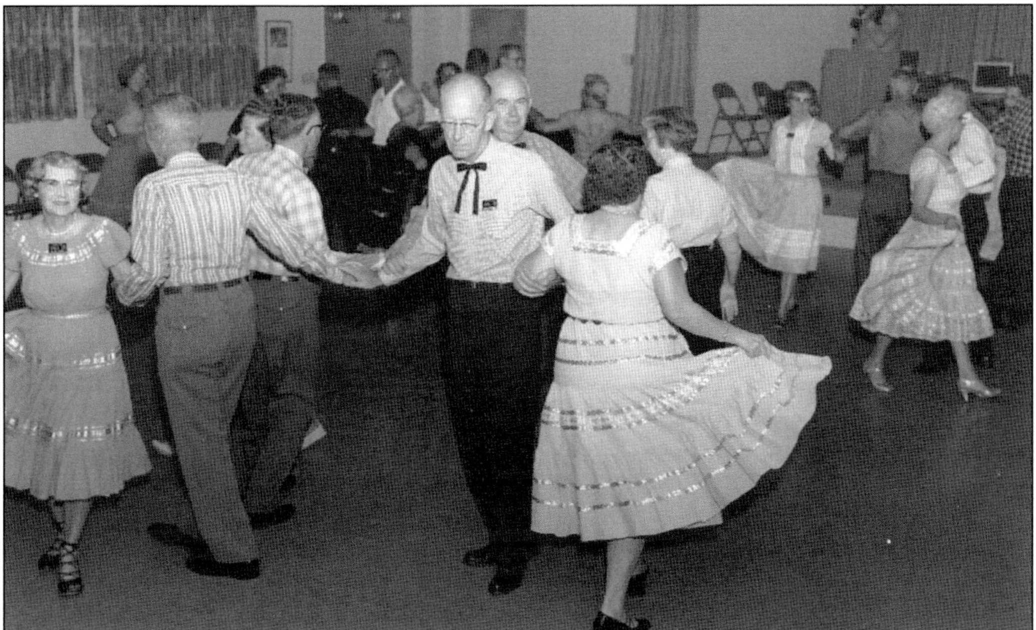

Dance clubs have always been a popular pastime in the community. Over the years, residents have had their choice of square dancing, ballroom dance, tap, jazz, Hawaiian, country, swing, and more. The first square dance club was organized in 1961 and offered a weekly square dance every Wednesday at the Community Center.

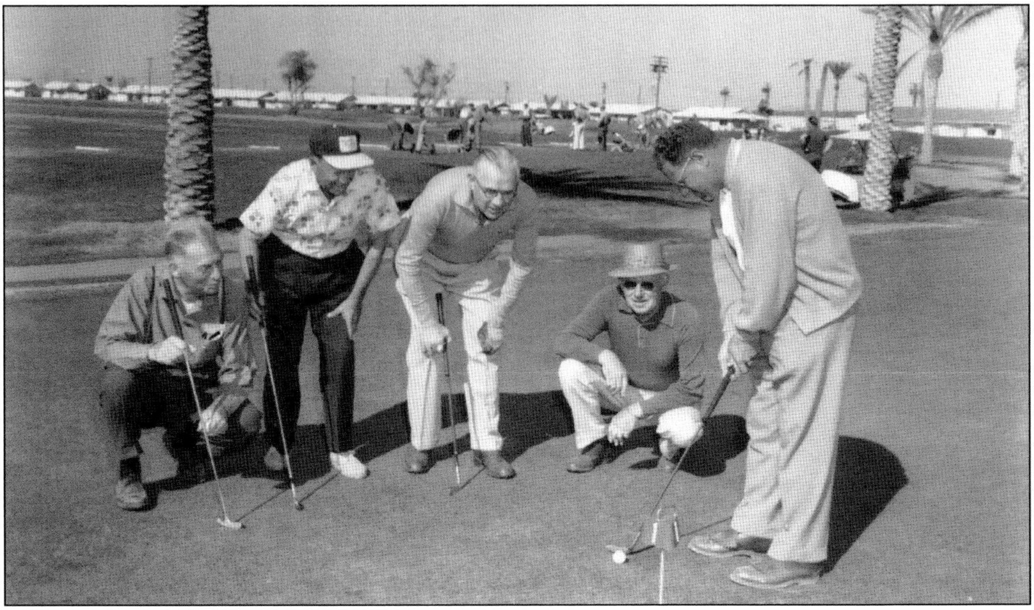

Sun City has always been known for its recreational amenities, social activities, and special-interest arts and crafts clubs. But of all the recreational activities offered, golf was then, and remains today, the No. 1 pastime of those who choose to retire to the nation's very first active-adult, master-planned retirement community. Pictured in February 1961 are, from left to right, Ed Johnson, ? Berglund, Harry Zinn, Gus Schroeder, and Sun City golf pro Fielding Abbott.

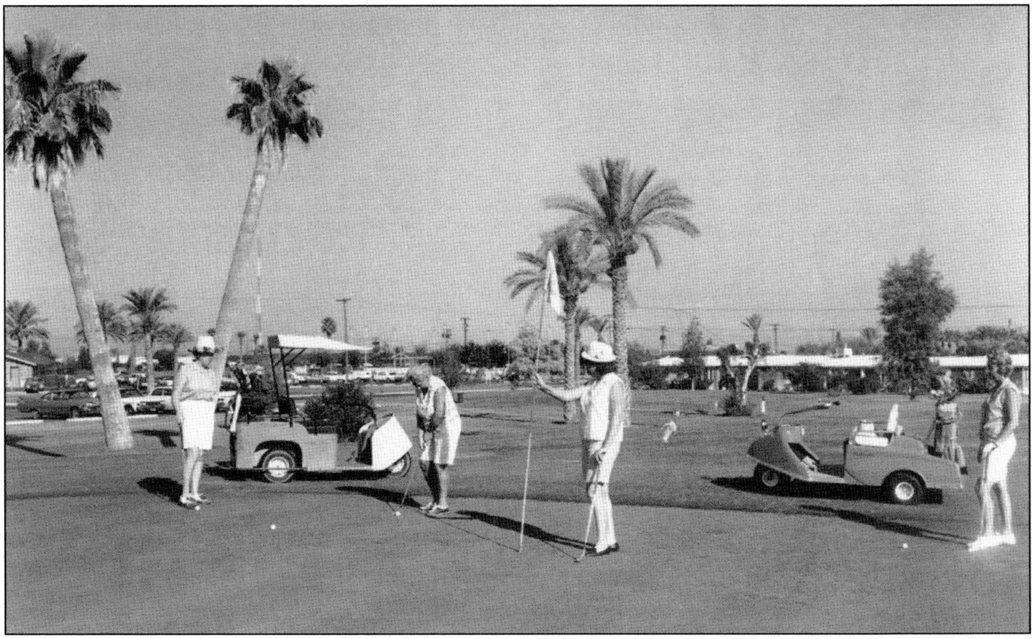

A ladies foursome tees off during the 1970s. Sun City's golf courses received national attention during the early days of the community. The All Star Golf television show kicked off its fifth season in 1961 with a match-skills game in Sun City. Competing in the four-week series were pro golfers Gary Player, Jerry Barber, Doug Sanders, Stan Leonard, and Peter Thomson. Sanders won with a course record score of 60.

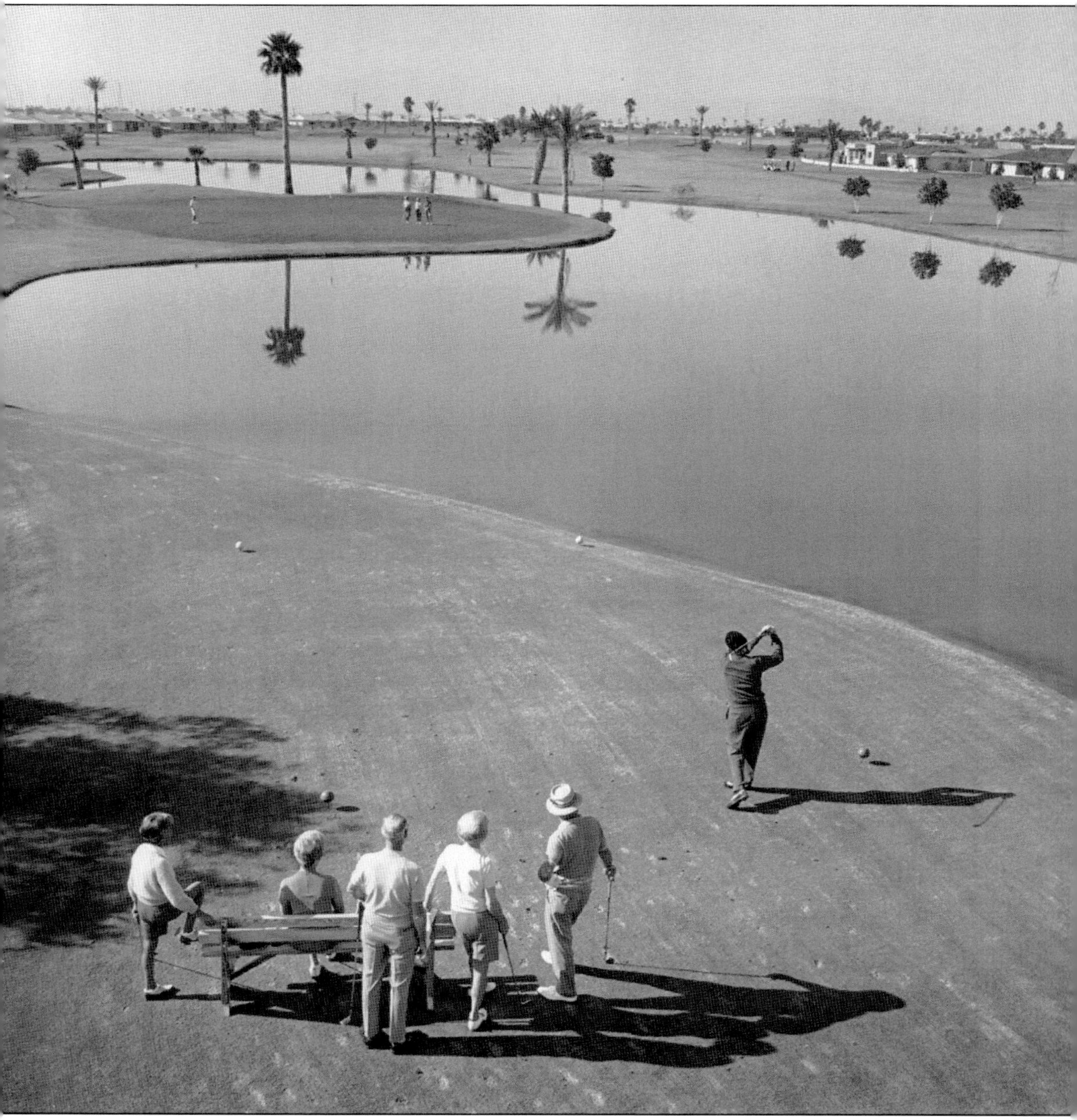

Sun City Country Club was the community's first private country club. Two other private clubs with golf courses—Palmbrook and Union Hills—eventually opened in Sun City. In this photograph, a foursome tees off at Sun City Country Club in 1968.

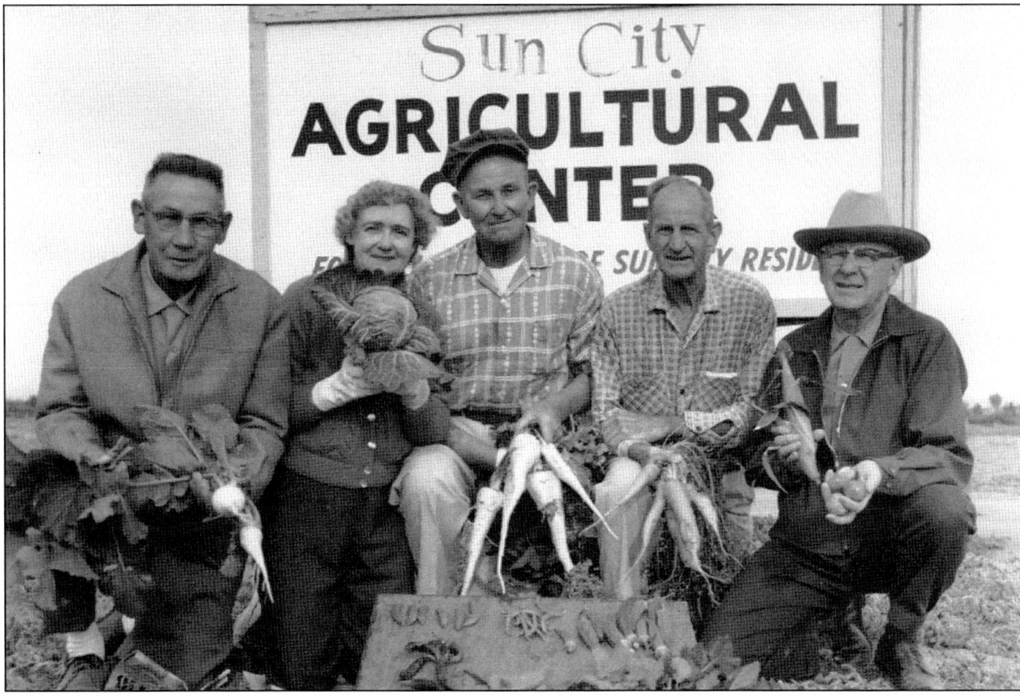


DEVCO created a garden center along Grand Avenue in 1960 and invited residents to use the facility to grow their own crops. A residents' committee overseeing the center eventually became one of the first clubs in the community, the Sun City Agricultural Club. DEVCO initially maintained the plots, but residents eventually took over. As the community grew, the garden was moved north to an area behind Sunland Mortuary.

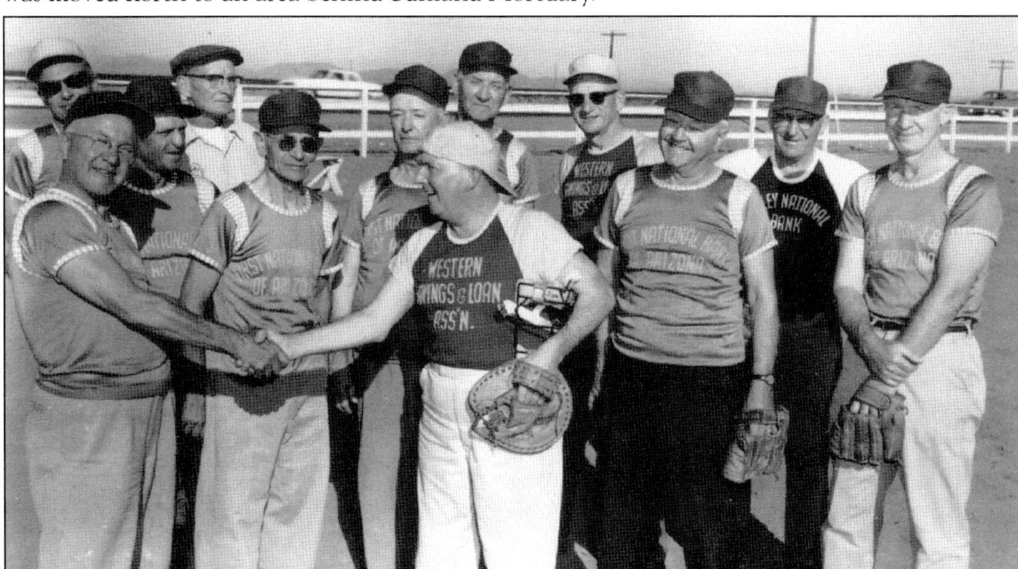

The boys of summer get to play all year long in Sun City, and softball has always been a popular activity. Shown here in February 1963, players celebrate the end of another hard-fought game. Today a modern state-of-the-art softball field is located next to the Sun Bowl and is home to the Sun Cities Senior Softball League.

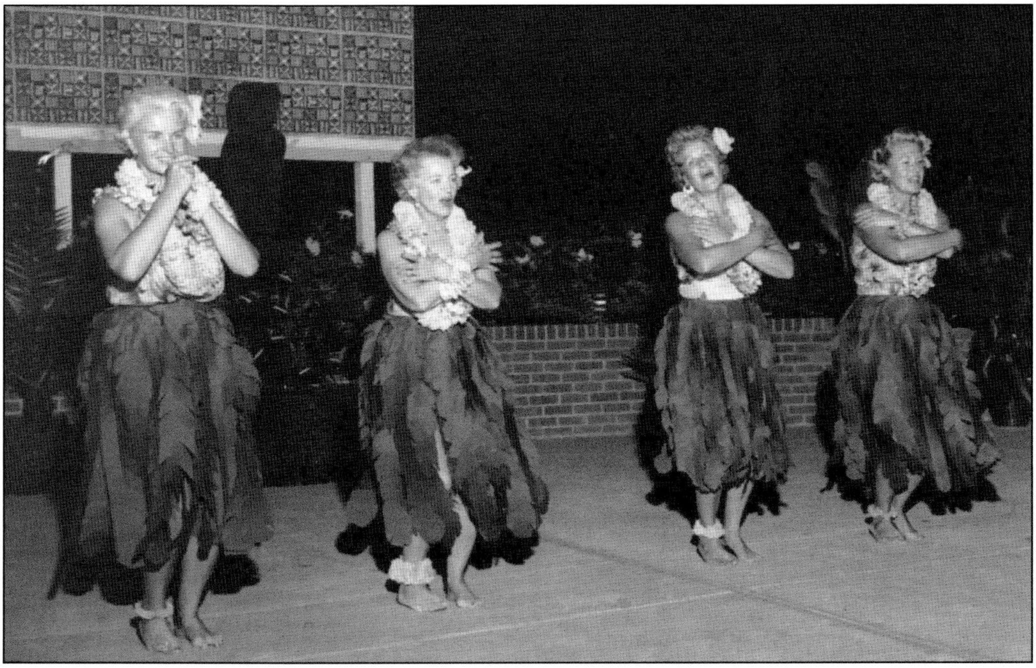

One of the first community festivals held in Sun City was a Hawaiian luau sponsored by the Town Hall Swim Club in October 1961. The festivals continued and featured skits and performances by local clubs. Participating in the 1962 event are, from left to right, Ina Dodt, Jo Gerig, Linnie Smith, and Elizabeth Ellis (McKinley). During the same show in 1962, the husbands, below, showed they could hold their own at a community luau.

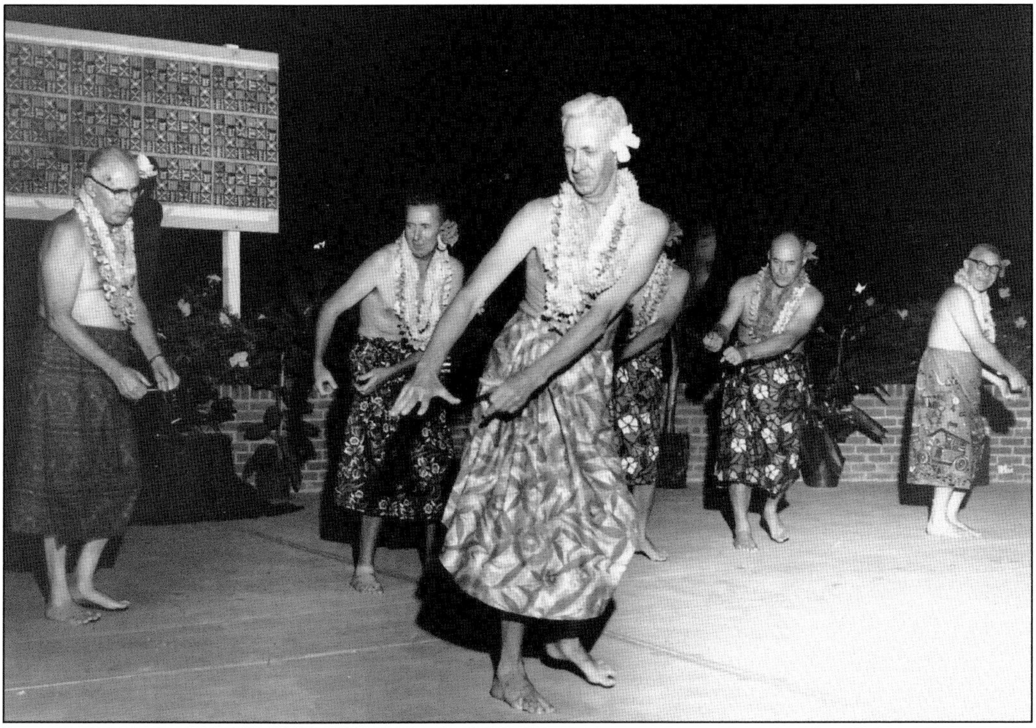

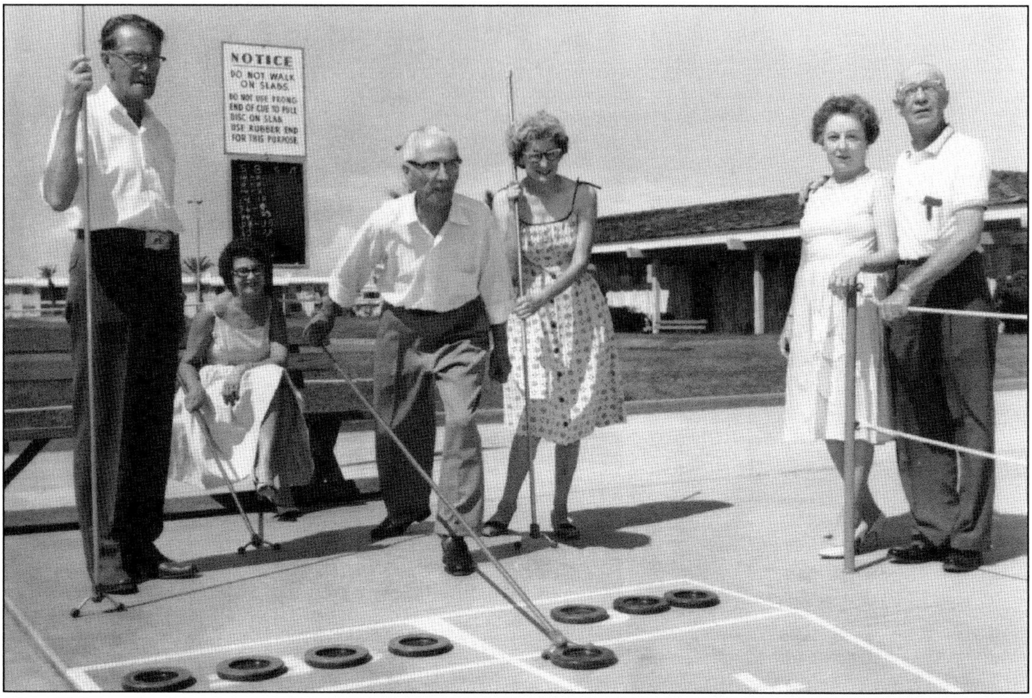


Shuffleboard players compete in 1963 at Town Hall North. The first shuffleboard club was organized in 1961 and often competed with players from Youngtown.

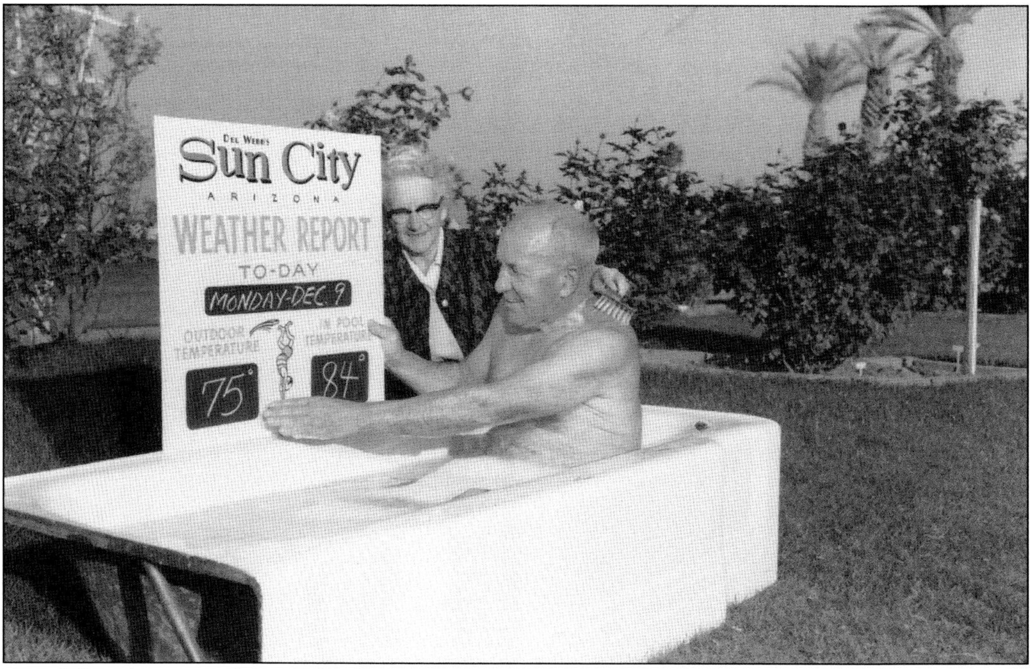


Wendell and Rae Noell enjoy the pleasant temperatures in 1964. Seventy-five degrees on December 9 certainly caught the attention of those back east struggling with cold weather and snow. The Del Webb marketing department specialized in these types of promotional photographs, and they often found their way into small newspapers throughout the Midwest and East.

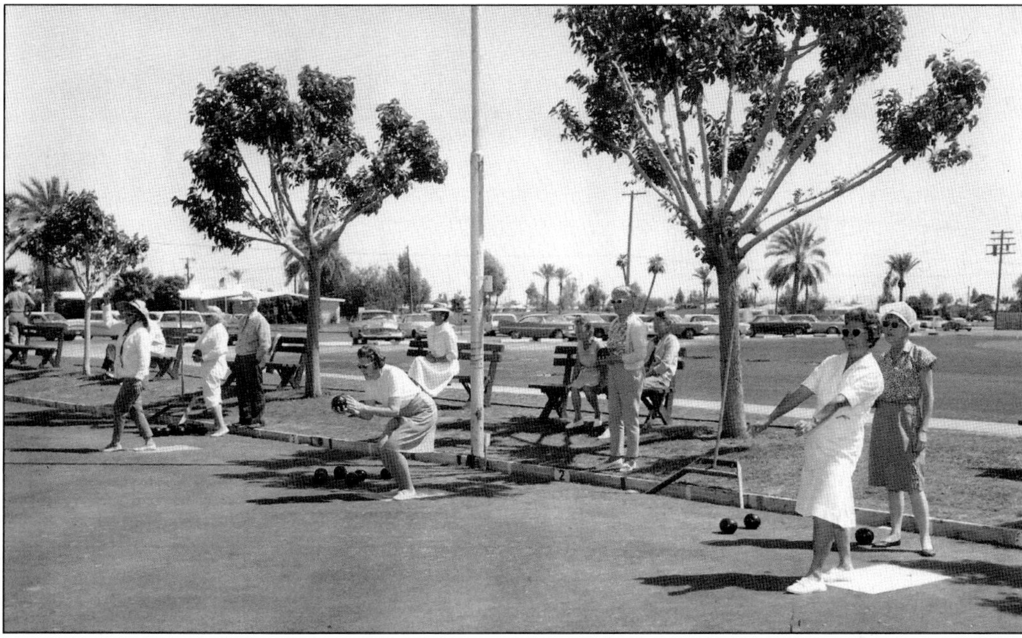

Sun City claimed to have the first organized lawn bowling competition in Arizona when its greens opened in 1960. Since no other competition existed outside of Sun City, local lawn bowlers were quick to proclaim themselves "state champions." Today there are five lawn bowling clubs in Sun City and seven greens. Sun City is considered to have the best greens in North America and in 2010 hosted the U.S. championships.

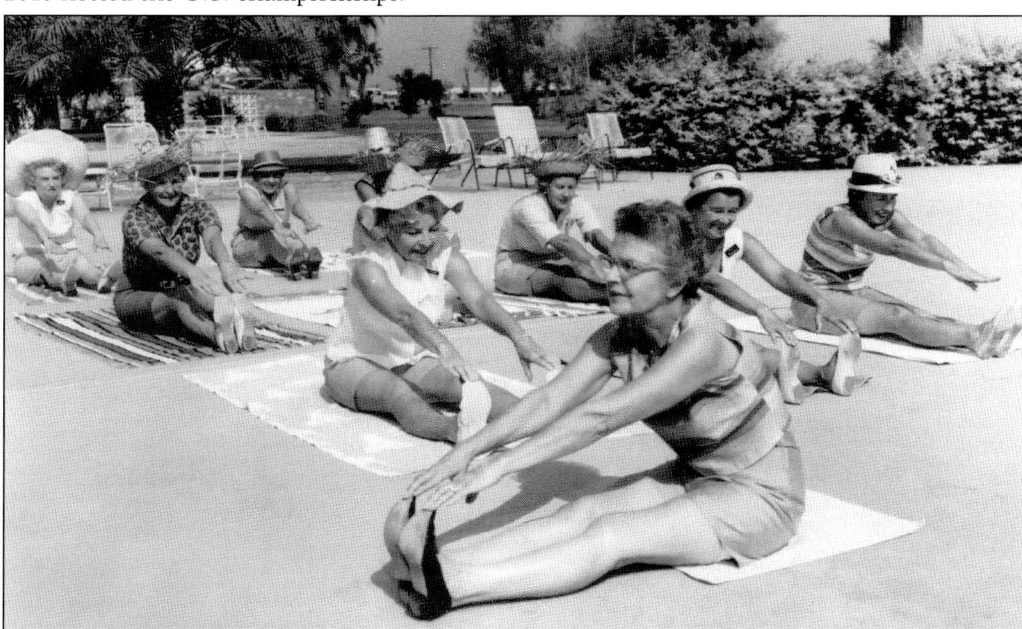

Sun City calls itself an "active" adult retirement community and staying in tip-top shape is a key ingredient to feeling, looking, and acting younger. Arizona's beautiful year-round weather allows many fitness classes to be held outdoors. Each of the seven recreational centers includes a state-of-the-art fitness center, popular from morning to night.

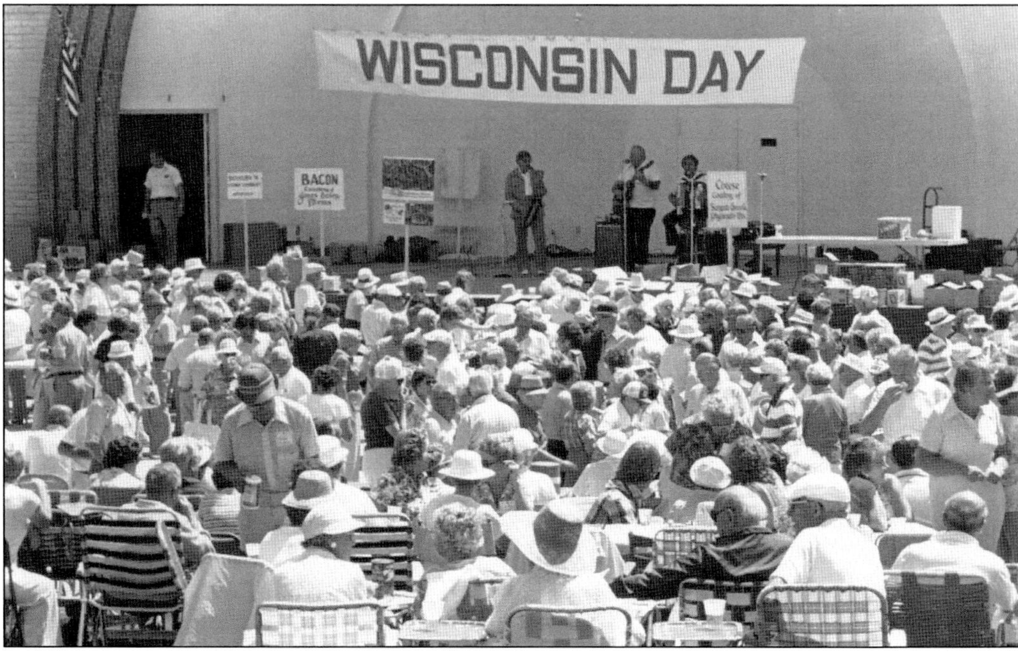


In the early days of the community, DEVCO organized "state clubs" so that residents from various states could meet each other and share common interests. A number of state clubs still exist and meet throughout the year, including the Wisconsin Club, which holds its annual Wisconsin Day celebration at the Sun Bowl. Residents from the Dairy State enjoy music, brats, and beer at the festivities. (Independent Newspapers, Inc.)

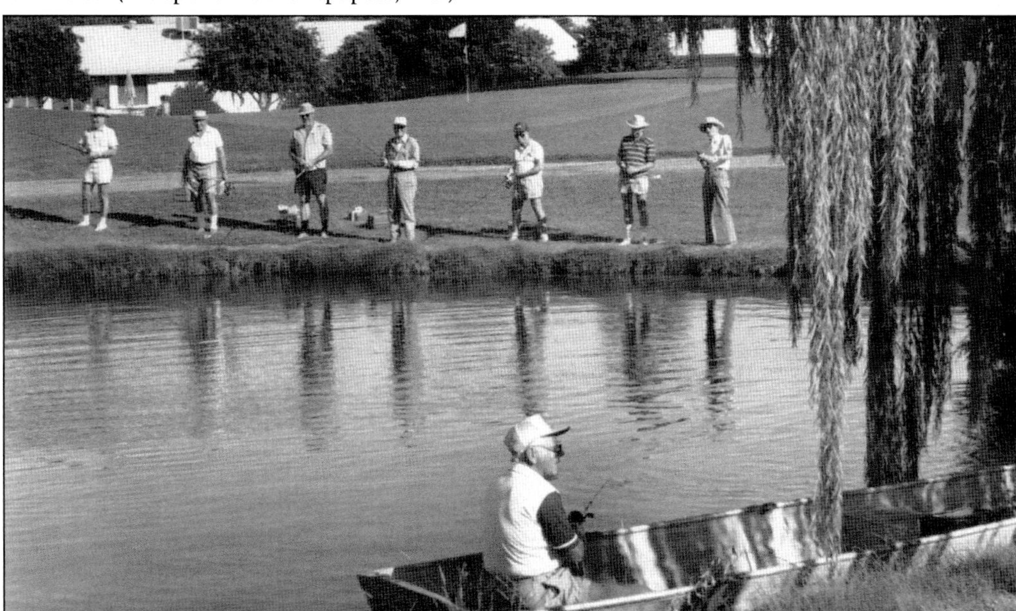

The fish are always biting in Sun City. Living in a desert does not mean local anglers are left out of the fun. Viewpoint Lake offers the best fishing opportunities in Sun City, but ponds at the local golf courses provide a challenge as well. This 1980s photograph is of a fishing contest at a pond at Lake West Golf Course. (Independent Newspapers, Inc.)

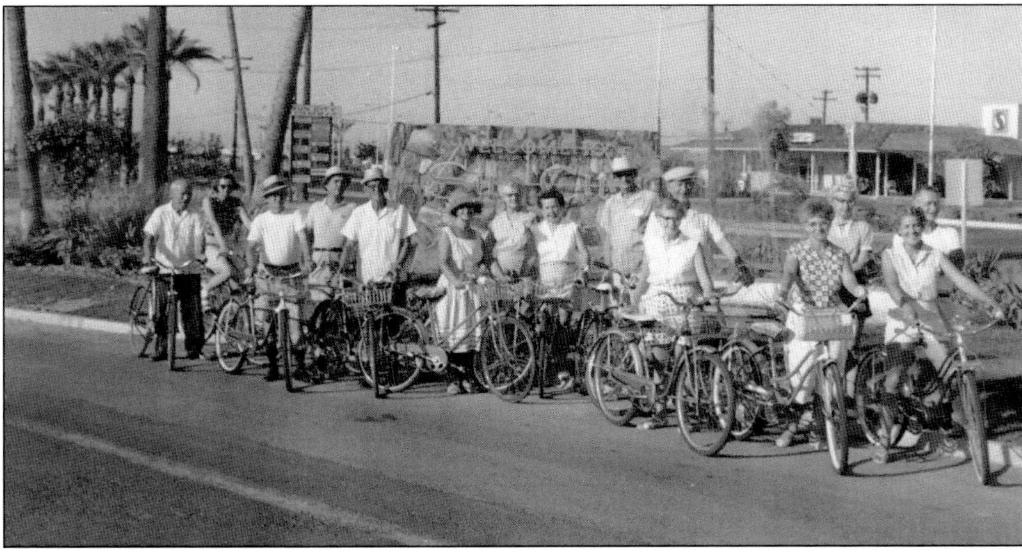

The Sun City Pedal Pushers was the first bike club to organize in Sun City. With Arizona's comfortable year-round temperatures, biking is a fun way to stay in shape and meet new friends. Shown here, a group of bikers take a break near the Sun City entrance at 107th Avenue.

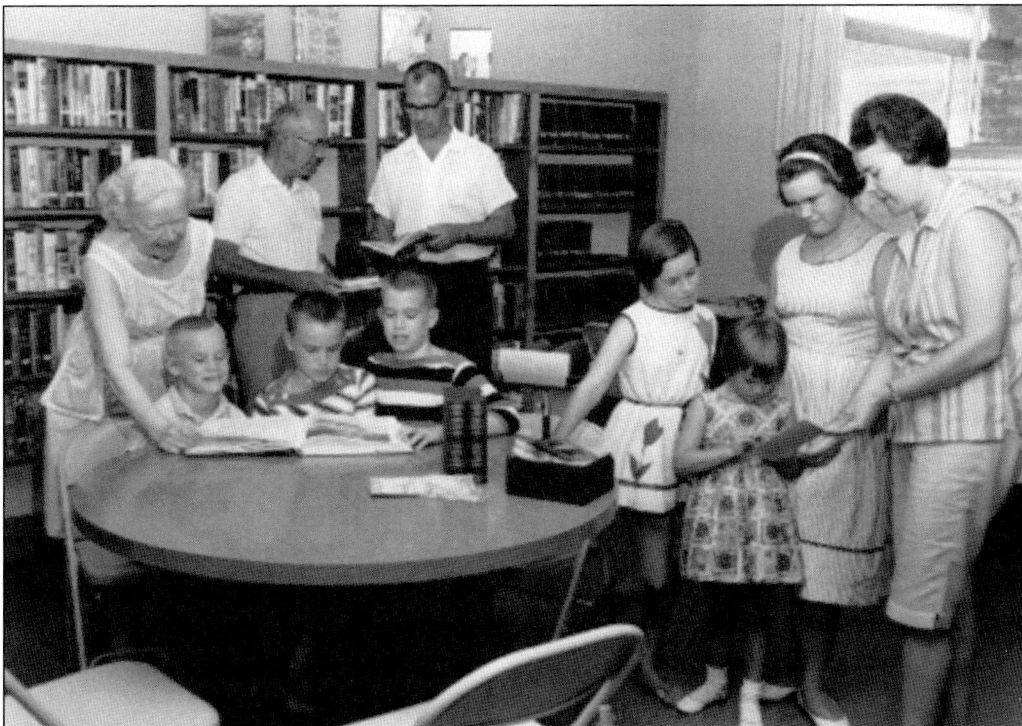

Sun City was designed as a community for those 55 and older, but children were always welcomed when visiting grandparents. The Philip Ahern family was profiled during a 1962 edition of Del Webb's *Sundial*, a community newsletter. Visiting the library at Town Hall Recreation Center were Ahern and his son-in-law John Fisher, Grace Ahern and her six grandchildren, and daughter Peggy at right. The Fishers lived in Phoenix.

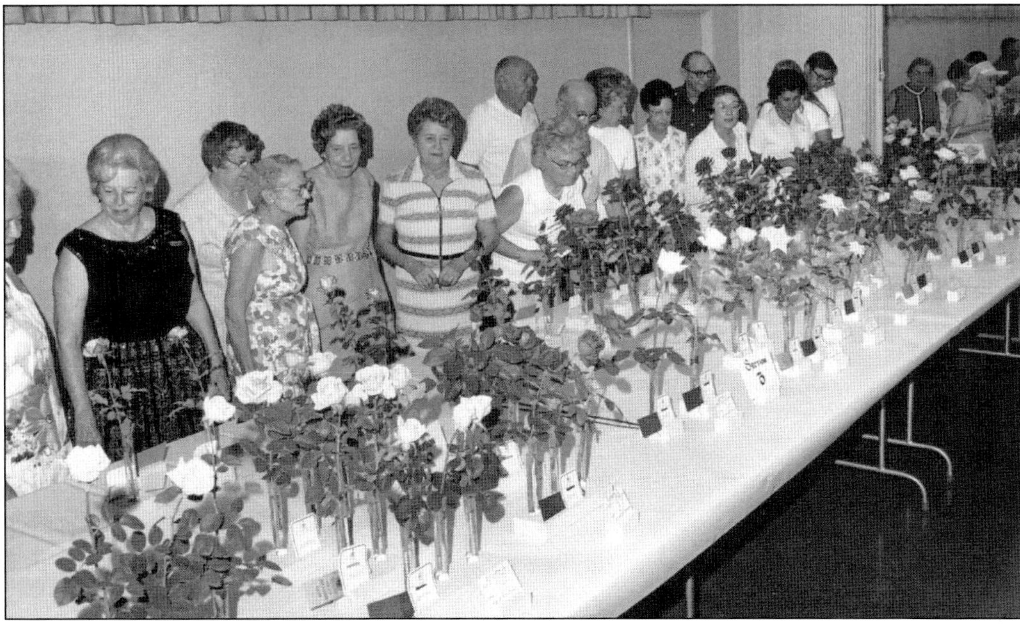

Members of the Sun City Rose and Garden Club displayed their best during a rose show held in 1974. The Rose and Garden Club was also responsible for maintaining a rose garden dedicated in January 1982 at the Sun Bowl.

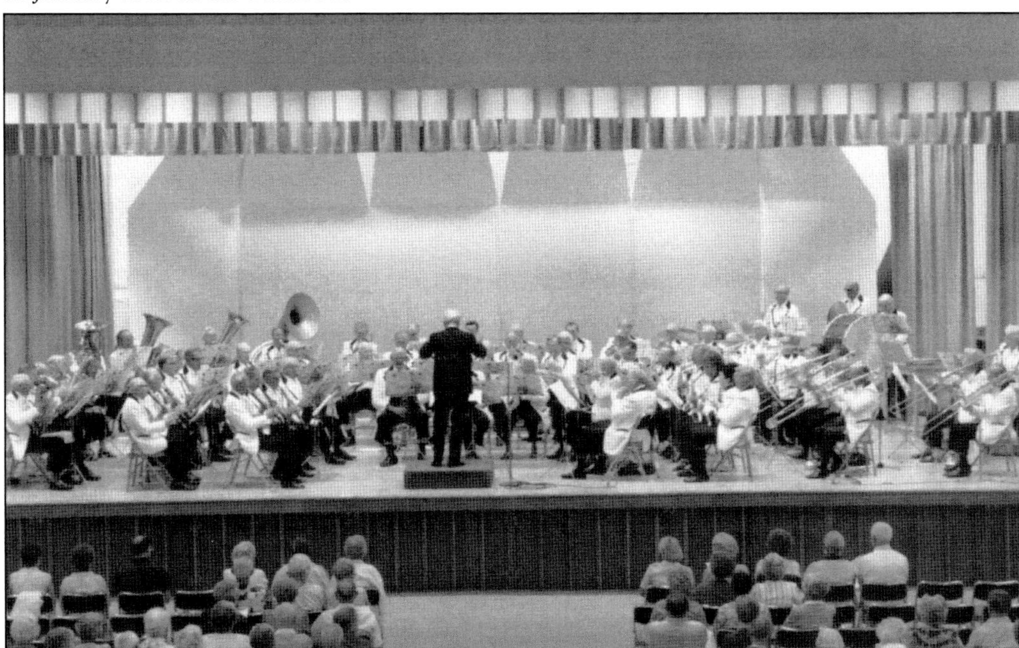

Music has always played an important role in Sun City. The Sun City Woman's Chorus was one of the very first clubs to organize in Sun City and over the years a number of other musical organizations evolved—choral groups, jazz bands, barbershop quartets, and more. Sun City once boasted its own professional symphony. Shown here, the Sun City Concert Band performs at Sundial Recreation Center in 1988. (Independent Newspapers, Inc.)

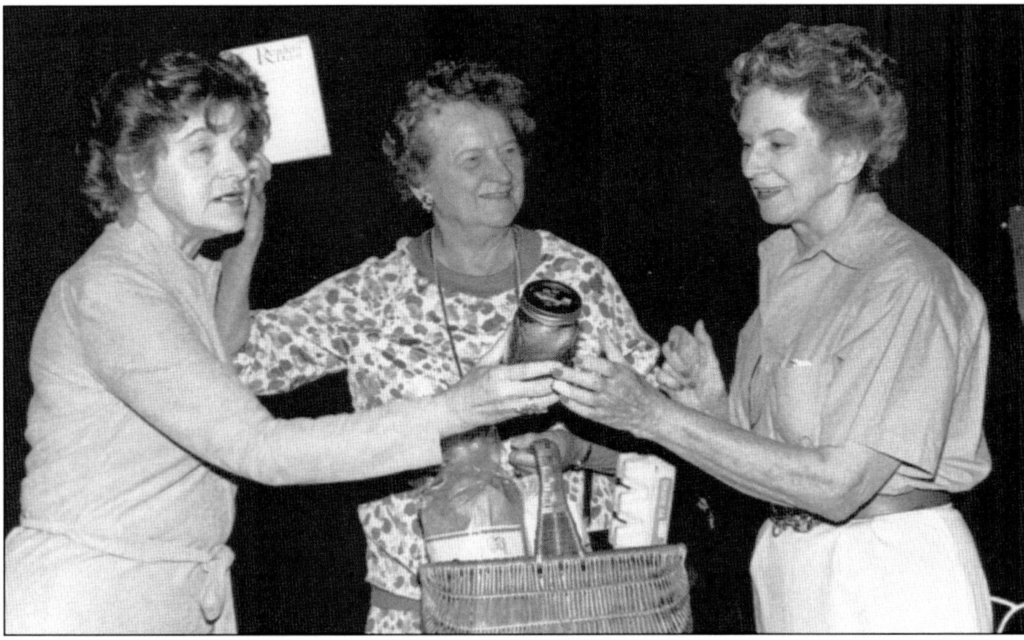

Sun City has been home to a number of performing arts organizations over the years, with none more popular than the Sun City Players. The troupe was organized in 1961 to perform at the first Sun City Jubilee show in May of that year. Rehearsing years later for the play *A Bad Year for Tomatoes* are, from left to right, Romona Riemer, Sue Irons, and Fran King. (Independent Newspapers, Inc.)

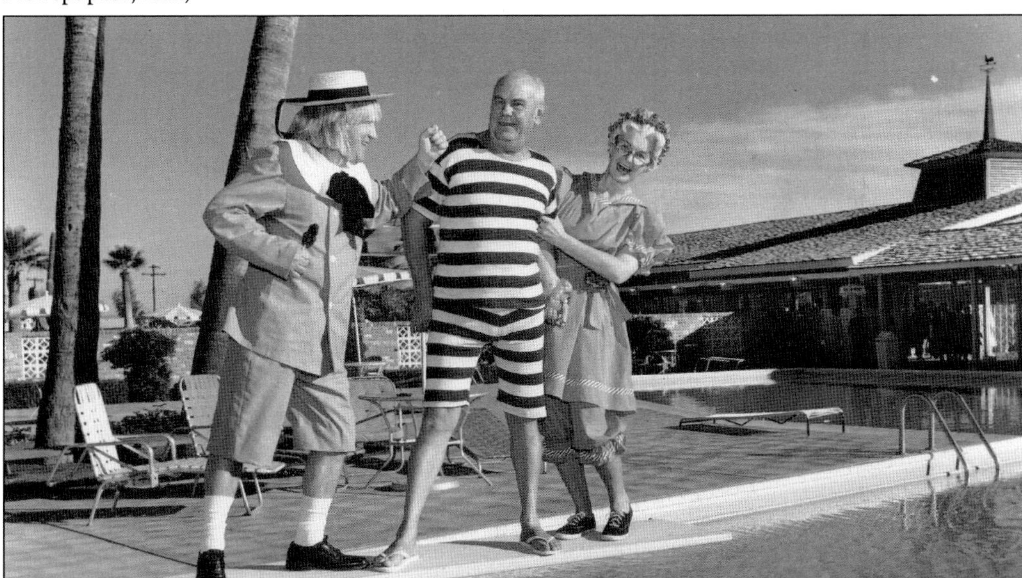

Here is another publicity photograph taken by the Del E. Webb public relations team to promote the "Sun City lifestyle," this one taken at Oakmont Recreation Center. The caption for this photograph when it appeared in the *Webb Spinner* newsletter was, "A lot of fun, exercise and hi-jinks take place in and around Sun City's four swimming pools. Fashion shows, luaus and swim parties are regular functions."

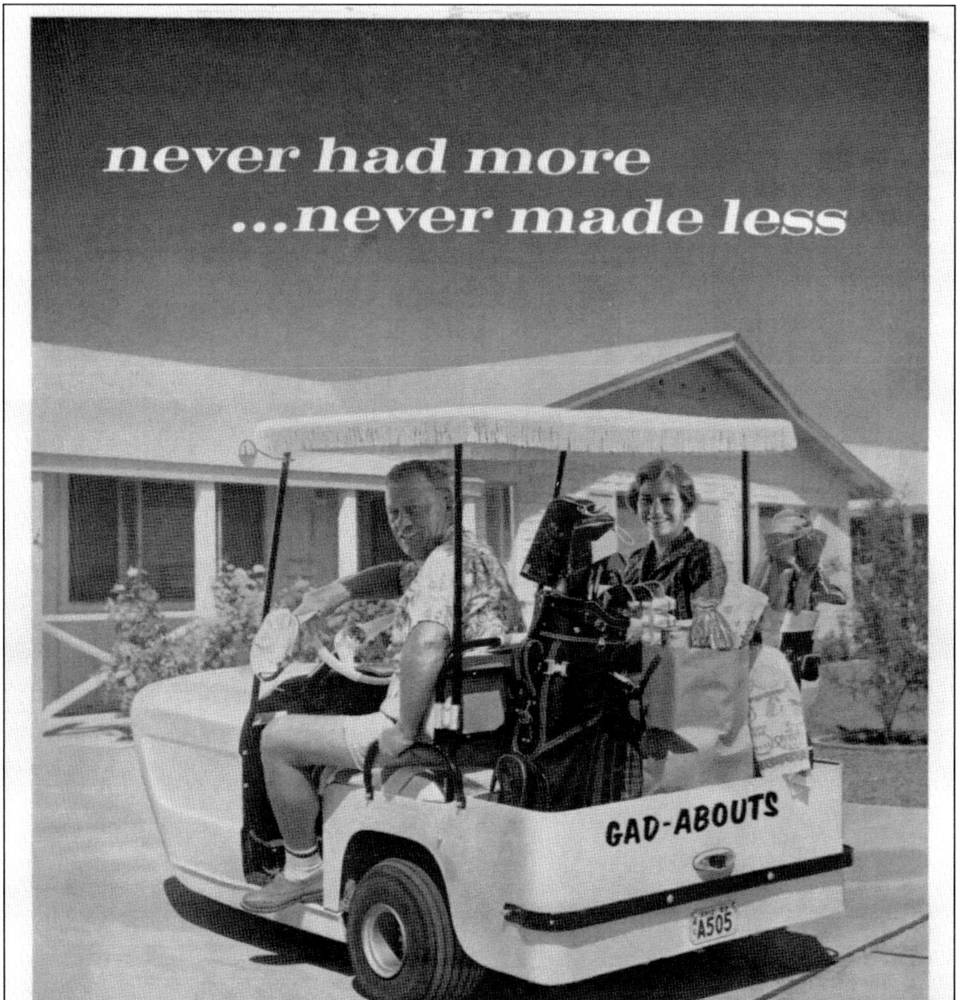


The "Sun City lifestyle" was the primary focus of nearly all of Del E. Webb's advertisements during the early days of the community. Photographs and stories reflected the fun lifestyle that awaited retirees in Sun City. Pictured here is a sample of one of the many advertisements developed by the creative minds in the Webb marketing department, this one from the 1960s. The advertisements, as well as a number of other pamphlets, newsletters, and promotional campaigns created over the years by the Del Webb marketing team, were recently showcased at the Del Webb Sun Cities Museum in an exhibit titled Creating the Perfect Retirement: How America was Sold on Sun City. (Pulte Homes/Del E. Webb Corporation.)

# *Eight*

# City of Volunteers

When the Del E. Webb Corporation built its final home in Sun City, there were many who questioned whether or not the community could survive without its benefactor.

The developer built the amenities, serviced the facilities, and was quick to resolve challenges. Even more important was the fact that Webb promoted Sun City on a national scale. There was concern future retirees would choose newer, more modern communities over Sun City.

Once again defying the odds, Sun City not only survived, but flourished. Its success as a thriving, self-sustaining, active-adult community is a result of strong civic pride and commitment to take care of one another.

The developer was quick to turn ownership of recreational amenities over to residents. Today the Recreation Centers of Sun City, Inc. (RCSC), is a nonprofit corporation owned by the residents and governed by a volunteer board of directors elected by members. The RCSC manages over $50 million in property, oversees activities at the centers, and provides a variety of events and programs for residents.

Other volunteer organizations were created over the years to fill other needs.

The Sun City Home Owners Association oversees the community's deed restrictions and works closely with elected officials on issues involving local laws, public safety, and street maintenance.

Cleaning the streets, assisting the sheriff with public safety, providing public transportation, supporting local health care institutions, promoting the community to a worldwide audience, and contributing to the less fortunate are just a few of many services provided by volunteers.

And charity does not stop at home. Clubs and service organizations contribute time and money to those outside the community. Whether it is volunteering in nearby schools, donating clothing to needy charities, raising money for worthy causes, or supporting veterans' hospitals, Sun City residents have made volunteering as much a part of their golden years as playing golf or bridge.

Today Sun City is officially known as the "City of Volunteers," and visitors to the community are greeted at all entrances with signs affirming the benevolent spirit found within the community's walls.

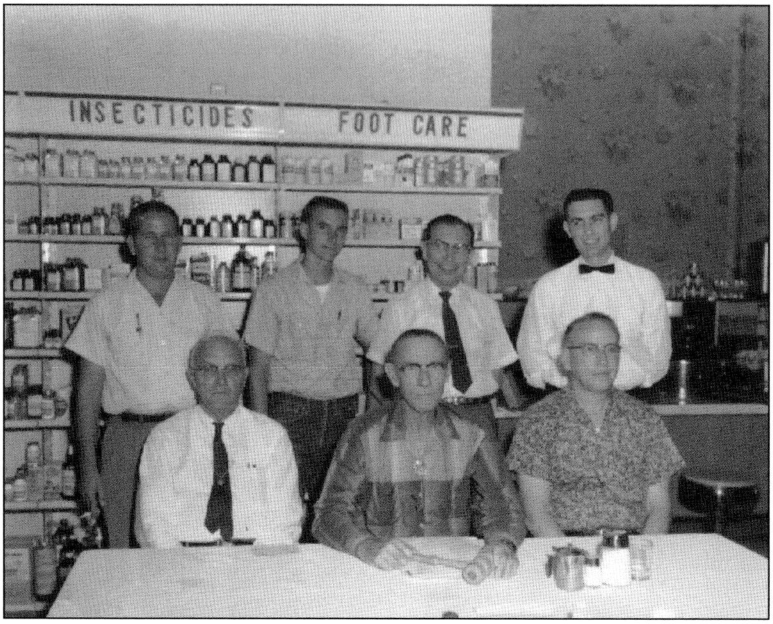


Civic groups have always played an important role in promoting community spirit and fostering charitable endeavors. The very first Lions Club met September 7, 1960, at Greenway Drug Store. Sun City's population was less than 2,000 when the club, later to be called Host Lions Club, was organized. Eventually, eight Lions Clubs would be chartered in Sun City.

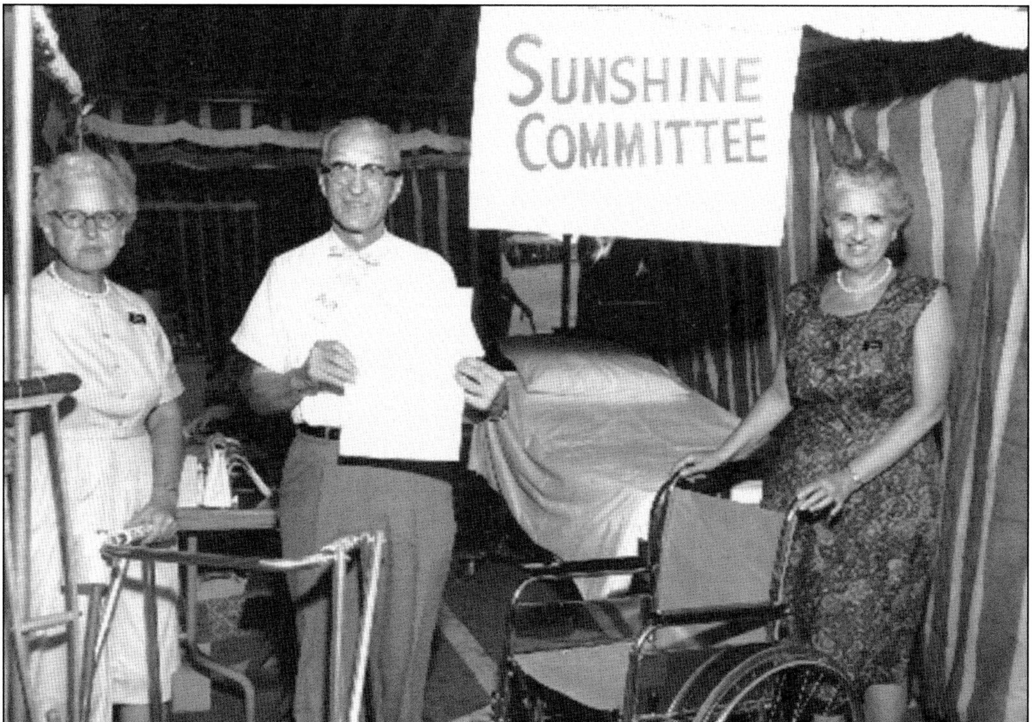


Sunshine Services was created in 1961 to help residents unable to pay their annual recreation dues. The organization expanded and soon started loaning medical equipment on a temporary basis to local residents. Sunshine Services, located at 9980 Santa Fe Drive, has won numerous awards over the years for its role and remains a vital institution in the community. Shown here, the organization is promoting itself at a booth during the community's Western Days Festival in 1963.

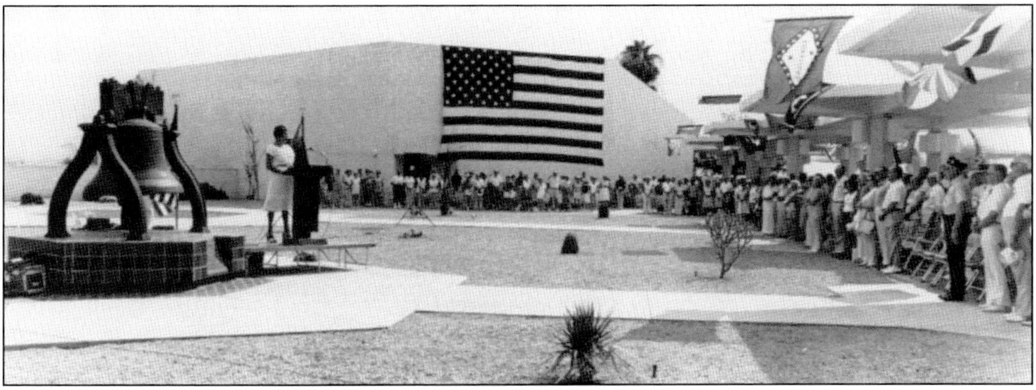

The Recreation Centers of Sun City, Inc., oversees the community's amenities and activities, such as the annual Fourth of July Ring the Bell ceremony at Bell Recreation Center. The multimillion-dollar corporation is governed by an elected board of volunteer directors. All homeowners are required to pay annual dues that provide for the maintenance and upkeep of the amenities. Its Web site is www.sunaz.com. (Independent Newspapers, Inc.)

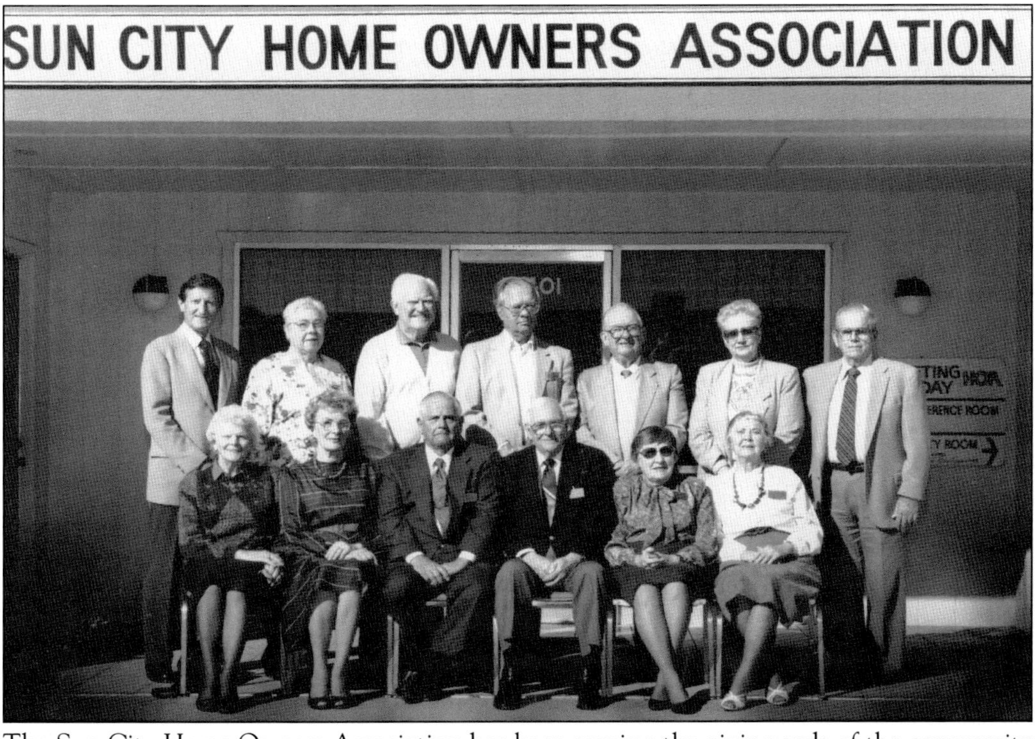


The Sun City Home Owners Association has been serving the civic needs of the community since 1963. A spin-off of the Sun City Civic Association, SCHOA works closely with county and state officials on such issues as enforcement of deed restrictions, street maintenance, and more. The organization is managed by an elected volunteer board of directors. The 1994 board is shown here. The SCHOA Web site is www.suncityhoa.org. (Independent Newspapers, Inc.)

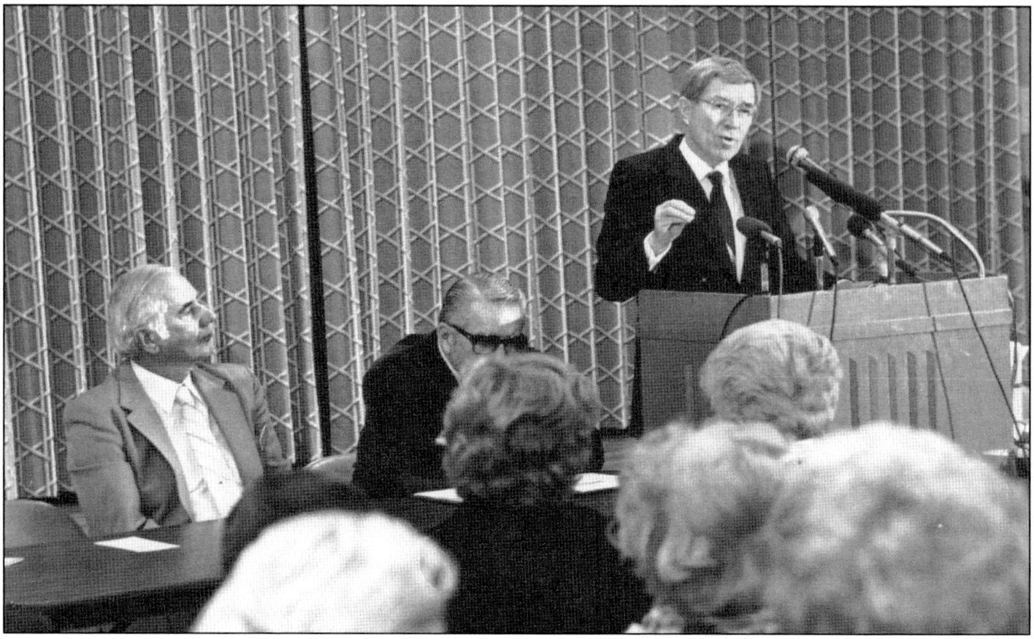

The Sun City Taxpayers Association, founded in 1969, keeps a close eye on issues that impact financial matters. The association often represents community interests in utility rate cases and tax-related matters, and works with some of the state's most important political figures. Former governor Evan Mecham, speaking, visited Sun City in 1987. Also in the photograph are SCTA officials Ken Larkin, left, and Murray Karsten. (Independent Newspapers, Inc.)

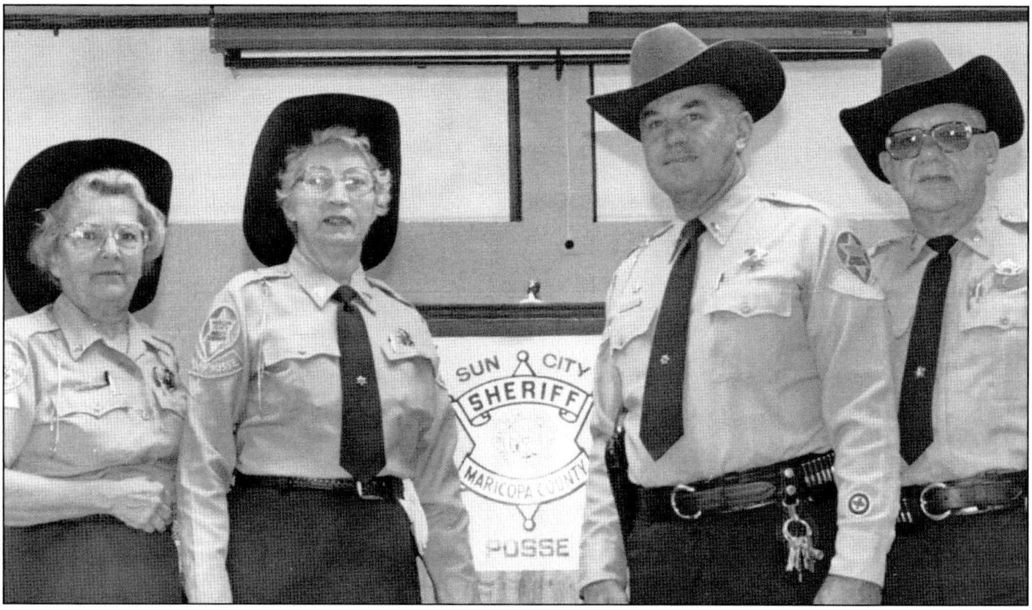


The Sheriff's Posse of Sun City was officially launched in 1973 and today serves as the "eyes and ears" of the Maricopa County Sheriff's Office. Volunteer posse members assist the sheriff by patrolling the streets, helping with traffic control, and conducting thousands of vacation watch home checks throughout the year. Similar volunteer posse groups now exist in other Arizona communities. (Independent Newspapers, Inc.)

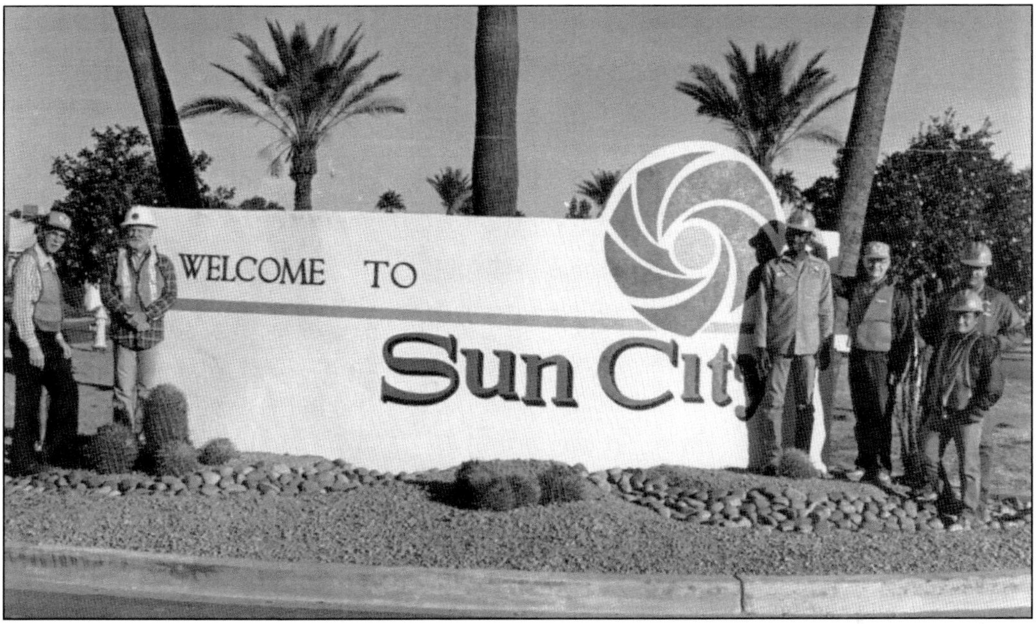


Sun City's pristine appearance is due in large part to a group of volunteers known as the Sun City PRIDES—Proud Residents Independently Donating Essential Services. Volunteers wearing the easily identifiable orange vests clean Sun City's 210 miles of streets and medians and collect fallen fruit from area trees to donate to the local food bank. Shown here, members spruce up one of the community's entrance signs. (Independent Newspapers, Inc.)

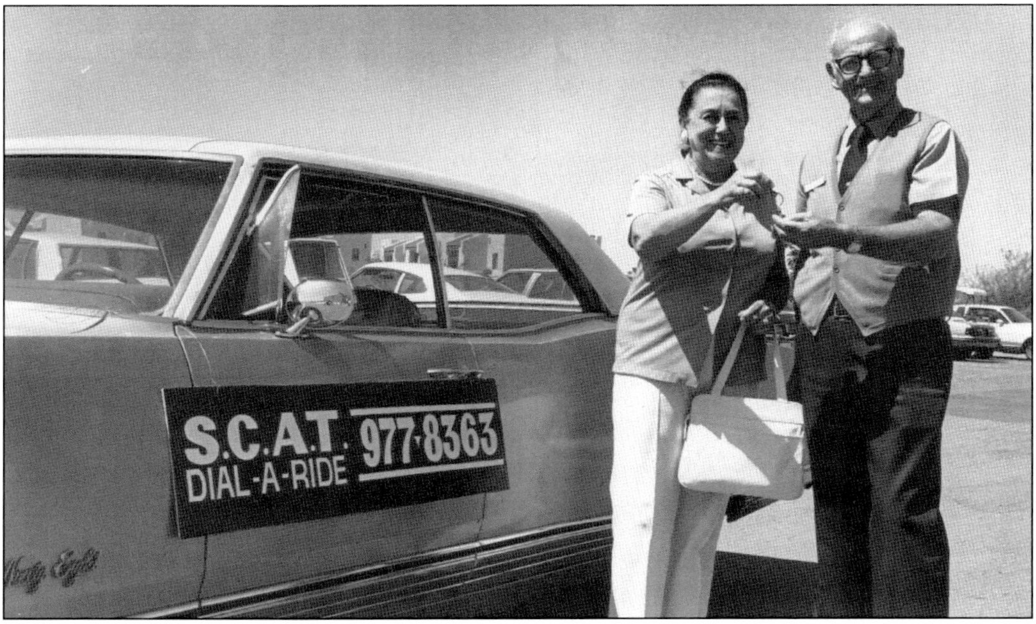


Sun Cities Area Transit, created in 1982, provided residents a dial-a-ride service to local shopping centers, medical facilities, and recreation centers. SCAT was a nonprofit organization and initially funded by local residents. Most donations were in the form of money, but in 1985, Sun City resident Beverly Caron went one step further and donated her 1968 Oldsmobile to the organization. SCAT president Chuck McKinnis accepted the gift. (Independent Newspapers, Inc.)

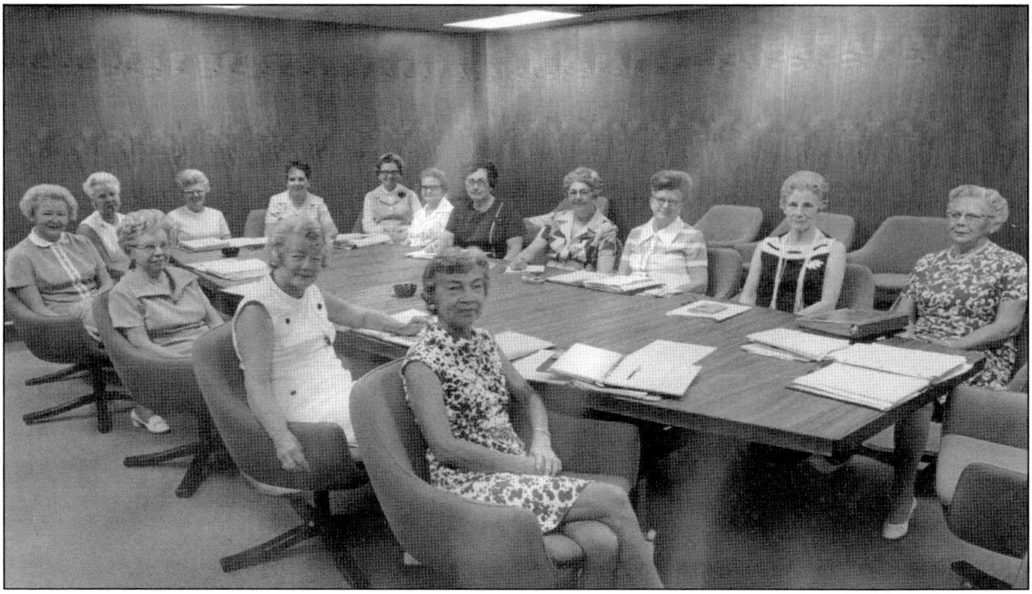

In 1968, Bill Chapman, board president of the yet-to-be built Boswell Hospital, called together a small group to organize an auxiliary to raise funds for hospital construction. Margaret Newby was appointed the first chairman and the Sun Health Auxiliary was born with 31 members its first month. The auxiliary has assisted the local health care community by raising millions of dollars and donating thousands of volunteer hours. The auxiliary's 1972 board of directors is pictured here. (Banner Boswell Medical Center.)

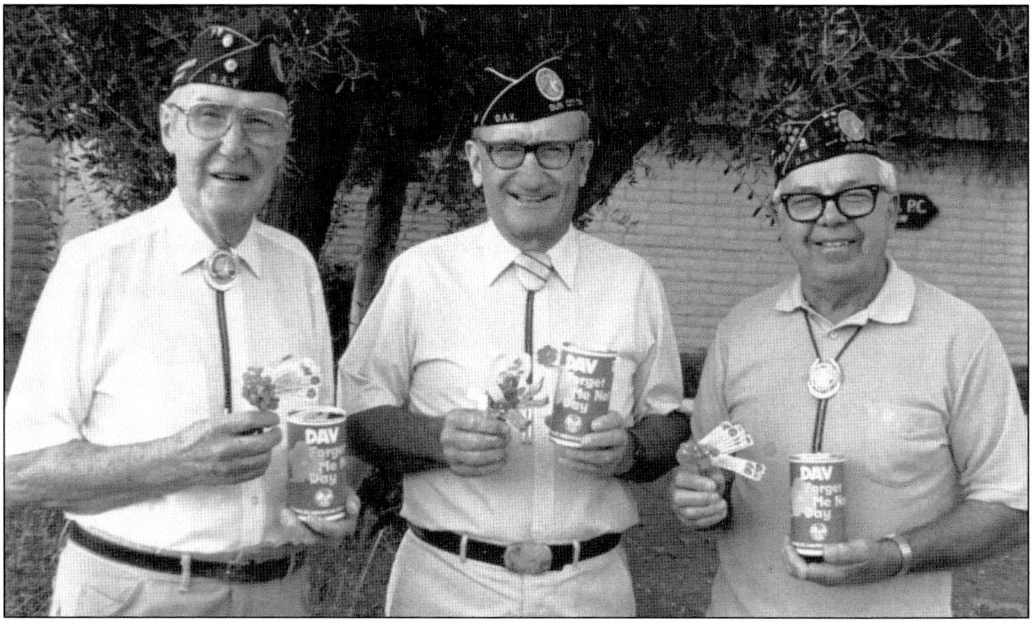

Charity begins at home, and taking care of friends and neighbors—or in this case fellow veterans—is a way of life in Sun City. Shown here, members of the Disabled American Veterans Sun City Star Chapter 24 conduct their annual Forget-Me-Not drive at Sun City shopping centers. From left to right are Victor Burkhart, commander; Ralph Squires, junior vice commander; and Al Radlinski, service officer. (Independent Newspapers, Inc.)

For many years, the Sun City Community Fund was the sole organization collecting contributions to support Sun City services. Conducting one large drive each year eliminated the need for separate groups to conduct their own campaigns and made it easier for residents to make one donation to support many associations. A thermometer was traditionally posted at Lakeview Recreation Center to keep residents up-to-date on the campaign's progress. (Independent Newspapers, Inc.)

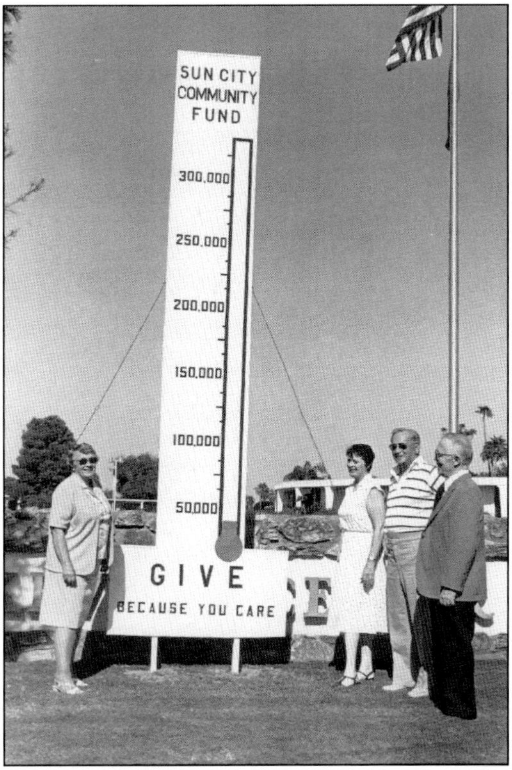


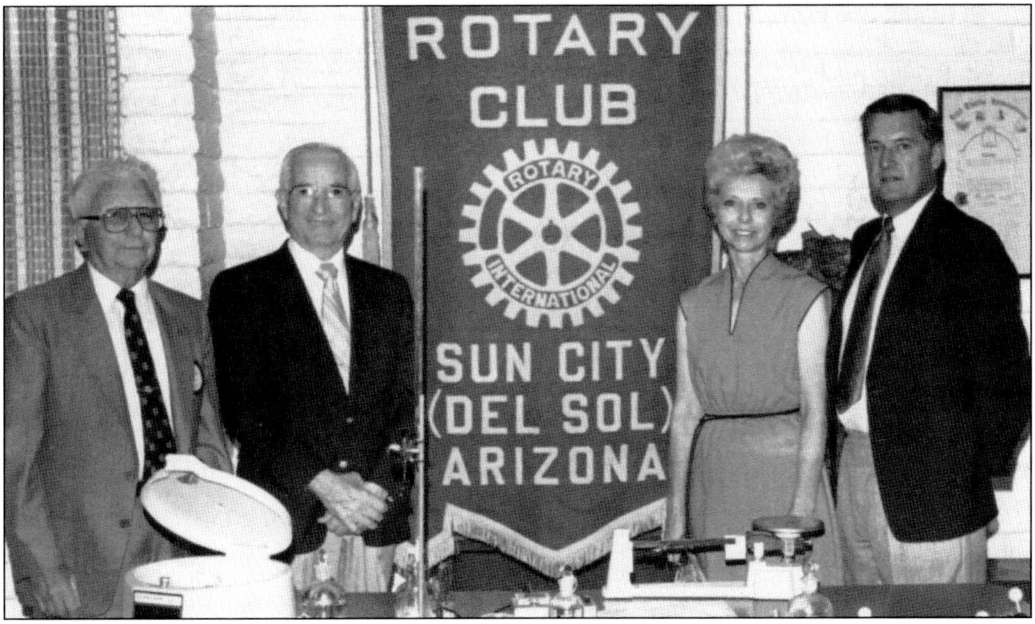


Sun City is home to several Rotary Clubs that through the years have contributed a tremendous amount of volunteer time and financial donations to projects that benefit children. Members of the Sun City del Sol Rotary Club in 1991 inspect chemistry equipment to be donated to Dysart High School in Surprise, Arizona. Pictured are, from left to right, club president Roy Health and high school officials Vince Marquese, Jayne Theis, and Bill Banden. (Independent Newspapers, Inc.)

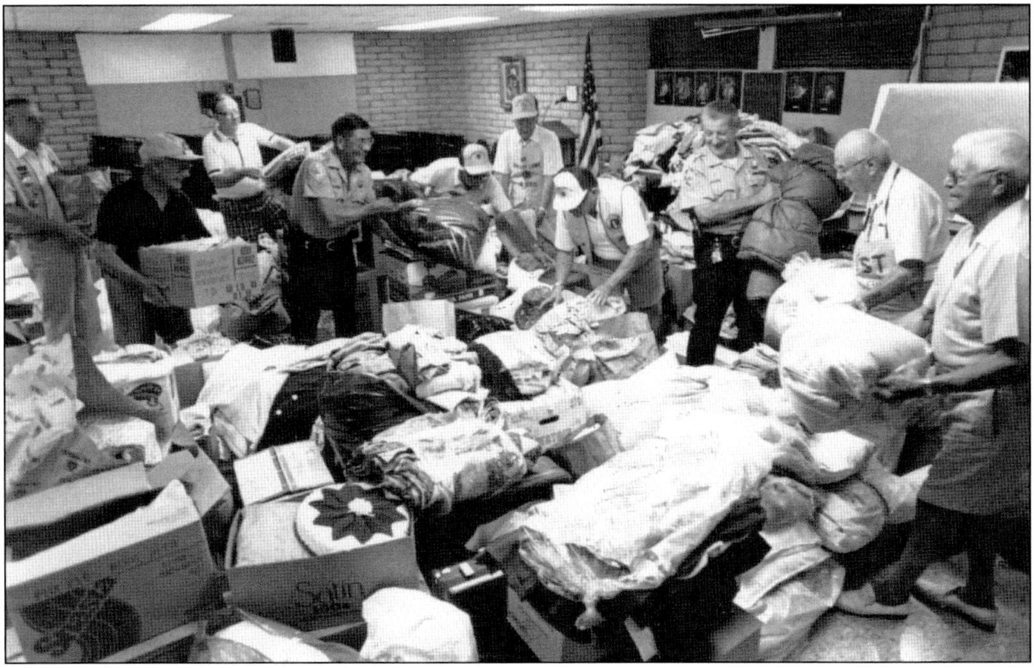

Sun City residents have always been generous in their efforts to help those in dire need. When a massive flood impacted residents of northern Arizona in the late 1980s, local residents were quick to donate food and clothing to assist displaced families. The Sheriff's Posse of Sun City accepted donations at its headquarters and members of the local Lions Club helped prepare items for shipping. (Independent Newspapers, Inc.)

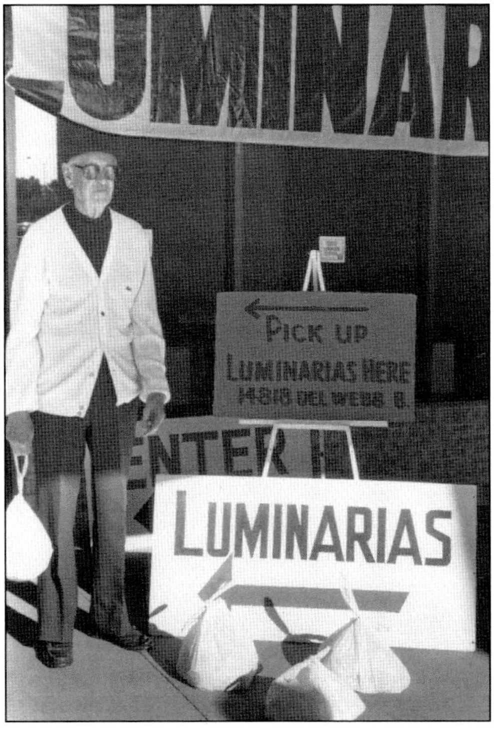


Interfaith Services, one of the oldest organizations in the community, offers programs designed to help disabled and aging residents remain in their homes as long as possible. One of the organization's biggest fund-raisers over the years involved selling luminaria kits for the holidays. Sture Johnson of the Sun Cities Physicians Club is shown helping with sales in this undated photograph. Today the organization is known as Benevilla. (Independent Newspapers, Inc.)

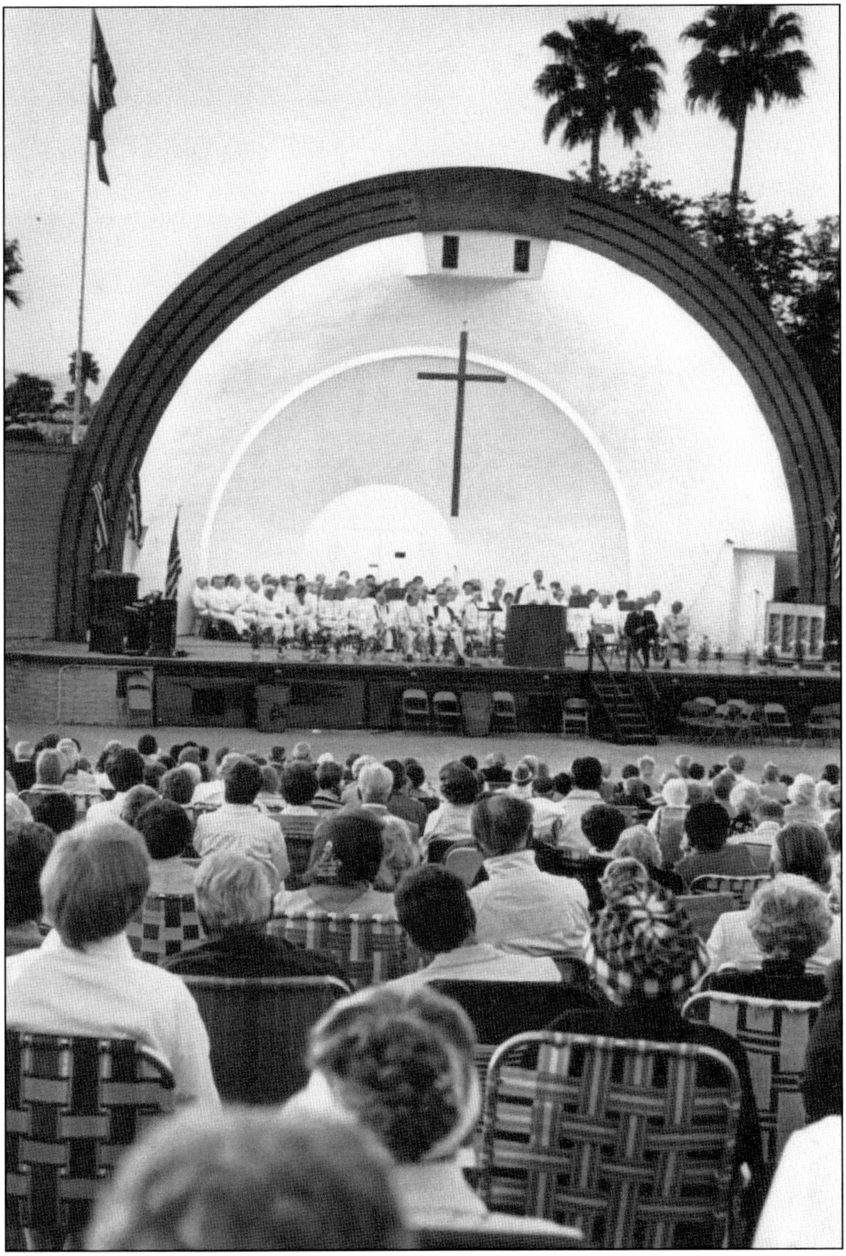

One of the community's oldest traditions is the Easter Sunrise Service held outdoors at the Sun Bowl. The very first sunrise service was held in 1961 on the patio of Town Hall Recreation Center. More than 1,000 residents attended the first service. The program was later sponsored by the Sun Cities Ministerial Association, an organization that brought together clergy from all faiths practicing in Sun City and Sun City West. The ministerial association also hosted an interfaith Thanksgiving service at the Sundome Center for Performing Arts in Sun City West. Sun City is home to nearly three dozen different faiths, and their influence extends far beyond simply offering religious guidance. Sun City's religious establishments have been quick to lend a helping hand to assist those in need, whether they are Sun City residents, nearby schoolchildren, or victims of a natural disaster. (Independent Newspapers, Inc.)

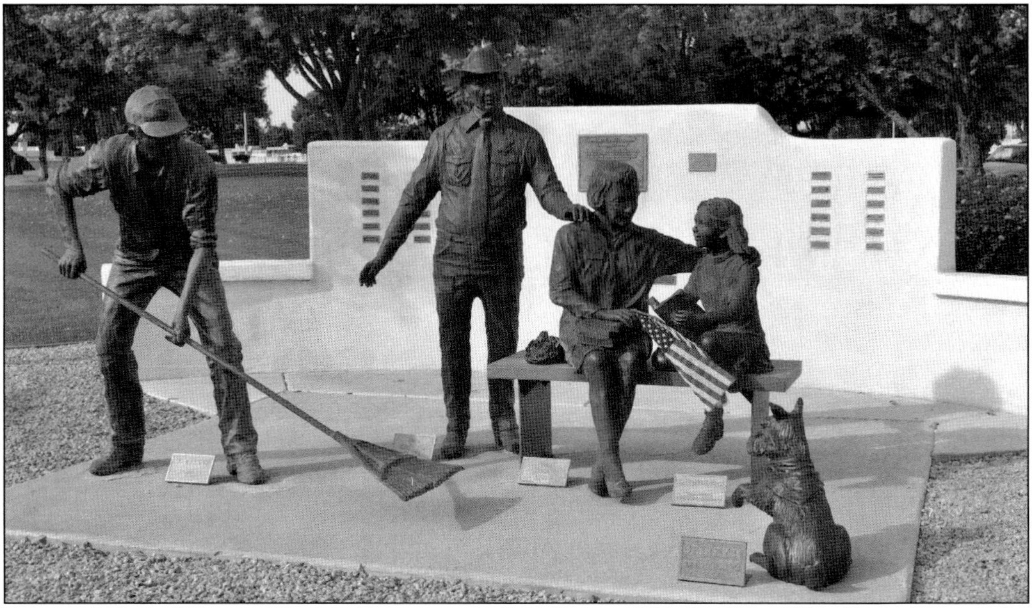

A bronze statue honoring the contributions of Sun City volunteers stands in front of Lakeview Recreation Center. The sculpture was created by Scottsdale artist Snell Johnson. Entitled *Sun City Volunteers: A Lifetime of Giving*, the memorial pays tribute to the PRIDES, the sheriff's posse, and members of those clubs and organizations that serve children and animals. The sculpture actually had two dedications—December 18, 2000, and March 17, 2011, when the small dog statue was added. (Bret McKeand.)

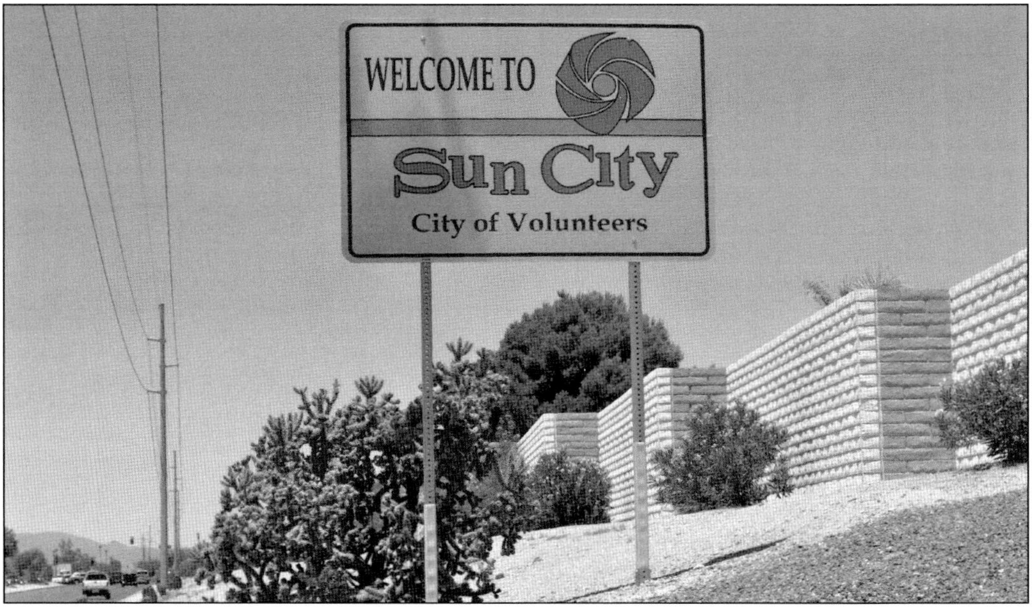


The Sun City Home Owners Association, led by George Hartman, in 1993 launched a campaign to encourage Sun City to adopt the slogan "City of Volunteers" to highlight the importance of volunteerism and recognize the efforts of local citizens. The campaign received strong support, and today visitors entering the community are reminded of Sun City's strongest and most endearing quality. (Bret McKeand.)

# *Nine*

# Life without Webb

The developer's departure created new challenges for the community, but it did not slow down or hamper Sun City's continued popularity. Indeed, without its benefactor solving problems, the community was forced to stand on its own two feet and provide for itself and its citizens.

An oasis in the desert when it first opened in 1960, by 1980 Sun City was being swallowed on all sides by dramatic growth occurring in neighboring Peoria and Surprise.

Sun City remains an unincorporated community, despite several attempts over the years to convince residents to establish a municipal form of government. The first incorporation campaign was launched in 1964 and several followed, although none ever received sufficient support to warrant a community-wide vote.

The most dangerous challenge to Sun City's existence came not from neighbors, but from the federal government. In 1988, changes to the Fair Housing Act all but prohibited seniors-only communities unless specific guidelines were met. After the minimum age requirement to live in Sun City was raised from 50 to 55, Sun City was "approved" and allowed to retain its retirement status (a status lost by Youngtown, the community that inspired Webb to build Sun City).

Many landmarks are gone, while others remain. The original recreation centers have been maintained, renovated, rebuilt, and at times, rebuilt again.

The first residents, too, slowly disappeared. The Sun City Pioneers Club, a club consisting of original residents who first moved to the community in 1960, was down to its last members by 1990 and would soon cease to exist.

Sun and fun may have been the initial attraction to Sun City 50 years ago. But the willingness of Sun City's residents to devote time and energy to running the community and staffing its many volunteer organizations have proven to be the keys to the community's continued success.

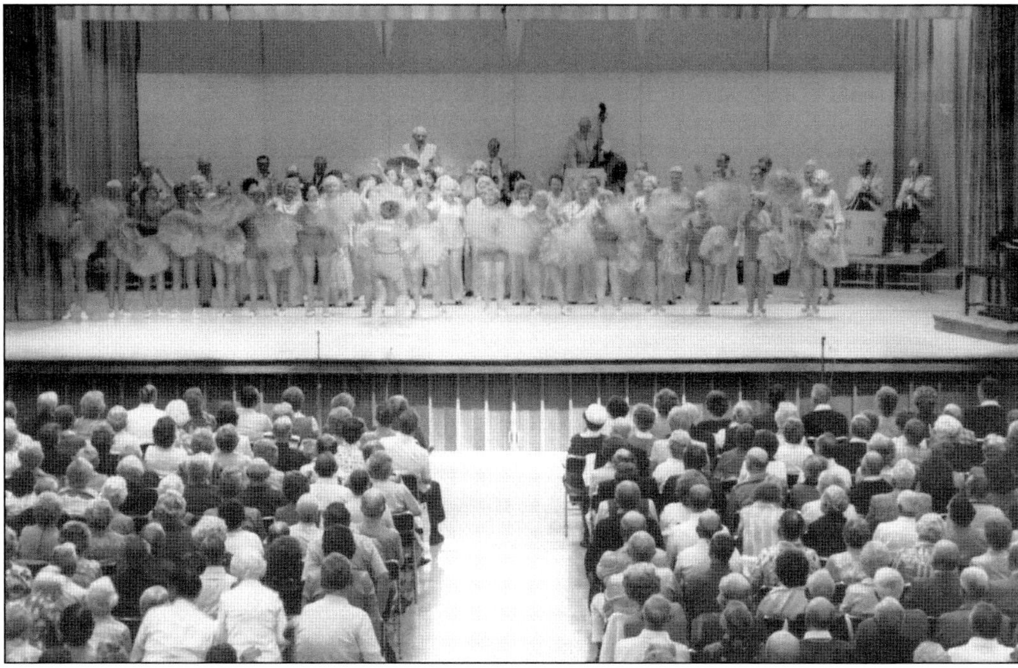

Sun City residents celebrated the community's 20th anniversary in January 1980 with an all-resident vaudeville show at Sundial Recreation Center.

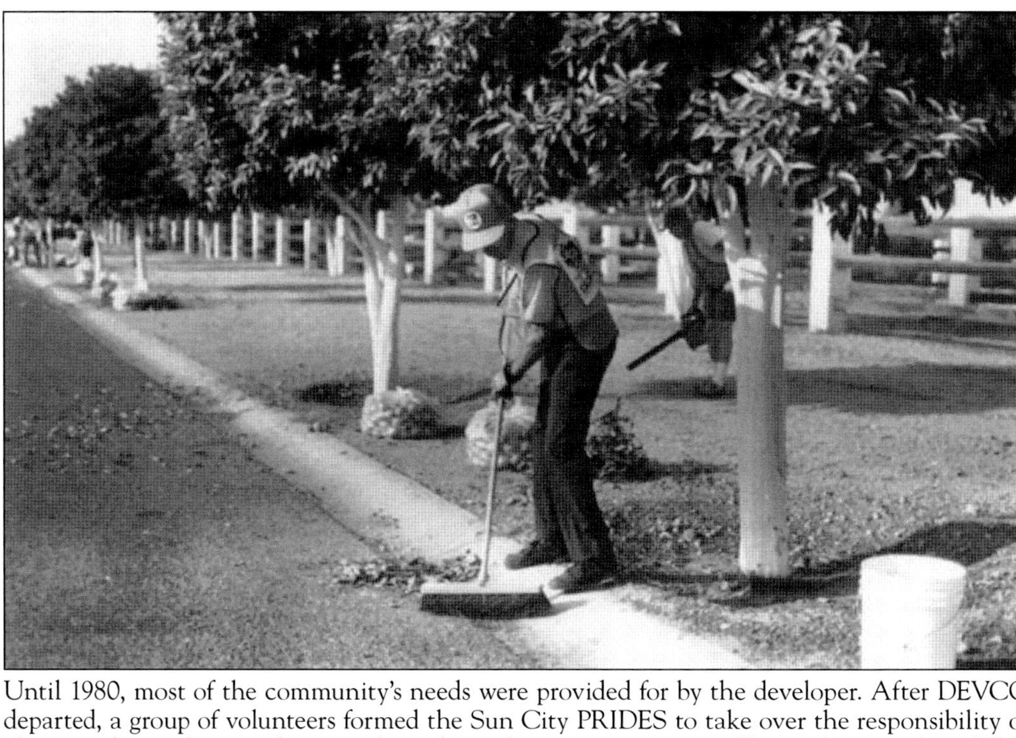

Until 1980, most of the community's needs were provided for by the developer. After DEVCO departed, a group of volunteers formed the Sun City PRIDES to take over the responsibility of cleaning the medians and streets throughout the community, as well as picking up fruit fallen from local trees. The PRIDES (Proud Residents Independently Donating Essential Services) have become a community institution. (Independent Newspapers, Inc.)

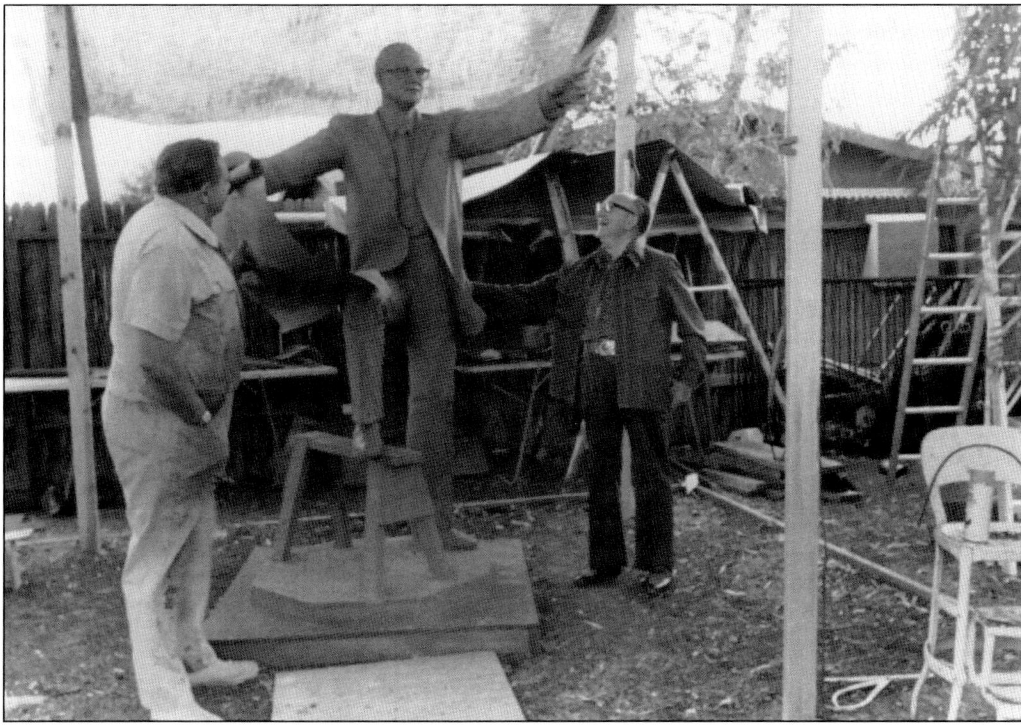

A statue committee headed up by Sam Higginbotham, right, was formed in 1980 to pay homage to Sun City's founder, Del E. Webb. The committee selected Scottsdale sculptor James O. Farley, left, to create the statue based on the theme of Webb as "a planner, builder, and a man of vision." A fund drive to raise $25,000 for the project was launched in 1981. (Independent Newspapers, Inc.)

The Webb statue is lowered to its final resting place in Memorial Garden at Bell Recreation Center. The statue was a project spearheaded by the Sun City Pioneers Club—a club consisting of residents who lived in Sun City since the first year it opened—and supported by DEVCO and local Lions Clubs. (Independent Newspapers, Inc.)

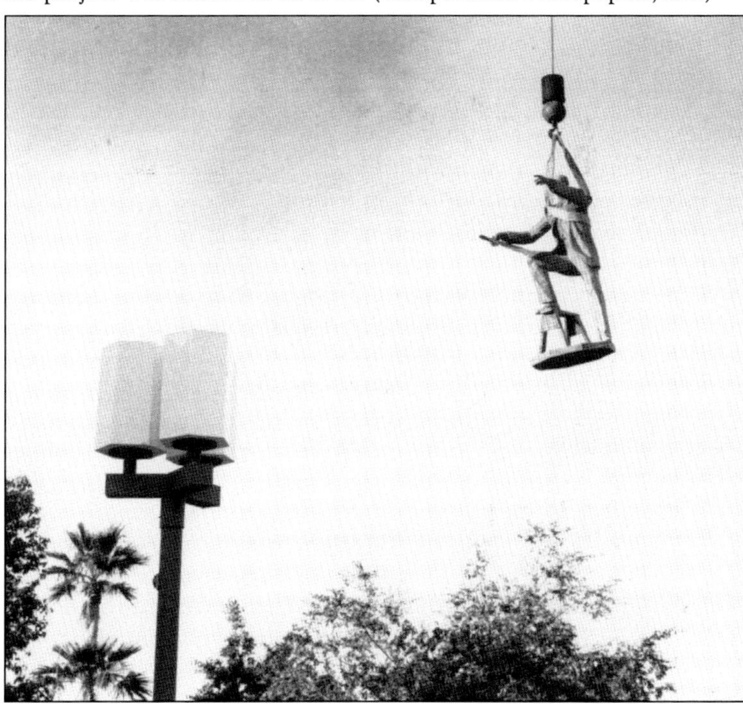

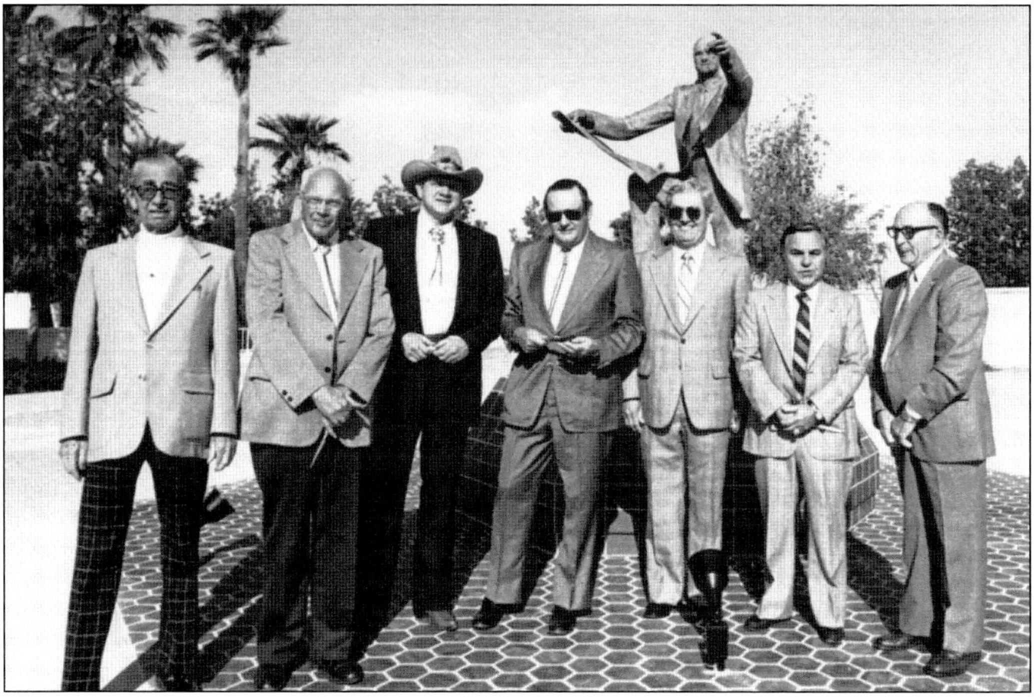

A dedication ceremony was held November 21, 1981. The statue committee included, from left to right, Doug Morris, editor of the *Sun City Citizen*; Norman Shrenk, Youngtown mayor; Jim Farley, sculptor; Burt Freireich, publisher of the *Daily News-Sun*; John Meeker, retired president of the Del E. Webb Development Corporation; Joe Aubin, general manager of DEVCO; and Sam Higginbotham, committee chairman. (Independent Newspapers, Inc.)

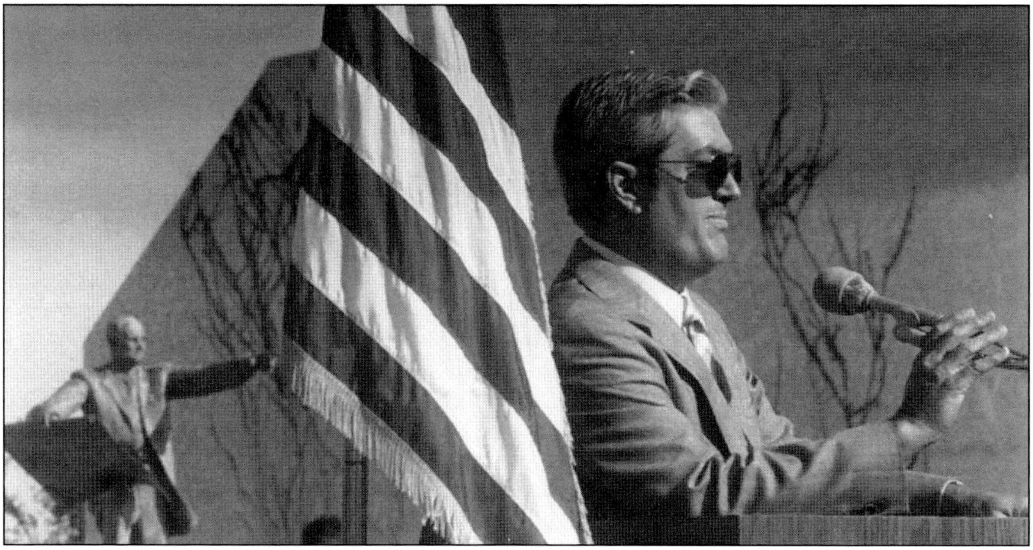

John Meeker, retired president of the Del E. Webb Development Corporation, was the featured speaker during the program to dedicate the Del E. Webb statue on November 21, 1981. Del Webb created Sun City, but it was Meeker who guided the community and managed the day-to-day operations during the first two decades. Often referred to as the "Father of Sun City," he died February 5, 2000. (Independent Newspapers, Inc.)

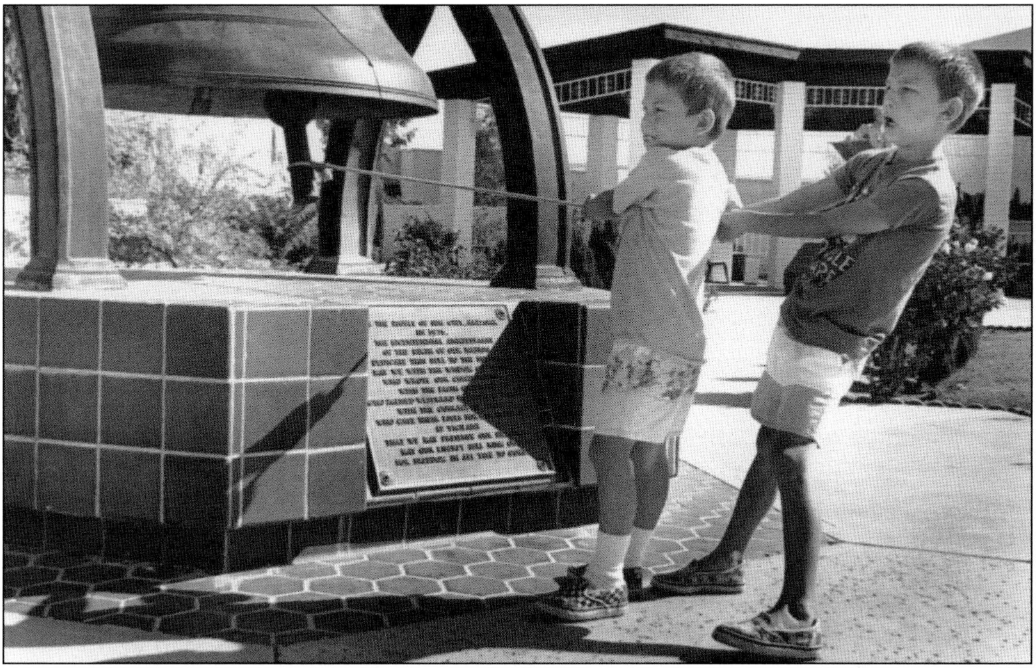

The annual Ring the Bell ceremony celebrates the nation's heritage, as well as the life of Sun City founder Del E. Webb, who died July 4, 1974. After patriotic songs and speeches, those in attendance are invited to grab hold of the bell's rope and give it a tug. In this 1987 photograph, visitors Ryan and Riley Winke were ready for their turn at the bell. (Independent Newspapers, Inc.)

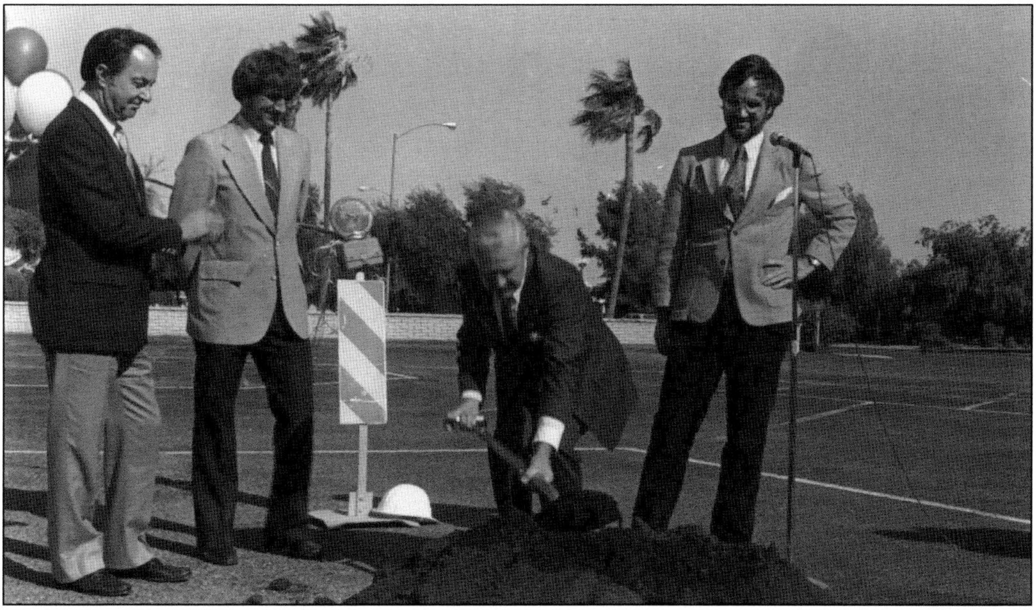

In 1980, the Sun Cities Art Museum would break away from its partnership with the Phoenix Art Museum and make plans to build its own facility. Eventually built on land located between Sun City and Sun City West, the museum's initial location was near 111th Avenue and Thunderbird Road in Sun City. Groundbreaking ceremonies were held, but plans were eventually scrapped in favor of a new location. (Independent Newspapers, Inc.)

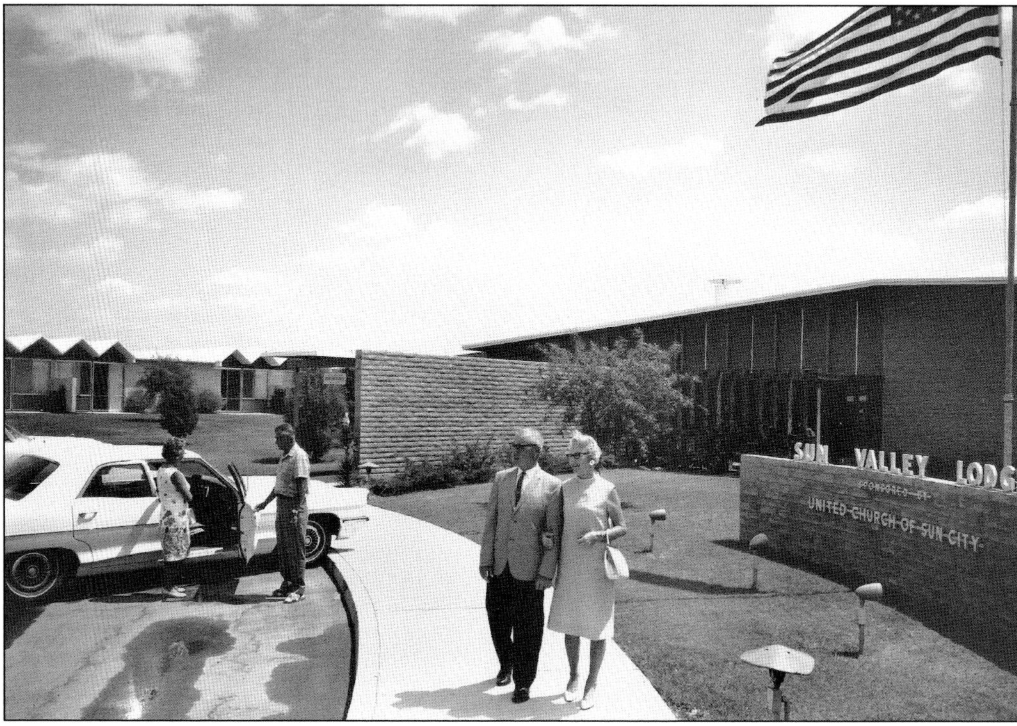


Sun Valley Lodge was the first extended care facility built in Sun City. Opened in 1965 by United Church of Sun City, the facility provided care to seniors who could no longer live independently. Sun City's second continuing care facility, Royal Oaks Lifecare Community, opened its doors in 1983 on 36 acres of land and is today home to more than 600 residents.

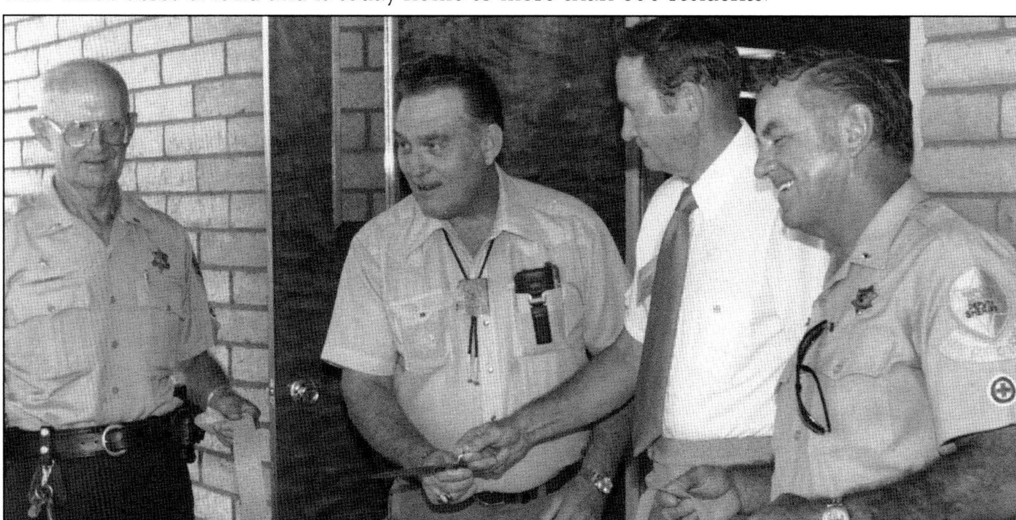

The Sheriff's Posse of Sun City officially opened its first headquarters in October 1980. County supervisor Hawley Atkinson, second from the right, was on hand for the event. The other three remain unidentified. The building was located on the corner of 111th and Peoria Avenues. The posse would later relocate to a larger building at 10861 Sunland Drive. (Independent Newspapers, Inc.)

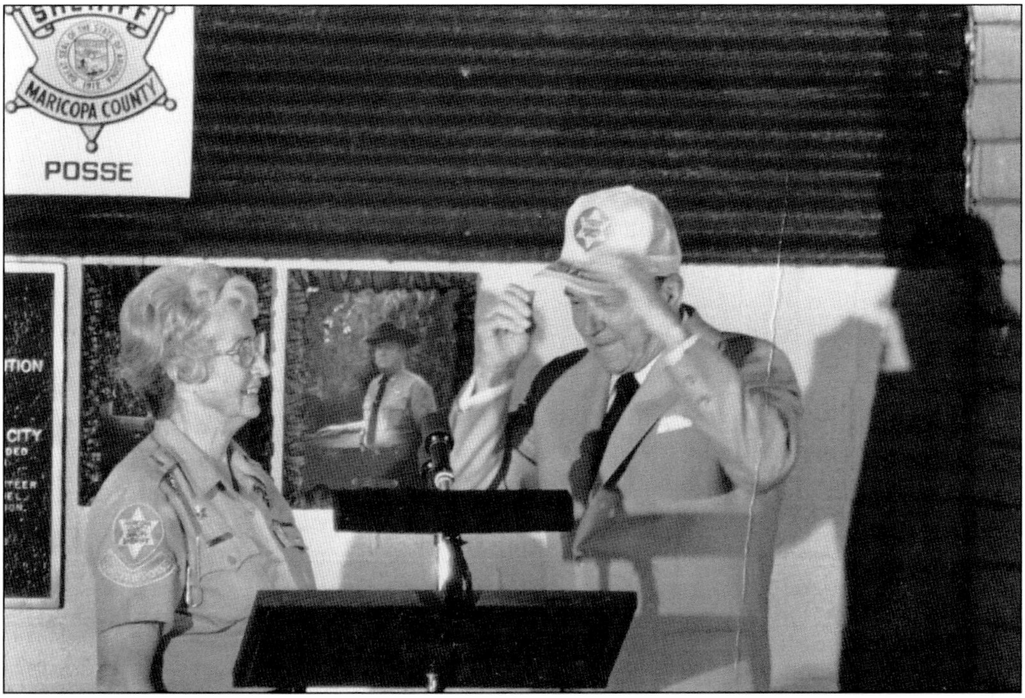


Ronald Reagan returned to Sun City in 1983, this time as president of the United States. President Reagan visited the community on May 6 to salute the work of the Sheriff's Posse of Sun City. In return, the president was made an honorary member of the organization.

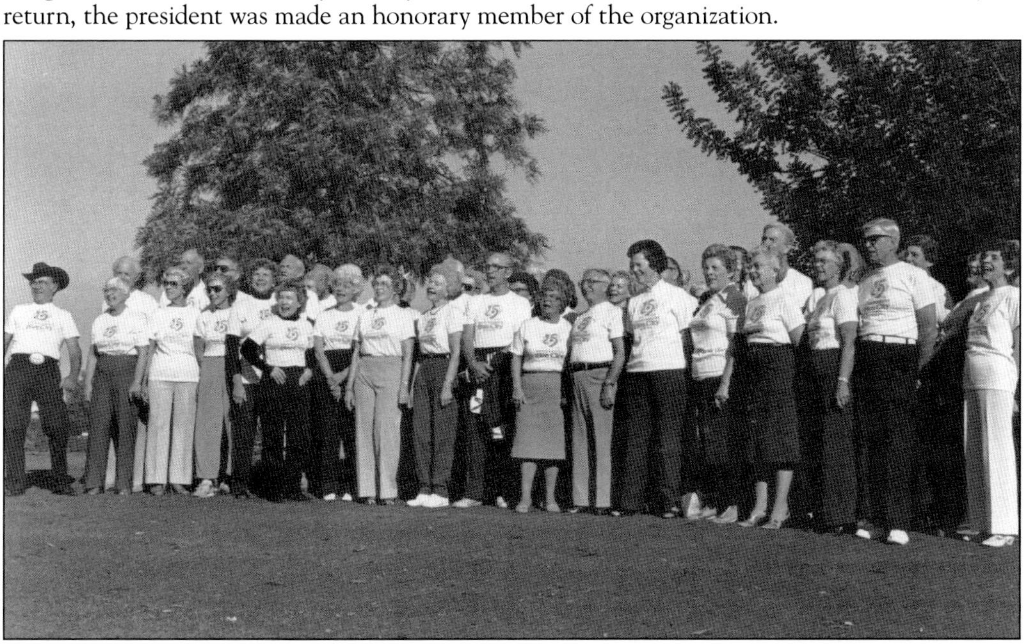

Of all the milestones marked in Sun City, the 25th anniversary in 1985 took on special significance and was the largest anniversary celebration held up to that time in the community. Festivities kicked off in early January with a special salute to the community on the ABC television show *Good Morning, America.* Residents gathered on the front lawn of Boswell Memorial Hospital to greet the national audience. (Independent Newspapers, Inc.)

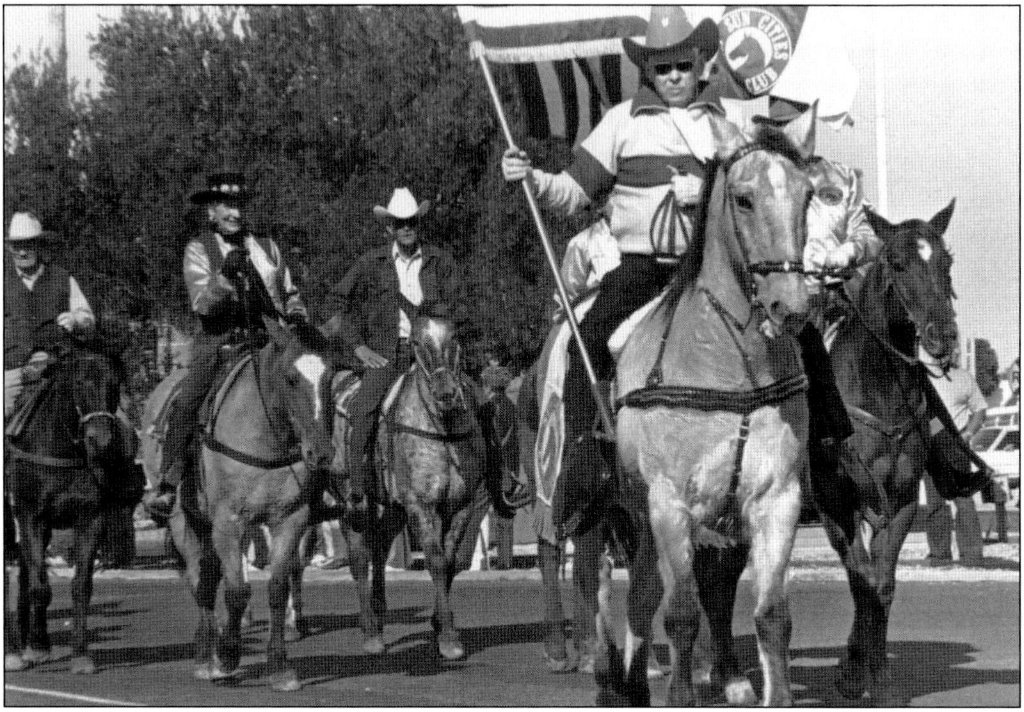

As was done in the early days of the community, a parade was held on January 30, 1985, to mark the 25th anniversary. Dozens of local clubs and organizations took part, as well as a number of area high schools and businesses. The Sun Cities Saddle Club was among those who participated. (Independent Newspapers, Inc.)

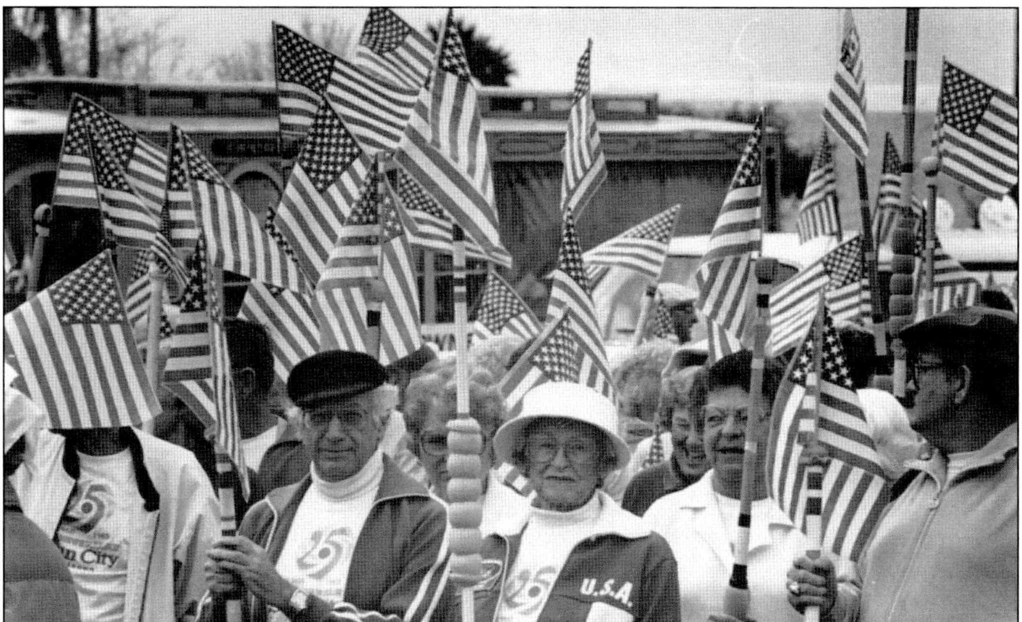


Members of the Sun City Italian-American Club show their pride in their community and their nation as they participate in the 25th anniversary parade in January 1985. (Independent Newspaper.)

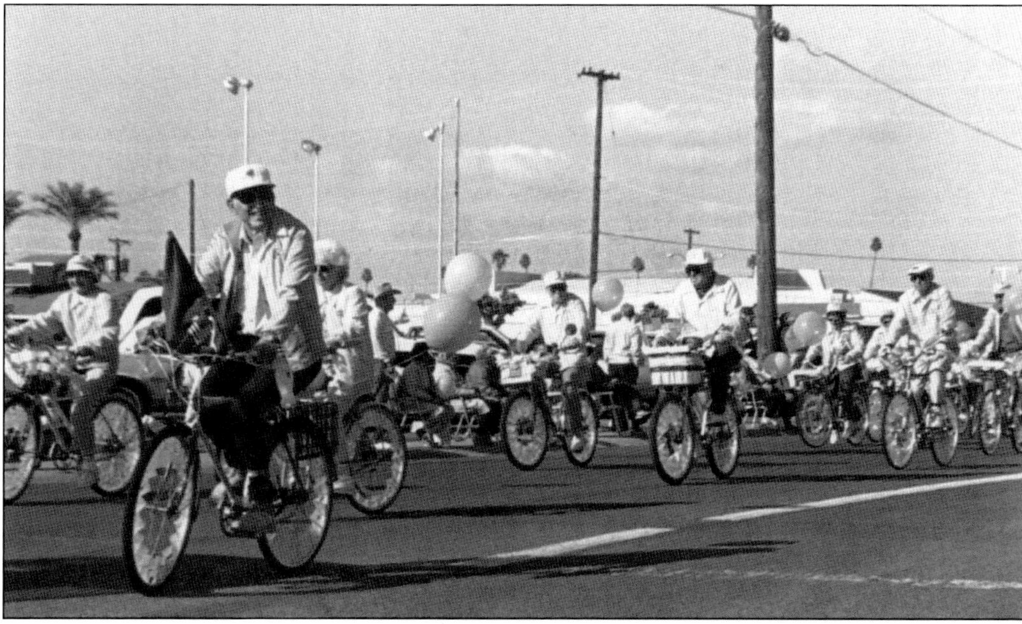

Members of the Sun City Pedal Pushers, the first bicycle club organized in the community, took part in the parade. Sun City Pioneers Eugene and Rose Butler established the club in the early 1960s and were among those in the parade. "Pioneers" were those residents who moved to Sun City in 1960; their final meeting was in 1990. (Independent Newspapers, Inc.)

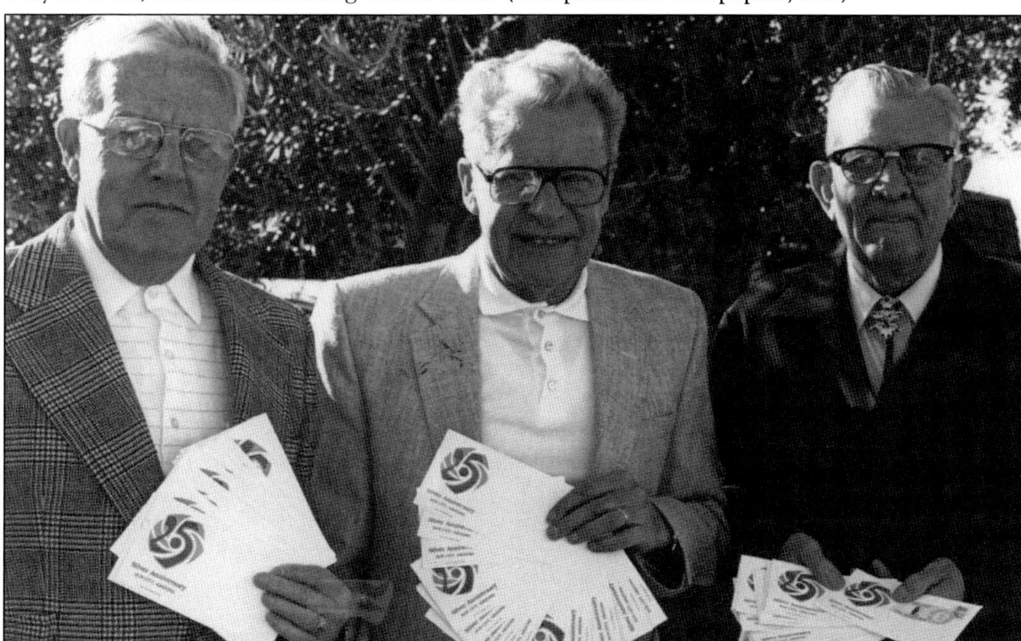

Members of the Sun City Stamp Club display a special envelope they created and sold to commemorate the 25th anniversary of Sun City and a special "first-day" postmark courtesy of the Sun City Post Office. The special edition cachet covers sold for $1. Shown from left to right are Frederick Swanson, 1984 president of the club; Robert M. Reed, chairman of the project; and John Fotheringham, 1985 president. (Independent Newspapers, Inc.)

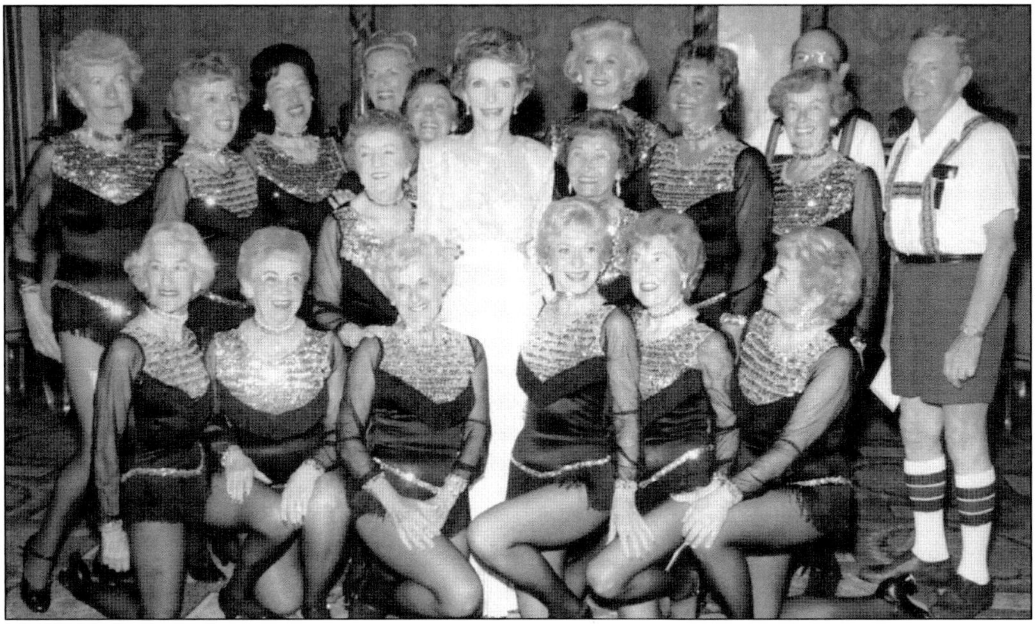

The Sun Cities Pom Poms, founded by Corinne Leslie, served as spirited ambassadors for Sun City and Sun City West and routinely performed at events throughout the nation. While on tour in 1985, the troupe performed in New York City at a fund-raiser for the National Fitness Foundation. During the performance, they were treated to a special meeting with First Lady Nancy Reagan.

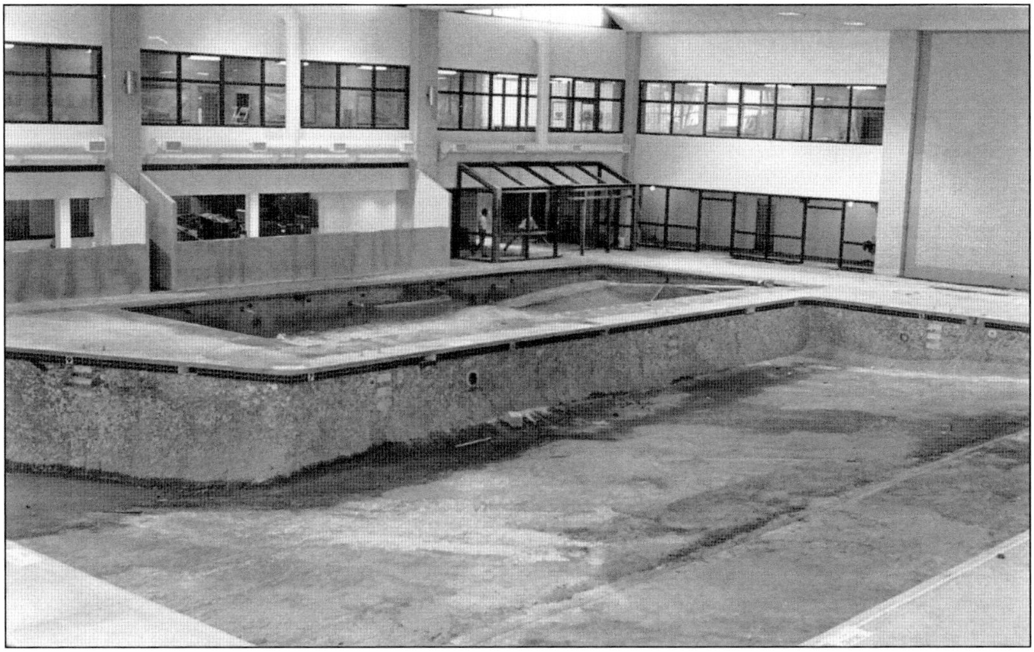

In 1986, weaknesses detected in the roof over the Sundial Recreation Center pool forced the center to be closed for nearly a year while repairs were made to the roof, as well as renovations to the pool and several craft rooms. The $1.3-million project forced the Recreation Centers of Sun City to dramatically increase yearly dues. The roof would again collapse 20 years later, causing major damage to the facility. (Independent Newspapers, Inc.)

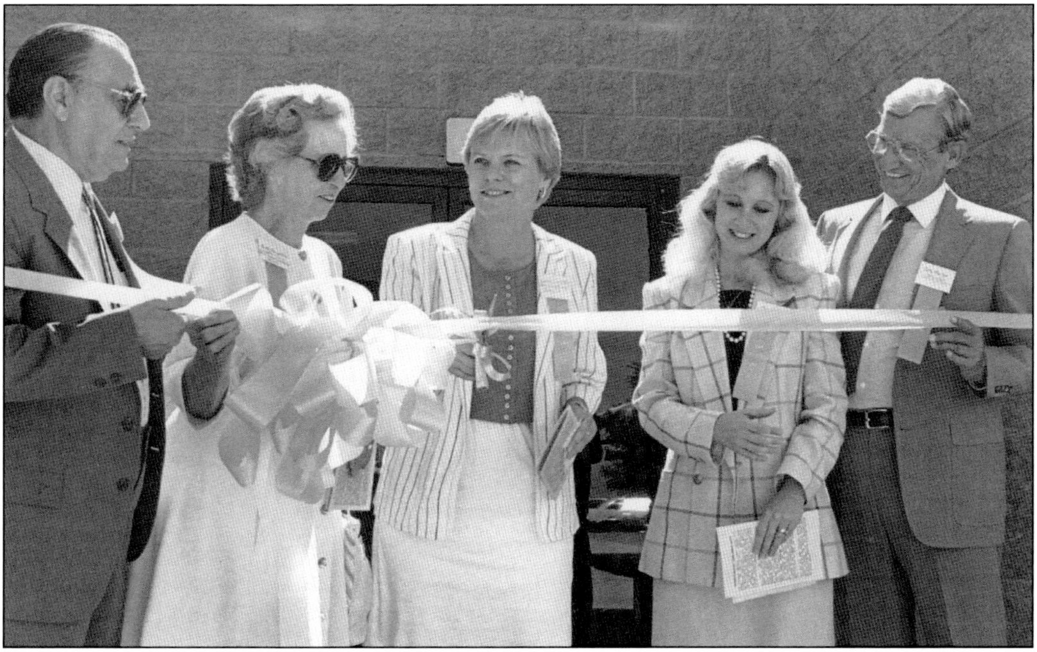

Sun City opened its first public senior center in the late 1980s. The Olive Branch Senior Center provided low-cost lunches and was partially funded by the county, Sun Health, and several other local organizations. The center was located at the Church of Christ before moving in the early 1990s to the Sun Bowl Shopping Center. The center today operates at United Church of Sun City. (Independent Newspapers, Inc.)

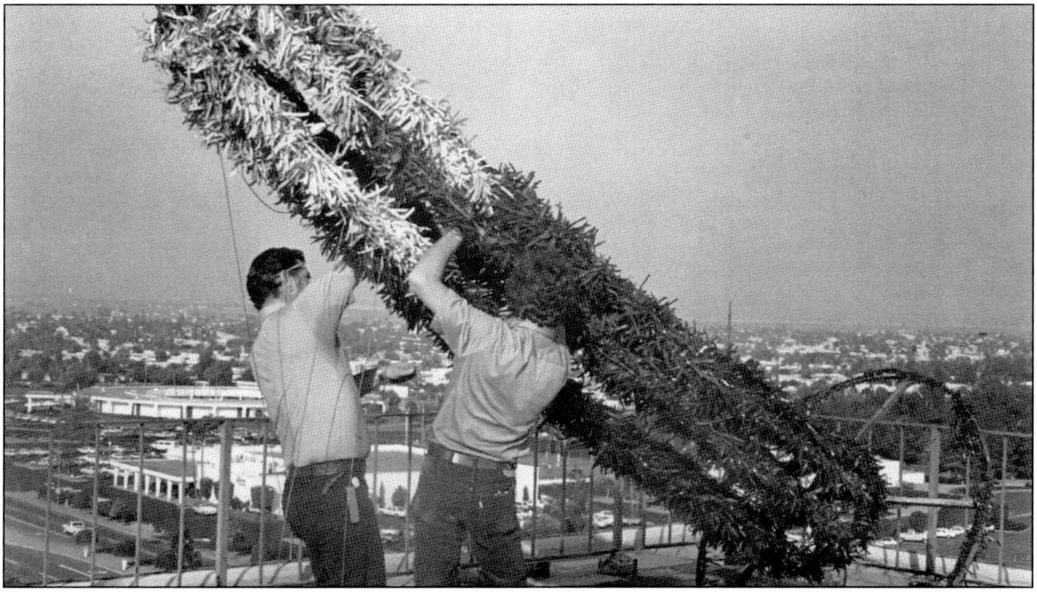

The official start of the holiday season in Sun City always began when Sun Health workers installed the huge holiday candles that sat on the roof of Boswell Memorial Hospital. The candles were a holiday tradition for nearly three decades in Sun City and could be seen from every corner of the community. One candle was 12 feet tall, the other was 16 feet tall. (Independent Newspapers, Inc.)

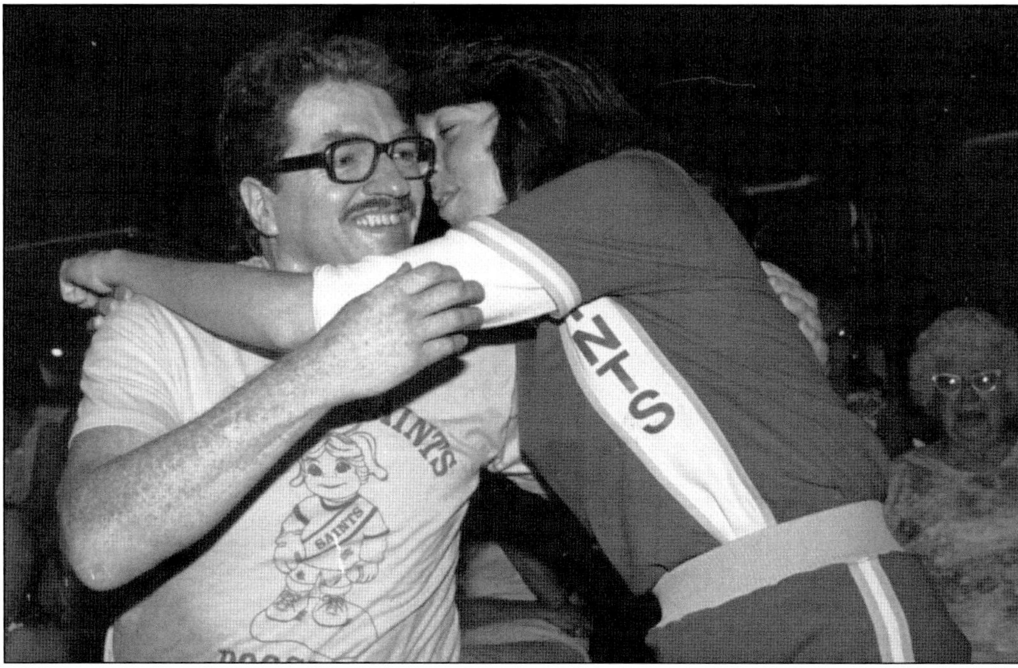

All-American fast-pitch softball player Debbie Doom, of the Sun City Saints, makes money by kissing fans for $1 during a Saints softball game. Larry Silverberg gets his dollar's worth during a game on June 30, 1982. The Saints enjoyed tremendous support and consistently attracted large crowds. DEVCO sold the stadium in 1983 to a private firm. An increase in rent forced the Saints to leave in 1984. (Independent Newspapers, Inc.)

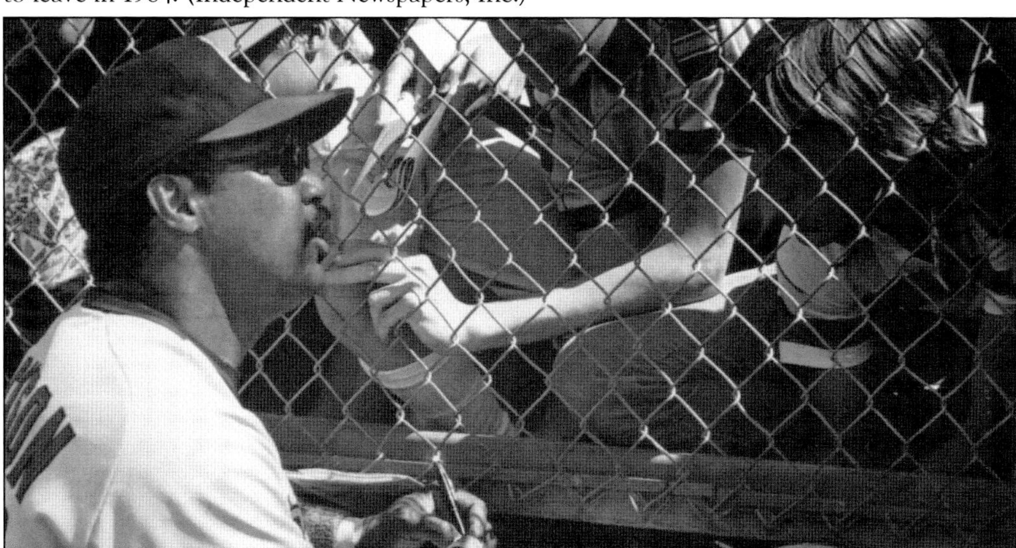

Hall of Famer Reggie Jackson was among the many baseball greats who played at Sun City Stadium during the 1970s and 1980s. In 1985, the Milwaukee Brewers moved from Sun City to a new spring training facility in Chandler. Despite efforts by local civic leaders, the community was unable to lure another team to the facility, and the stadium never again hosted a Cactus League game. (Bret McKeand.)

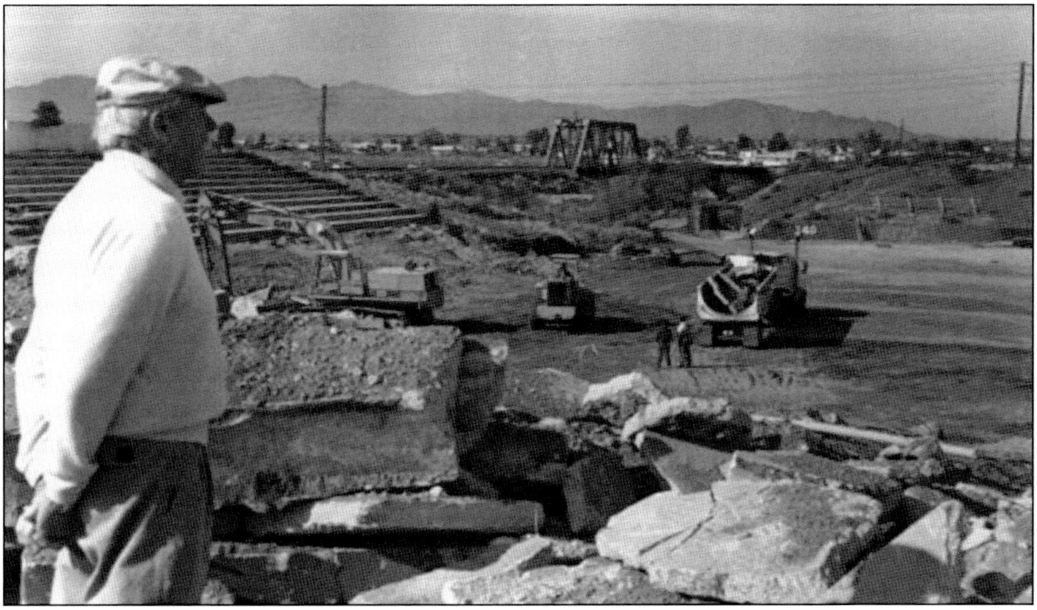

The Arizona Fall League's Sun Cities Solar Sox played two seasons at Sun City Stadium before moving to Peoria. In 1995, the stadium was demolished to make room for an apartment complex. All that remains of the stadium is the outfield wall, which can be seen in the complex's parking lot at 111th and Grand Avenues. (Independent Newspapers, Inc.)

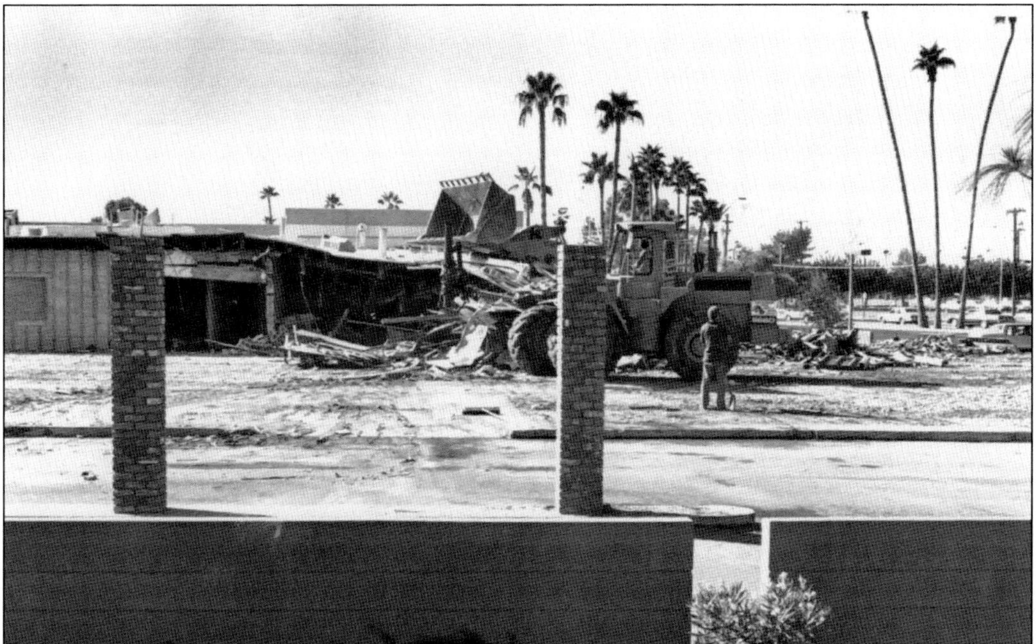

Another longtime Sun City icon was torn down in 1989. King's Inn Restaurant and Hotel, one of the first buildings ever constructed in Sun City, was demolished to make way for a grocery store. Originally called the Hiway House Motor Hotel, the facility was often the first place many early residents visited when they came to Sun City. The plaza that exists in its place is called the King's Inn Center. (Independent Newspapers, Inc.)

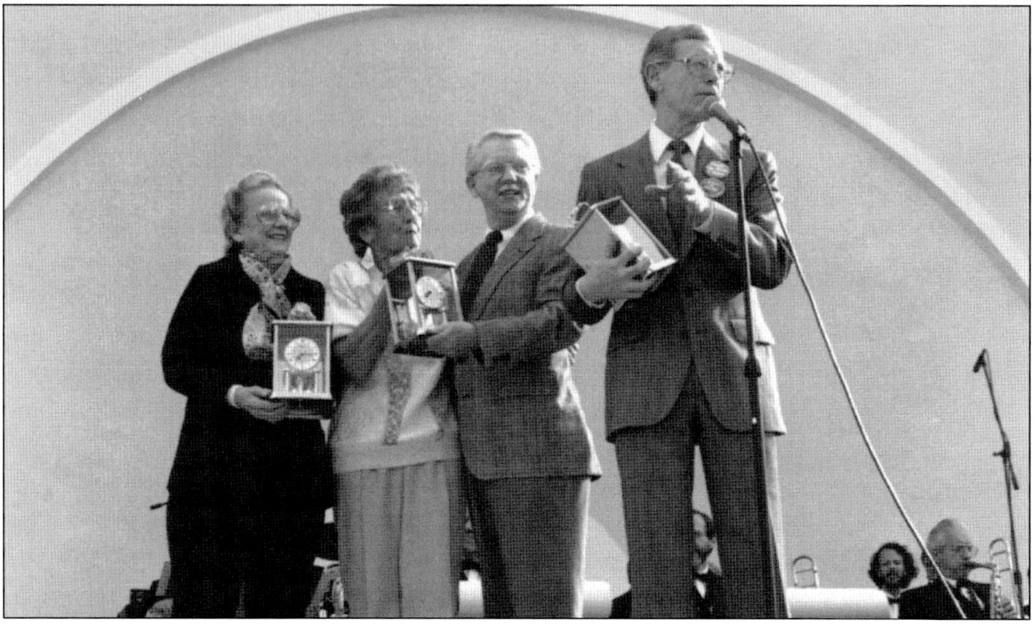

Sun City marked its 30th anniversary with a concert at the Sun Bowl in January 1990. Awards were presented to several community leaders. From left to right are Jane Freeman, one of the founders of the Sun Cites Area Historical Society; Corrine Leslie, founder of the Sun City Poms; Red Pope, of Valley National Bank; and Jerry Svendsen, former DEVCO public relations manager and then owner of *Sun Life* magazine. (Independent Newspapers, Inc.)

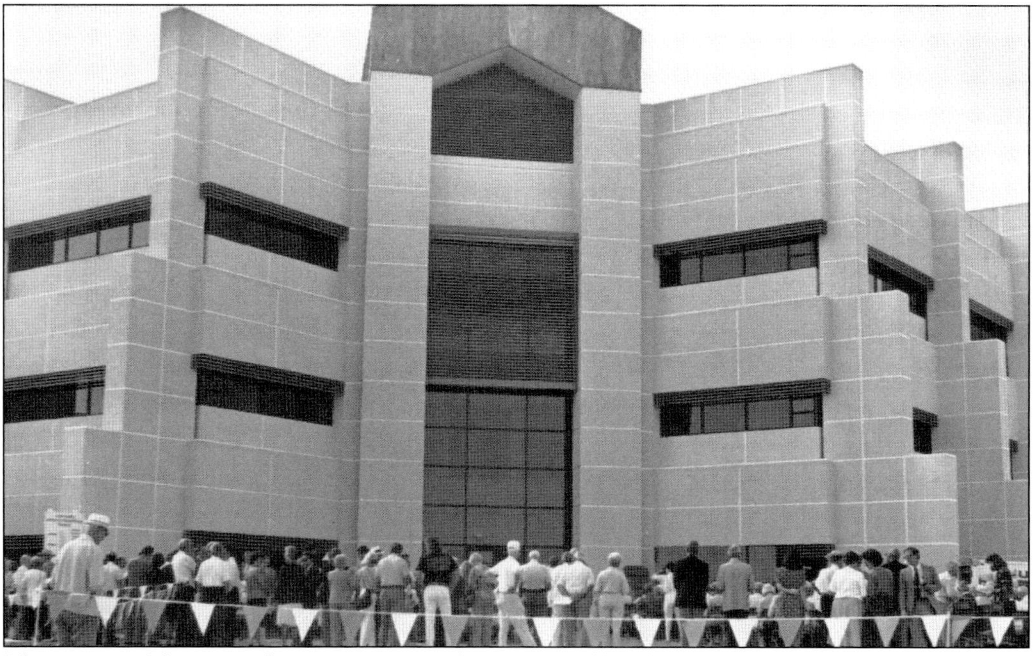

The Sun Health Research Institute opened in 1986 and has become a leader in research seeking cures for such age-related diseases as Alzheimer's and Parkinson's. The institute is one of the world's leading tissue banks and provides tissue to scientists across the globe. (Independent Newspapers, Inc.)

Since 1964, the issue of incorporation has been a highly debated issue in Sun City. Les Merydith, shown here, was president of Citizens for Self-Government and attempted three incorporation drives between 1985 and 1998 but was never able to collect enough signatures to force a community election. Merydith's primary adversary was Nat Jampel, president of the Town Meeting Association, a group that opposed incorporation. (Independent Newspapers, Inc.)

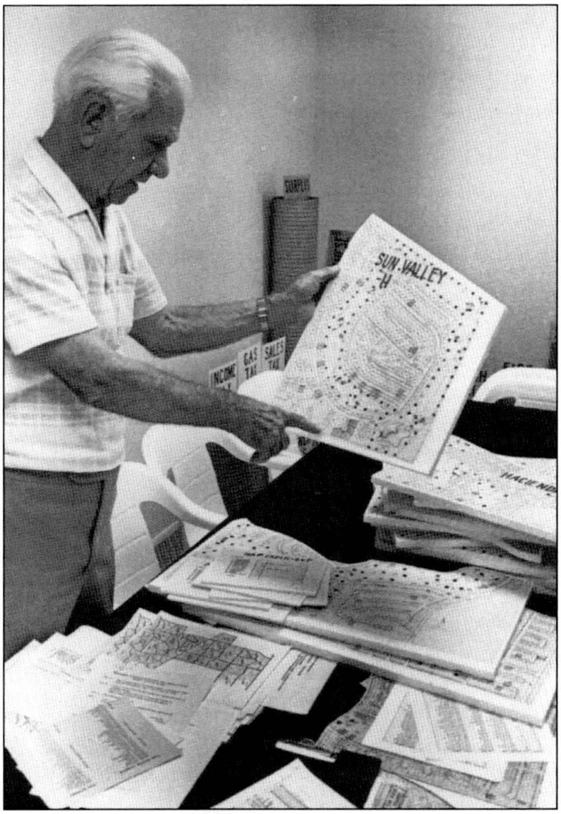


The 1996 presidential campaign passed through Sun City. Pres. Bill Clinton, the Democratic nominee and incumbent, was running against Republican candidate Bob Dole. Dole's running mate, Jack Kemp, visited Sun City later in the campaign. Clinton's venture into the Republican stronghold of Sun City paid off—he captured Arizona's electoral college votes on his way to reelection. (Bret McKeand.)

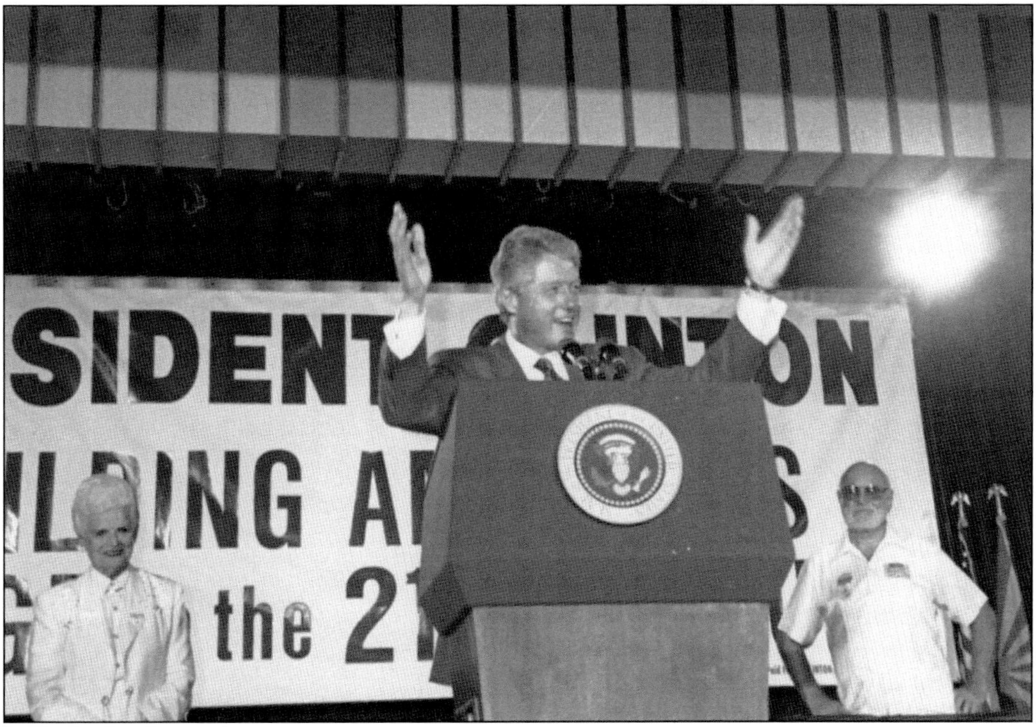

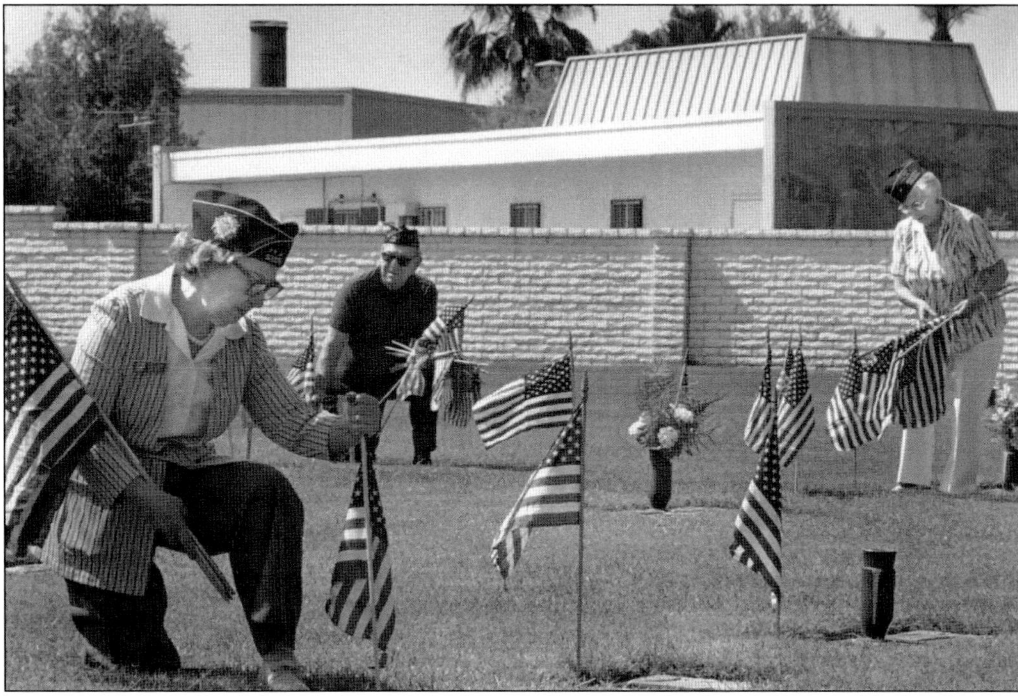

Sun City residents have never been shy in expressing their patriotism and love for their country. The community honors its veterans during the annual Memorial Day and Veterans Day ceremonies, held today in the Garden of Valor at Sunland Memorial Park and Mortuary. The Garden of Valor is the site of several memorials to veterans, military organizations, and the nation's military branches. (Independent Newspapers, Inc.)

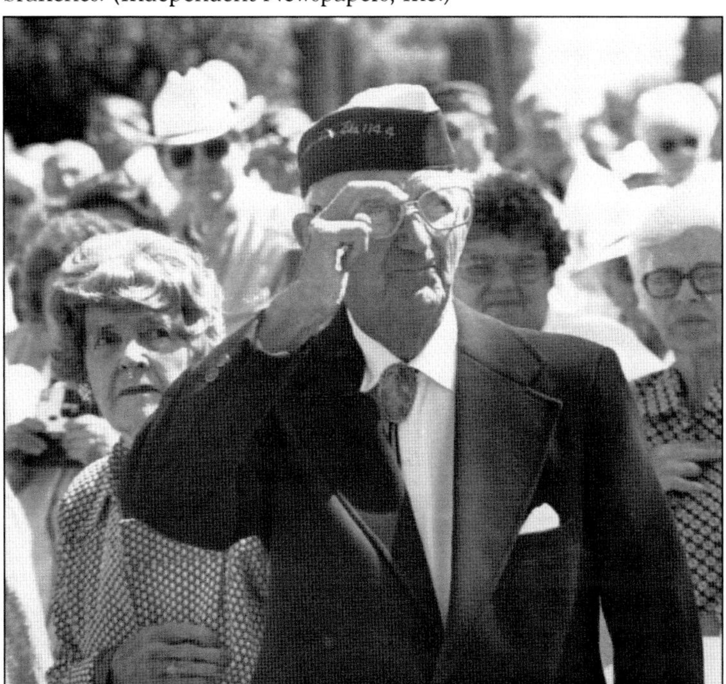

Sun City and Sun City West are home to a large population of veterans. There are more than a dozen military clubs and organizations serving the two communities, and they combine their efforts each year to sponsor Memorial Day and Veterans Day ceremonies. Pictured in this photograph of a Veterans Day ceremony in the late 1980s is Lt. Bernard Vogel, 95, the last surviving member of the Sun City-Youngtown chapter of the World War I Barracks. (Independent Newspapers, Inc.)

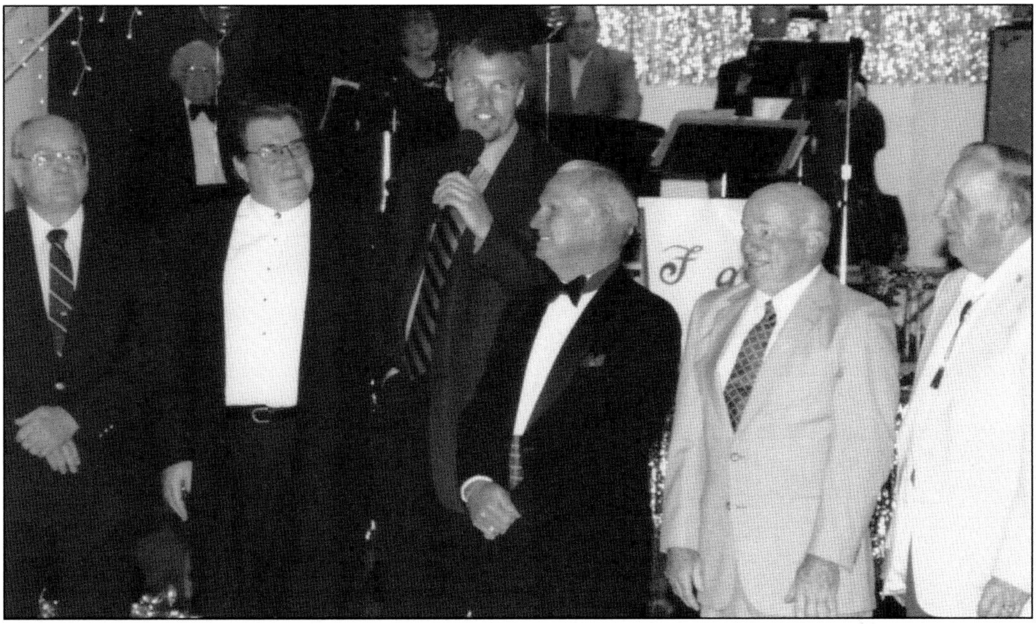

Sun City reached another milestone in 2000, as the community celebrated its 40th anniversary. A 40th Anniversary Committee organized the celebrations and donated all proceeds to a charitable foundation. The celebration kicked off with a dance held January 9, 2000, at Sundial Recreation Center. Tom Chambers of the Phoenix Suns served as master of ceremonies for the event. (Independent Newspapers, Inc.)

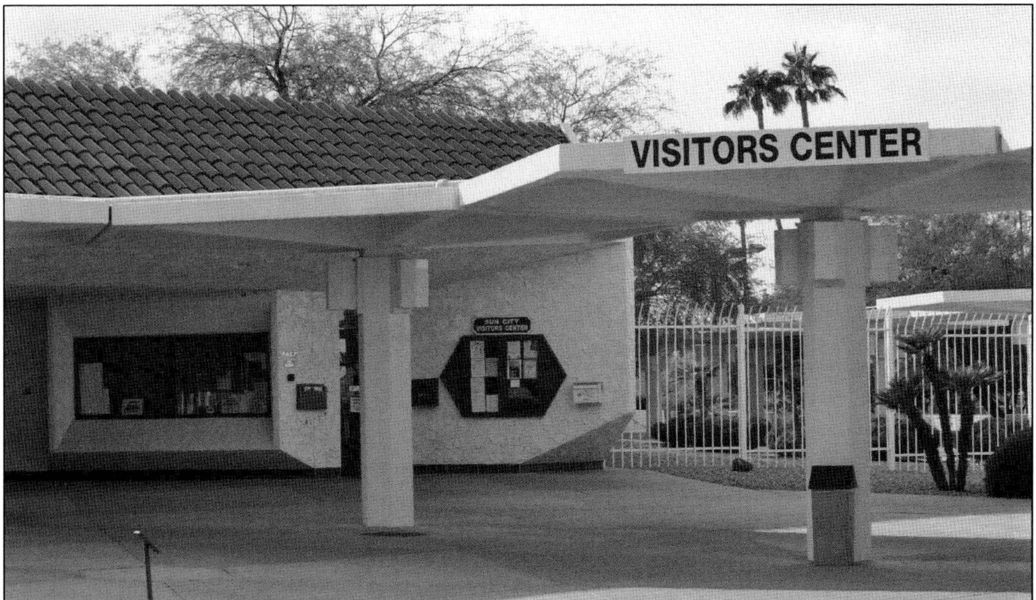


A group of residents and business owners created the Sun City Ambassadors in 1989 to fill the promotional void left by the departure of DEVCO. Facing competition from newer retirement communities, it was important the original Sun City continue to be promoted and advertised nationally. The nonprofit organization operates the Sun City Visitors Center at Bell Recreation Center. Its Web site is www.suncityaz.org. (Bret McKeand.)

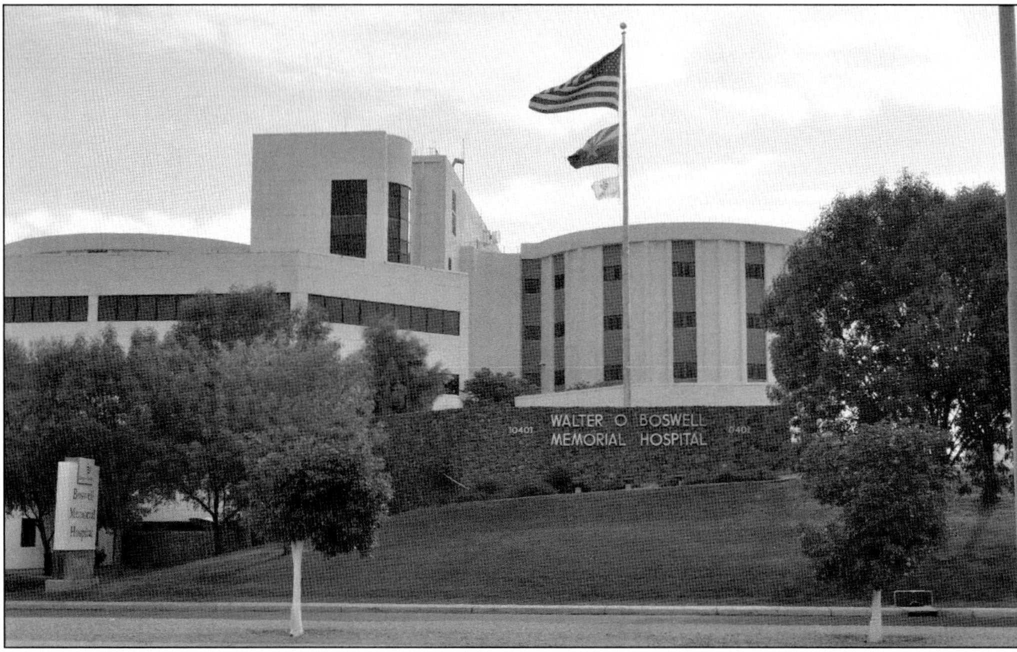


Boswell Memorial Hospital celebrated its 25th anniversary in 1995, and in 1997, the Sun Health Corporation launched a $24-million renovation and expansion of the facility. In addition to its vast health care and medical facilities in Sun City, Sun Health also operates the Del E. Webb Memorial Hospital in Sun City West. Banner Health acquired Sun Health in 2008. (Bret McKeand.)

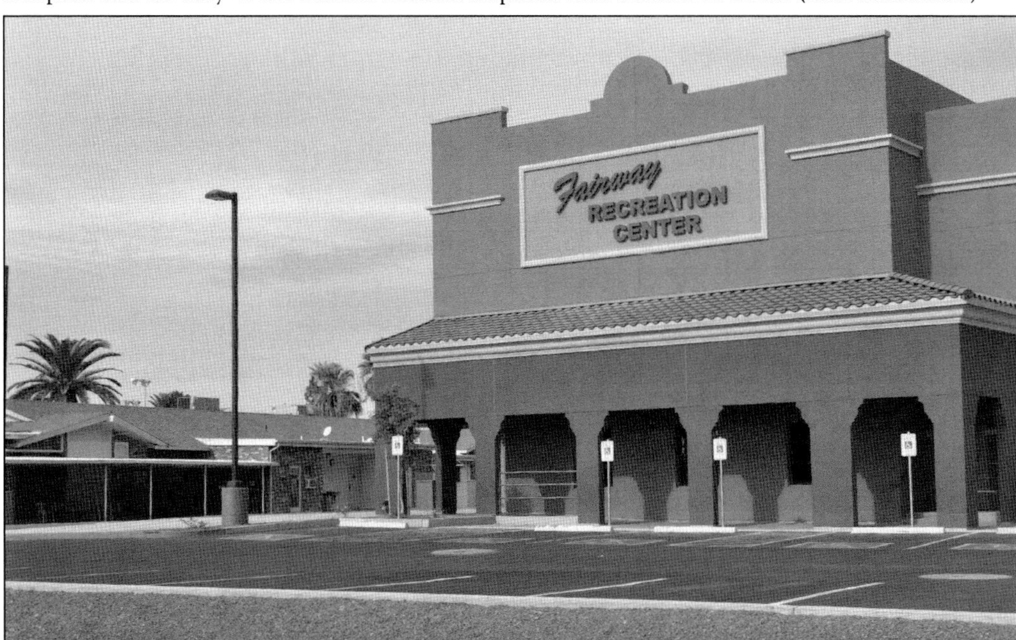


Homes and recreation facilities in Sun City have aged well over the past 50 years. Fairway Recreation Center, the second recreation center built in Sun City, was demolished in 2009–2010 and a new facility was erected in its place. The new center is on the right, while part of the original structure on the left waits to be torn down. (Bret McKeand.)

# *Ten*

# Golden Anniversary

Celebrating community milestones has always been a tradition in Sun City, and in 2009, residents began gearing up for the biggest and best celebration yet: the community's 50th anniversary. Experts once predicted Sun City was an experiment doomed to fail, but by 2010 those experts had long since been proven wrong.

Sun City had survived. It had grown and changed with the times. It had learned to coexist with neighboring communities whose boundaries now pressed up against its walls. It still attracts new residents, despite intense competition from newer developments. Residents had plenty of reason to celebrate.

A number of organizations took the lead in planning the year-long schedule of festivities. A special 50th Anniversary Committee was created to plan activities, and the Sun City Visitors Center played a pivotal role in promoting and conducting events.

To coincide with the anniversary and to pay homage to the community's founder, the Sun Cities Area Historical Society in 2009 renamed its museum the Del Webb Sun Cities Museum. The museum, which serves as the society's headquarters, is located in one of the first model homes ever built in Sun City.

The more things change, the more they stay the same. Drive around Sun City and many of the streets and buildings appear much as they did when they were first constructed decades ago. A scattering of homes and recreational facilities have received face-lifts, and the amenities and activities have changed over the years as the interests and desires of new retirees shifted.

The Del E. Webb Corporation merged with Pulte Homes in 2001, and the company continues to build communities for active adults. A testament to the original community is the fact that the "Sun City" moniker is still used in many of the company's newer projects.

Clearly, the name continues to resonate and create positive images in the minds of today's baby boom retirees.

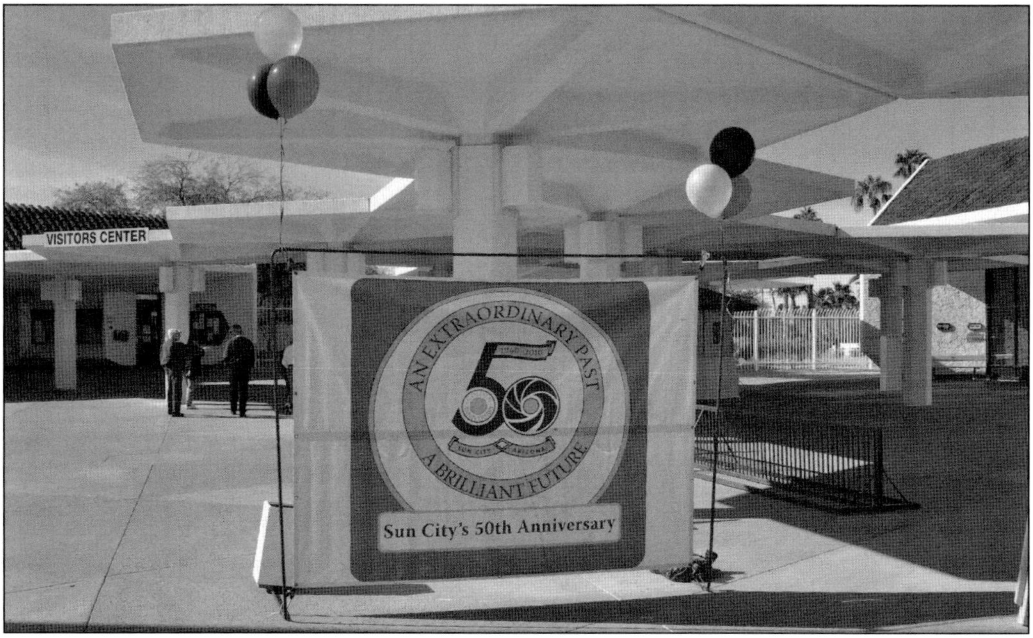


A special 50th anniversary party was held January 1, 2010, at Bell Recreation Center to mark the golden anniversary of Sun City. The event attracted several hundred residents who were treated to birthday cake and refreshments, speeches, and music by a barbershop quartet. It was the first of a number of celebrations held in 2010 by the 50th Anniversary Committee. (Bret McKeand.)

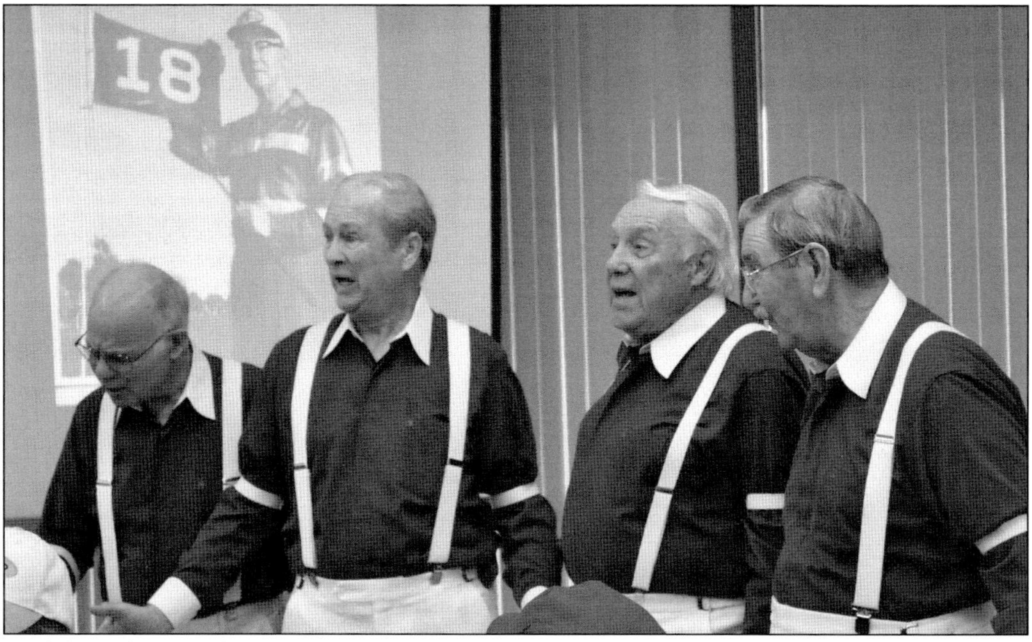


Birthday cake, speeches, and musical entertainment were all part of the 50th anniversary kick-off celebration at Bell Recreation. Entertainment was provided by the Sun Cities School Board Quartet while photographs of Del E. Webb and the early days of Sun City were highlighted. Members of the quartet are, from left to right, Dave Tague, Ken Corns, Doug Campbell, and Bud Heterman. (Bret McKeand.)

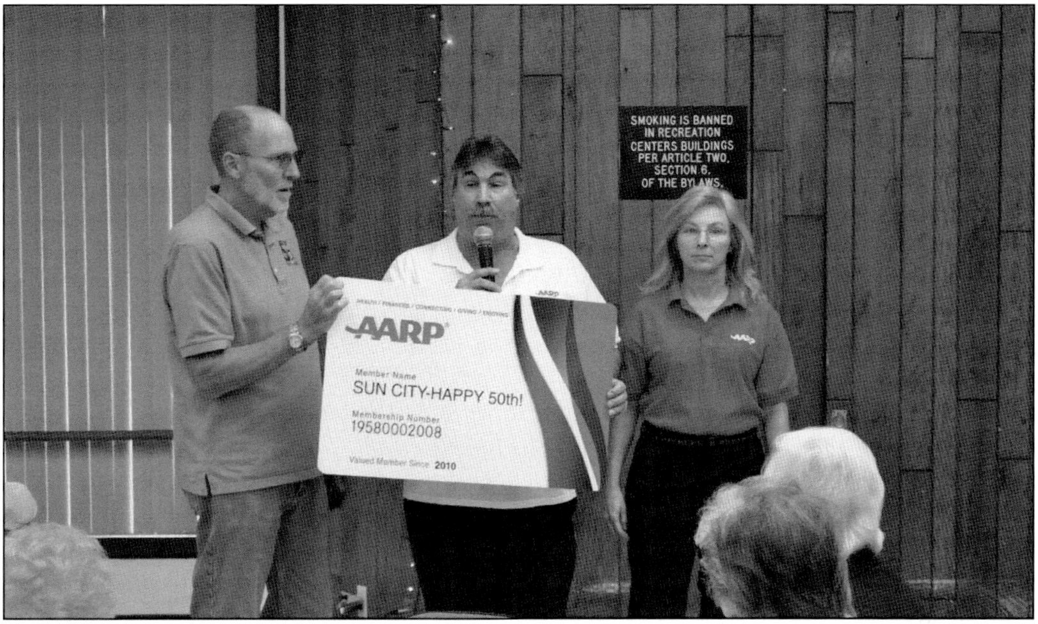


Representatives from the local AARP chapter marked Sun City's 50th birthday by officially presenting the community with its AARP membership. In this photograph, Paul Herrmann (left), executive director of the Sun City Visitors Center and host of the day's ceremonies, accepted the card from AARP officials. The very first AARP chapter ever established was in Youngtown, while Sun City is home to the fourth AARP chapter to organize. (Bret McKeand.)

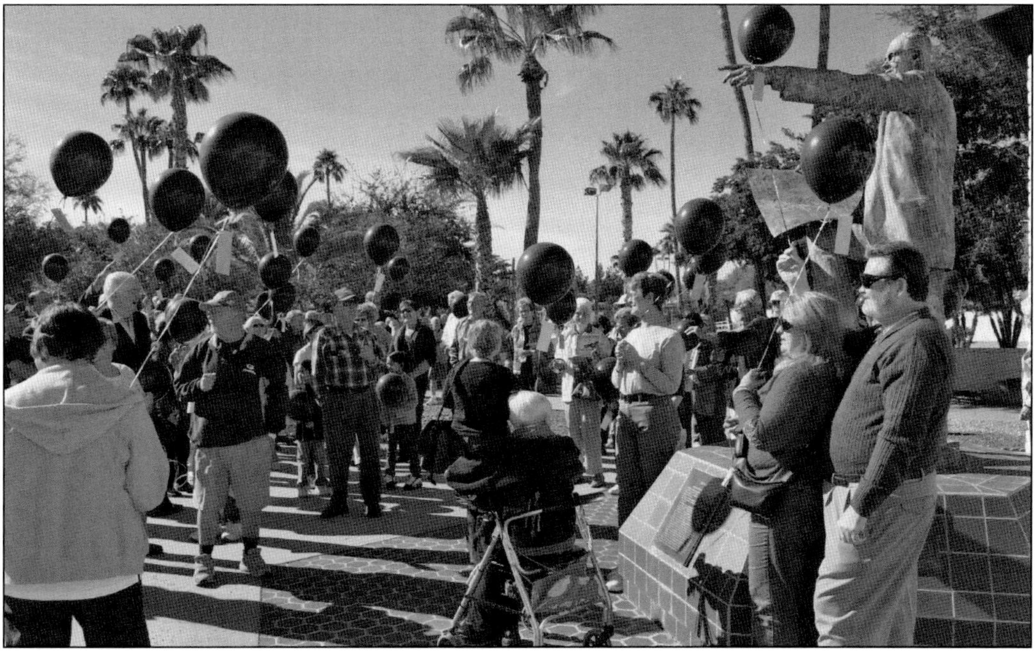

At the end of the January 1, 2010, birthday celebration at Bell Recreation Center, those in attendance were invited outside to Memorial Garden to take part in a massive "balloon release" near the statue of Del E. Webb. Memorial Garden is also home to the community's Liberty Bell replica and is adjacent to the Sun City Visitors Center. (Bret McKeand.)

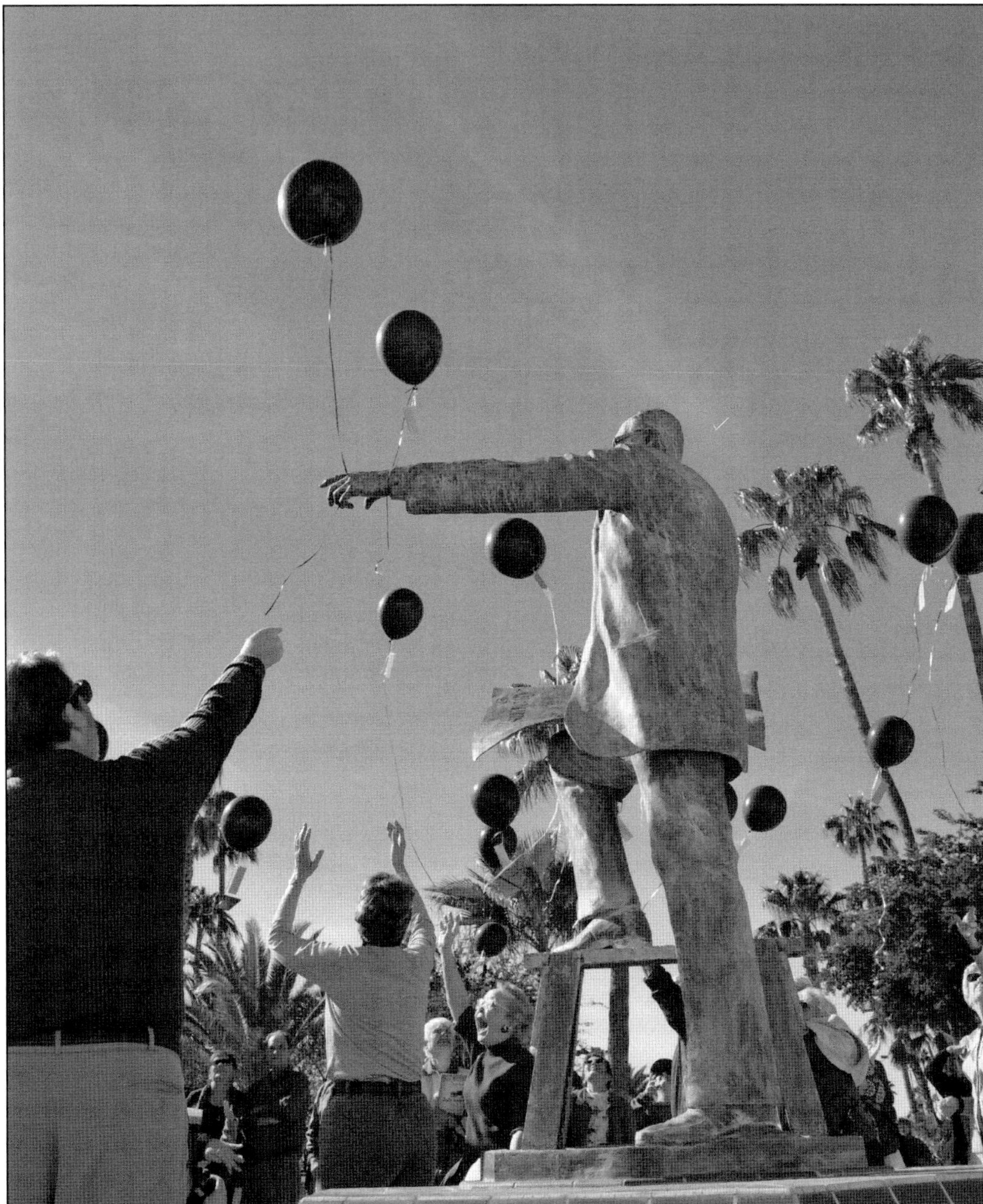

The 50th anniversary birthday party—held January 1, 2010, at Bell Recreation Center—culminated in a balloon release near the statue honoring Sun City's founder. A number of celebrations were held throughout the year to mark the community's golden anniversary. Most of them were coordinated or hosted by the 50th Anniversary Committee, the Sun City Visitors Center, or the Sun Cities Area Historical Society. (Bret McKeand.)

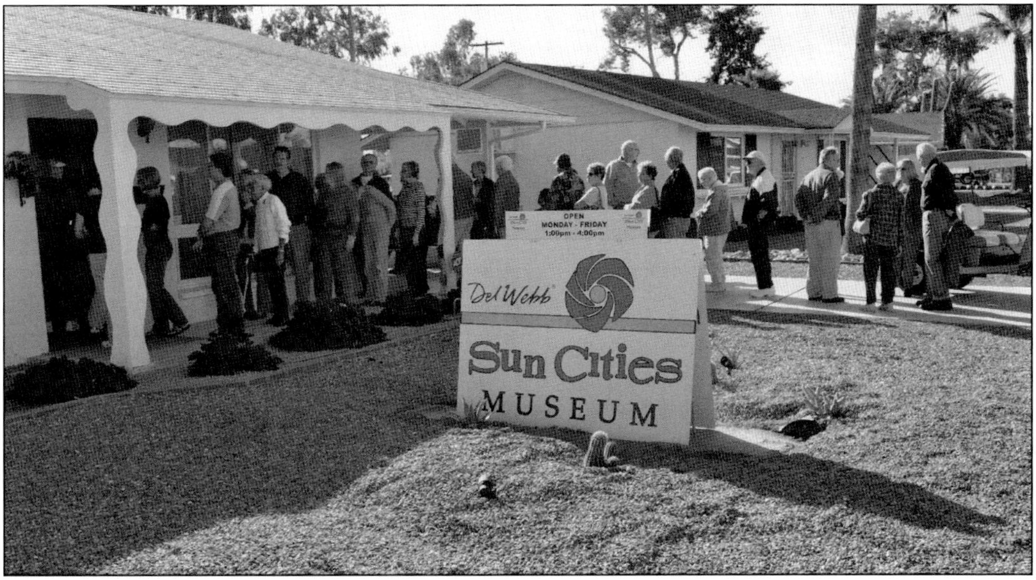


The Del Webb Sun Cities Museum held a 50th anniversary open house on January 1, 2010. The museum, located at 10801 Oakmont Drive, is located in the first of five model homes visited by curious buyers on opening day, January 1, 1960. The home has been restored to its original condition and today includes exhibits and artifacts showcasing the history of the Sun Cities. (Bret McKeand.)

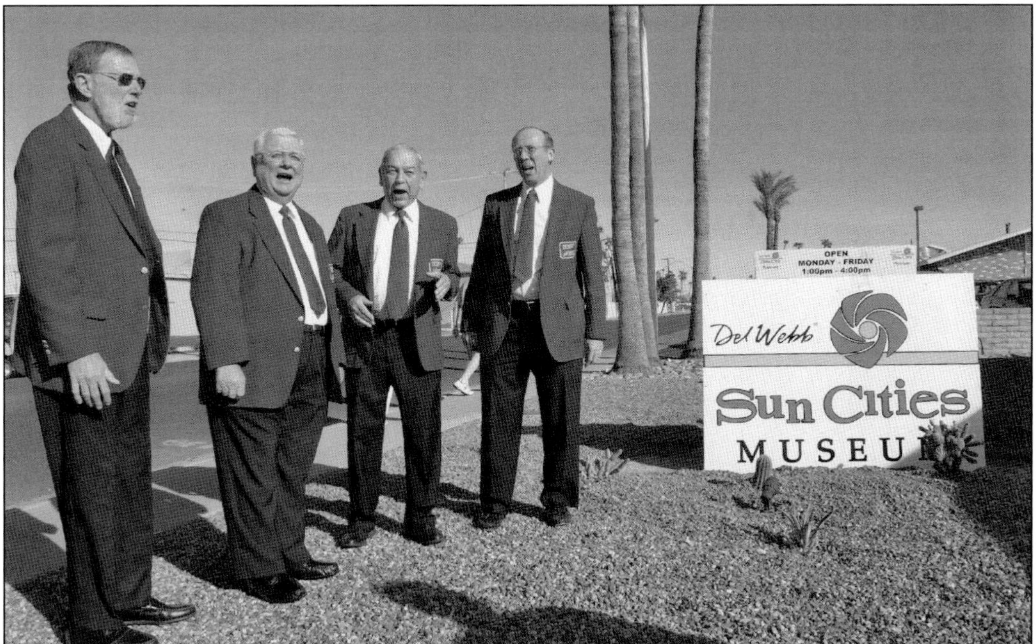


A crowd of nearly 400 attended the museum's open house on January 1, 2010. The Vintage Voices provided barbershop-harmony entertainment. Incredibly, quartet member Joe Salz, second from left, also performed with a quartet hired by the Del E. Webb Corporation to perform at the same house on opening day in 1960. The museum serves as the headquarters of the Sun Cities Area Historical Society. (Bret McKeand.)

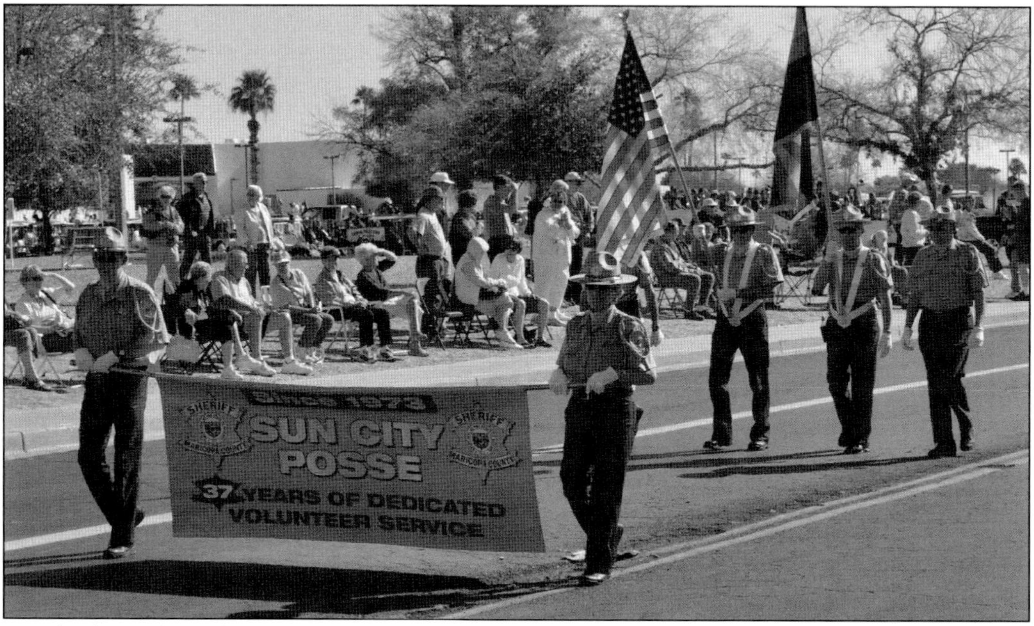


Parades have always been popular in Sun City and in February the community marked the 50th anniversary with one of its biggest and longest parades ever held. The parade was another in a series of celebrations planned by the 50th Anniversary Committee. For more information on the committee and the 50th anniversary, visit www.suncity50thanniversary.org. The Sun City Posse was part of the festivities. (Bret McKeand.)

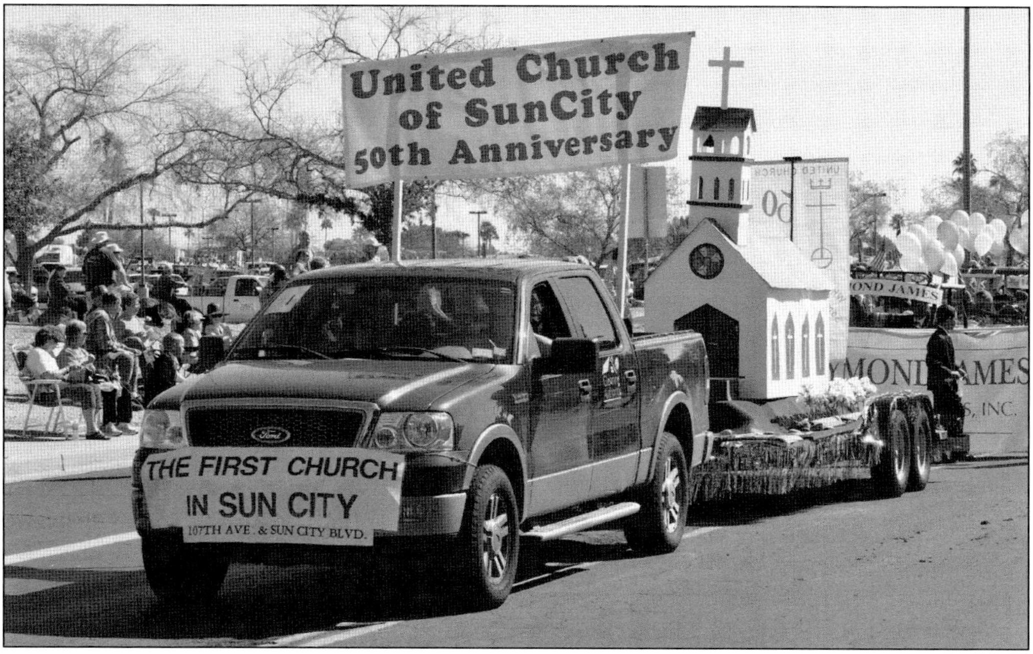


Members of the United Church of Sun City congregation celebrated Sun City's golden anniversary with a float in the February parade. The church's entry also highlighted the fact that it, too, was about to turn 50. The United Church of Sun City was the community's first church. (Bret McKeand.)

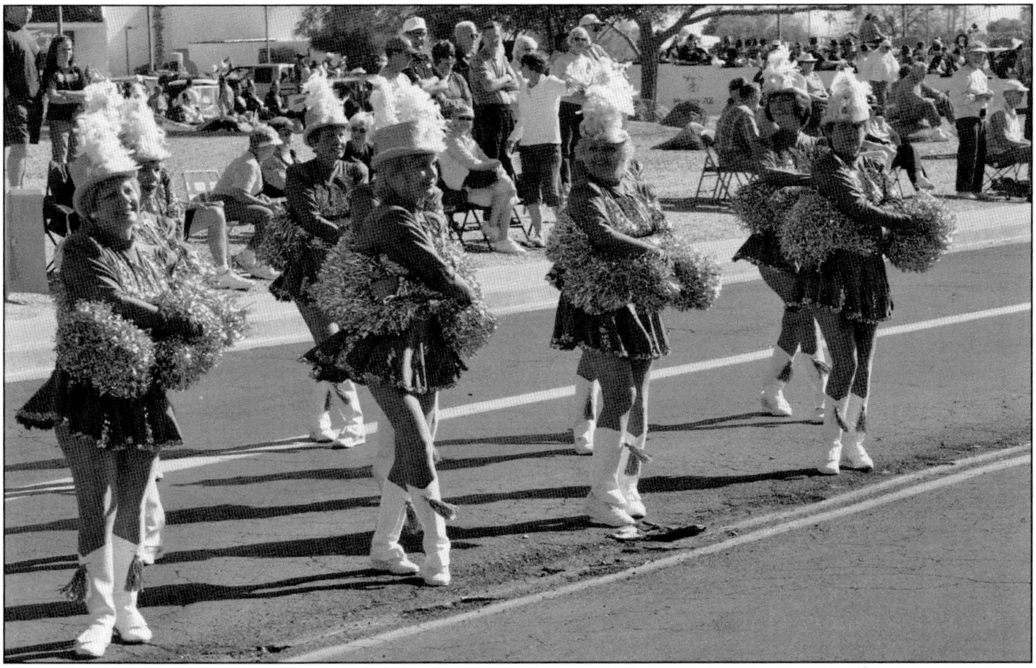

The Sun City Poms take center stage to entertain local fans during the parade. The Poms are veteran parade performers and over the years have represented the Sun Cities by participating in some of the nation's most popular parades. (Bret McKeand.)

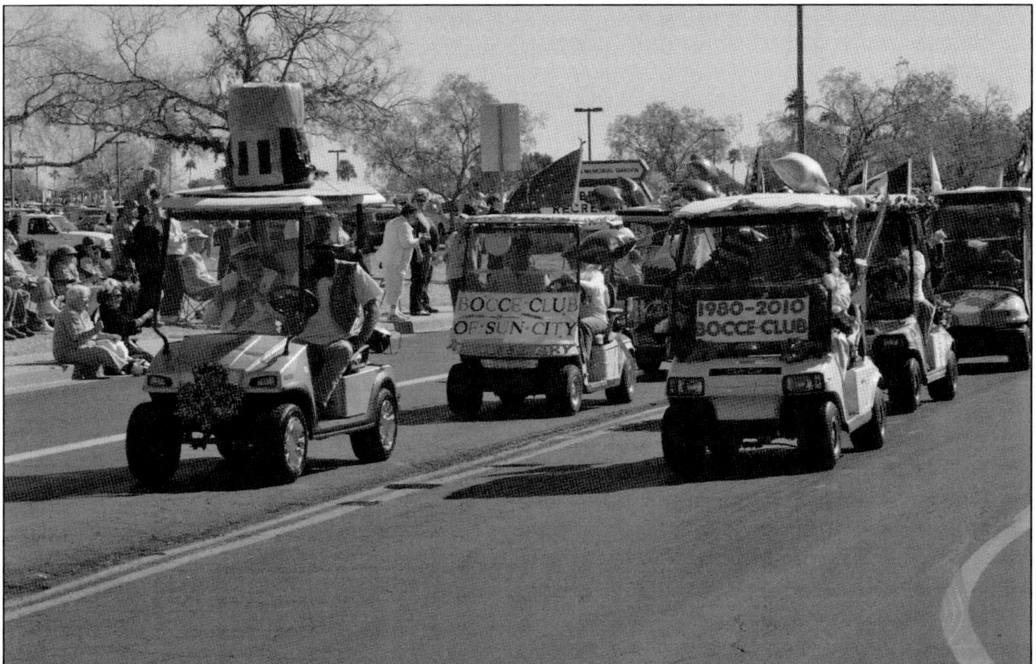


The Sun City Bocce Club was one of several recreational clubs to participate in the parade. Club members turned out in force with decorated golf cars, which are Sun City's preferred mode of transportation. (Bret McKeand.)

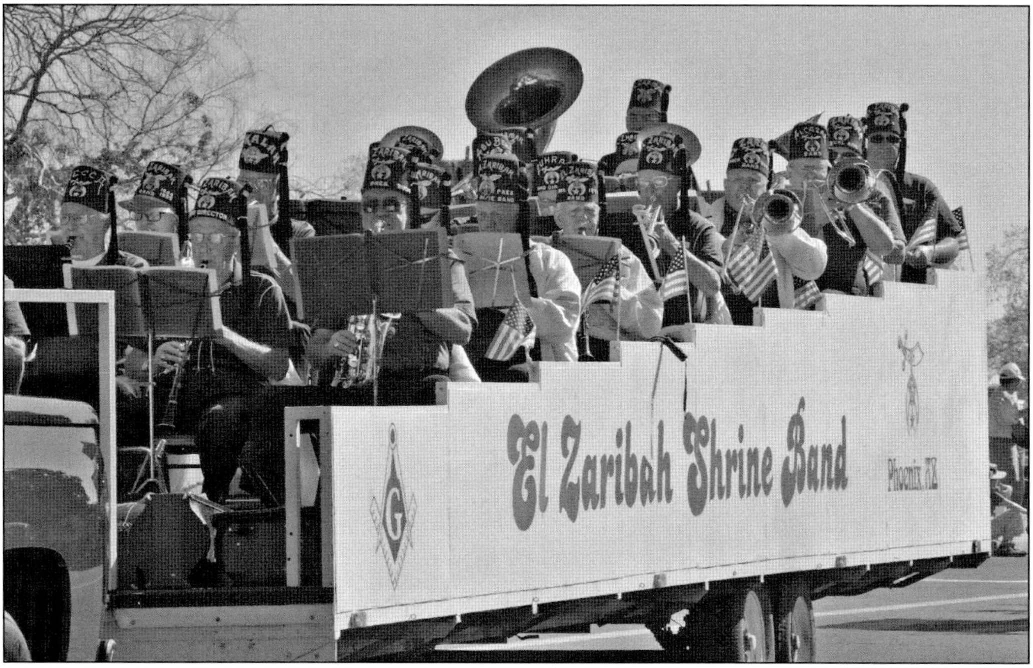


Members of the El Zaribah Shrine Temple provided musical entertainment during the 50th anniversary parade. (Bret McKeand.)

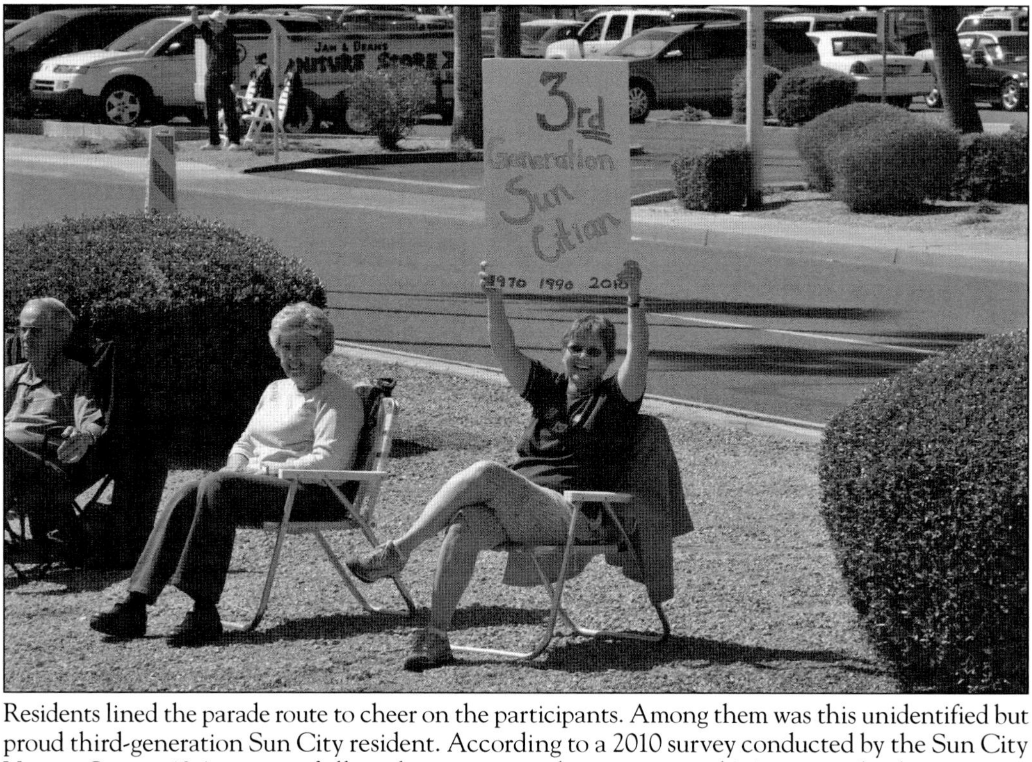


Residents lined the parade route to cheer on the participants. Among them was this unidentified but proud third-generation Sun City resident. According to a 2010 survey conducted by the Sun City Visitors Center, 18.4 percent of all residents are second generation and 1.6 percent third generation, meaning their parents and grandparents also lived in Sun City before them. (Bret McKeand.)

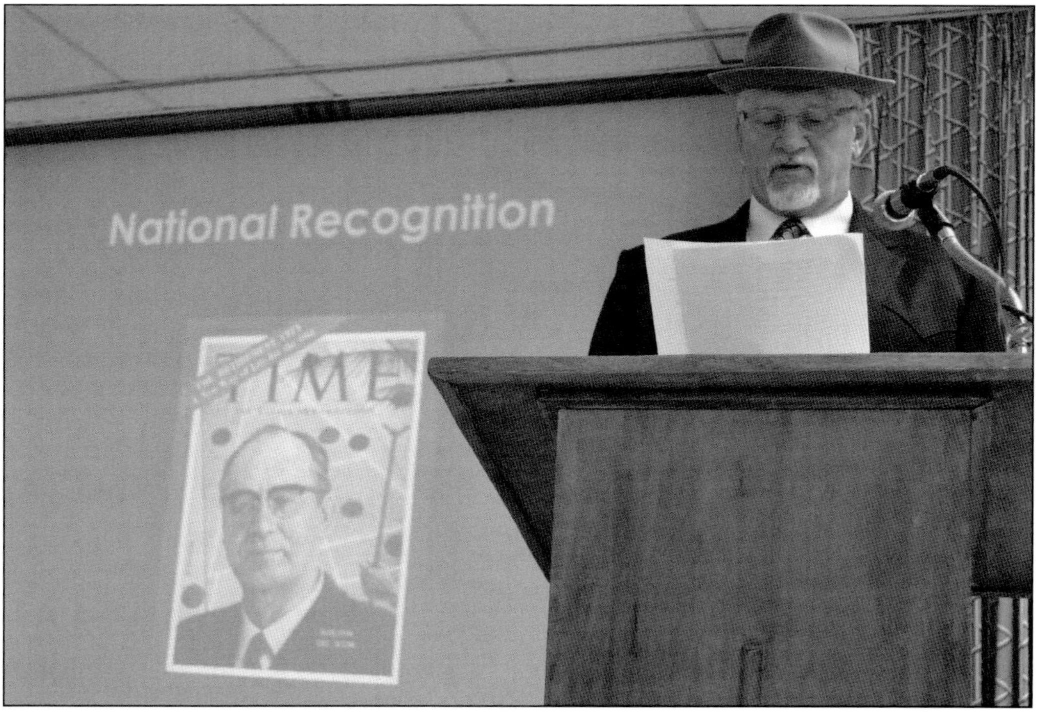


The Sun Cities Area Historical Society celebrated Del Webb's 111th birthday with an event May 16 at Oakmont Recreation Center. More than 200 people attended the program, which featured complimentary cake, recollections of the early days of the community by several former DEVCO employees, and a special biography on the life of Del Webb as told by Jim Gatscher of the Sun City Players Community Theater. (Bret McKeand.)

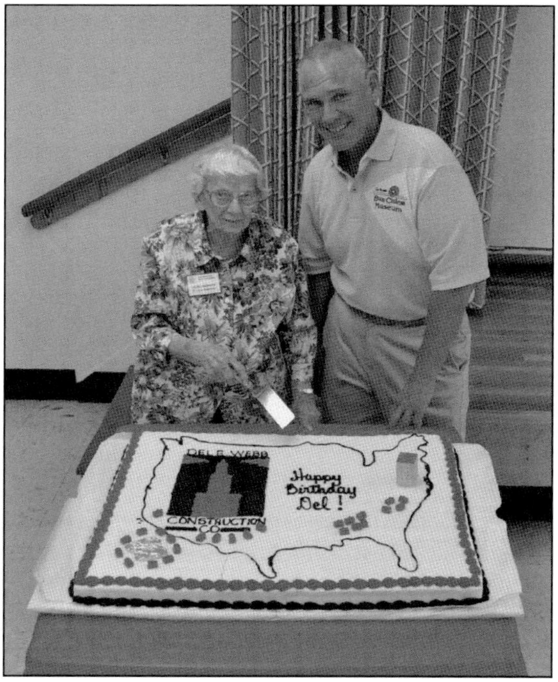


Jane Freeman, cofounder of the Sun Cities Area Historical Society, and Bill Pearson, SCAHS 2010 president, prepare to cut the ceremonial cake honoring the 111th birthday of Del E. Webb. In 1984, Freeman and Glenn Sanberg wrote the book *Jubilee: The 25th Anniversary of Sun City*, still considered to be the most authoritative history of the retirement community. (Bret McKeand.)

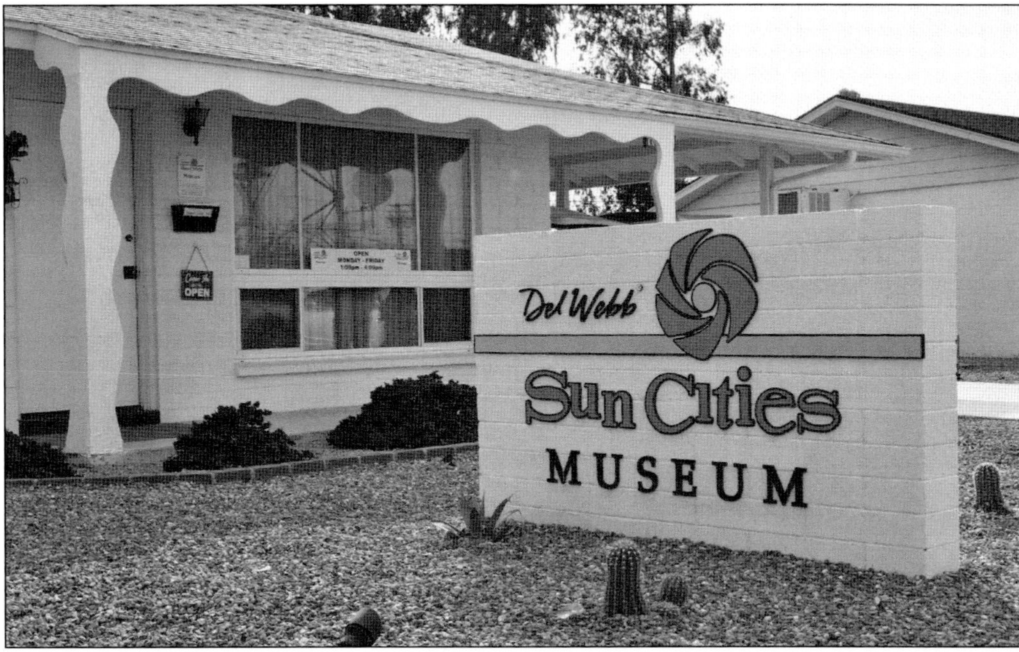


The Del Webb Sun Cities Museum is located in one of the first five model homes built in 1959 by DEVCO. The home closely resembles on the outside how it appeared in 1960. Visitors are treated to rotating exhibits and memorabilia showcasing the history of both Sun City and Sun City West. (Bret McKeand.)

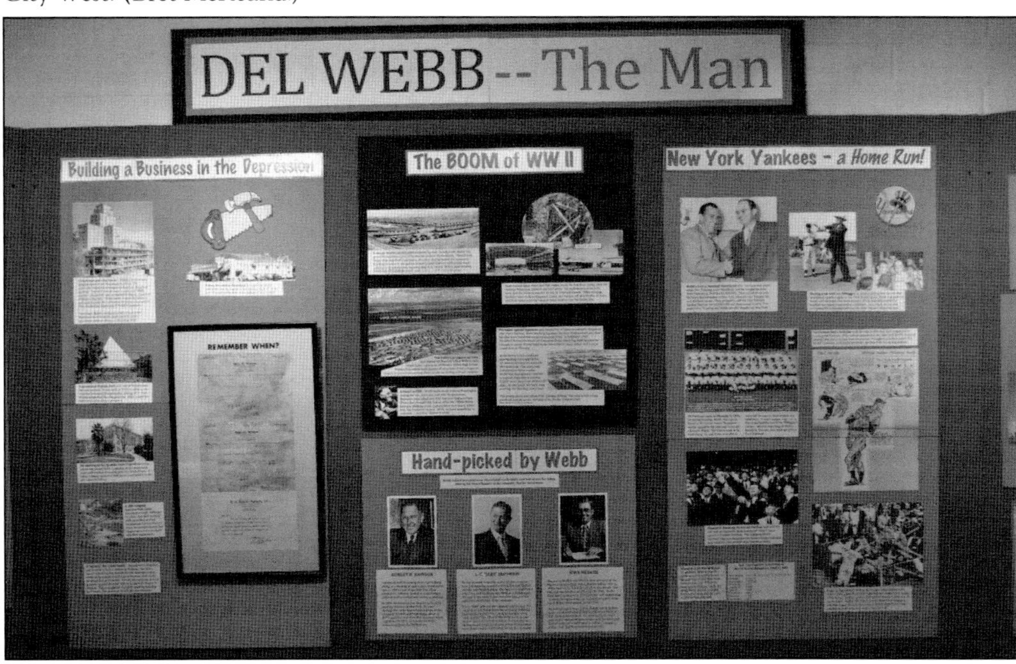


The museum was officially renamed in 2009 to honor the memory of the community founder, Del E. Webb. Since that time, a number of new exhibits have been introduced, including a special room dedicated to the memory and accomplishments of Del E. Webb. The exhibit features a number of Webb's personal items and artifacts on loan to the museum. (Bret McKeand.)

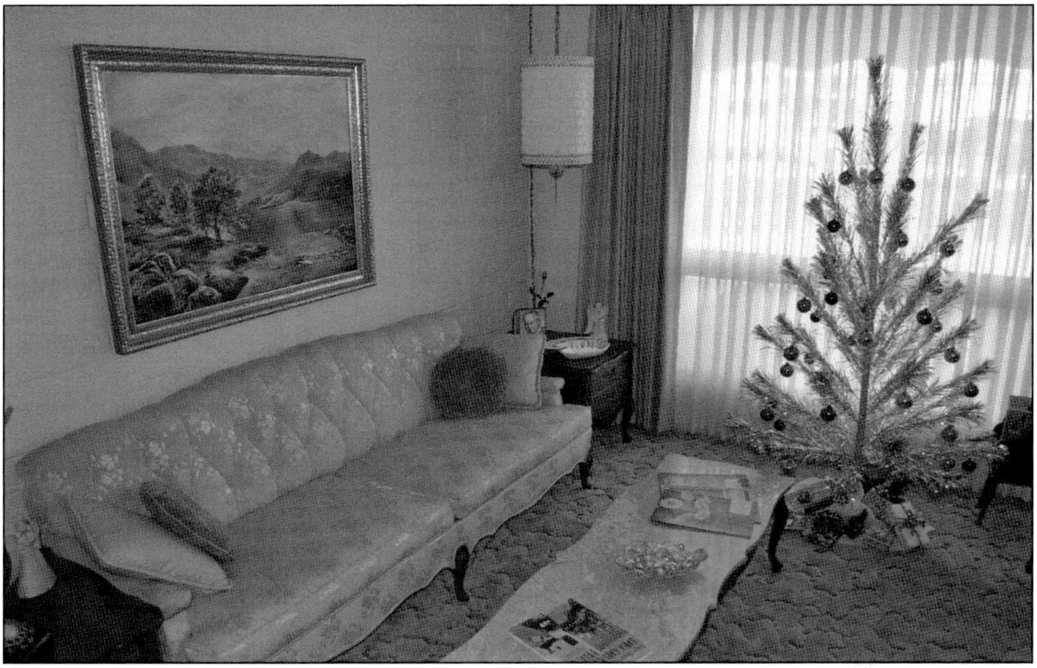

The museum offers a glimpse of what Sun City homes may have looked like in 1960. The living room is furnished in 1960s-era furniture. This photograph was taken on January 1, 2010, and the room on that day also featured a 1960s-era aluminum Christmas tree. For more information on the museum, visit www.delwebbsuncitiesmuseum.org. (Bret McKeand.)

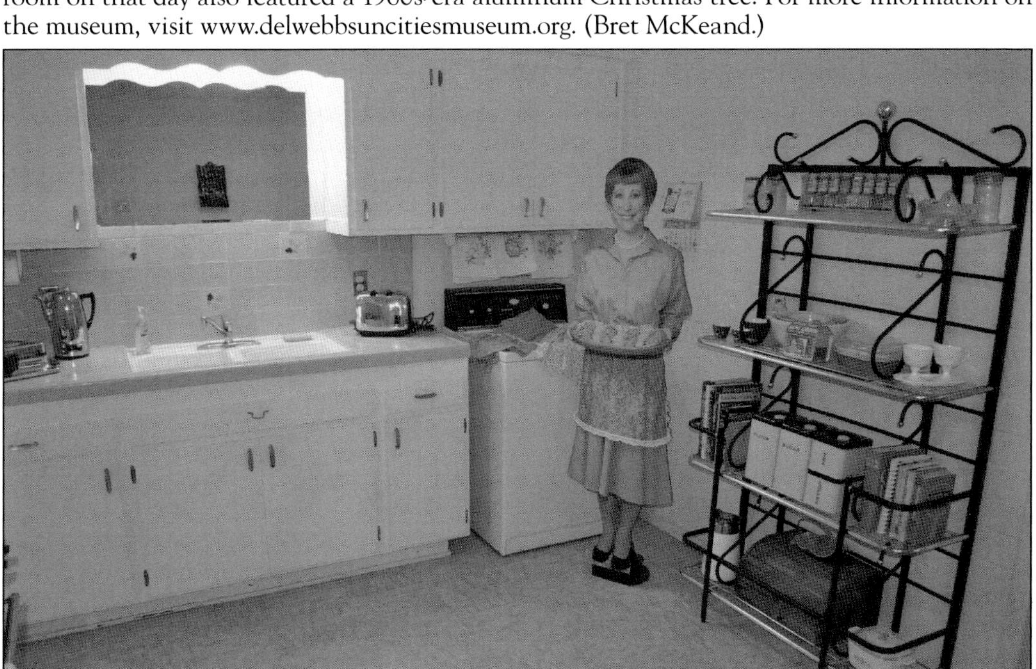

The museum's bright pink kitchen reflects how the house may have looked to those very first visitors and residents in 1960. The kitchen boasts appliances that were all the rage to new home buyers in 1960—and the refrigerator still works today! (Bret McKeand.)

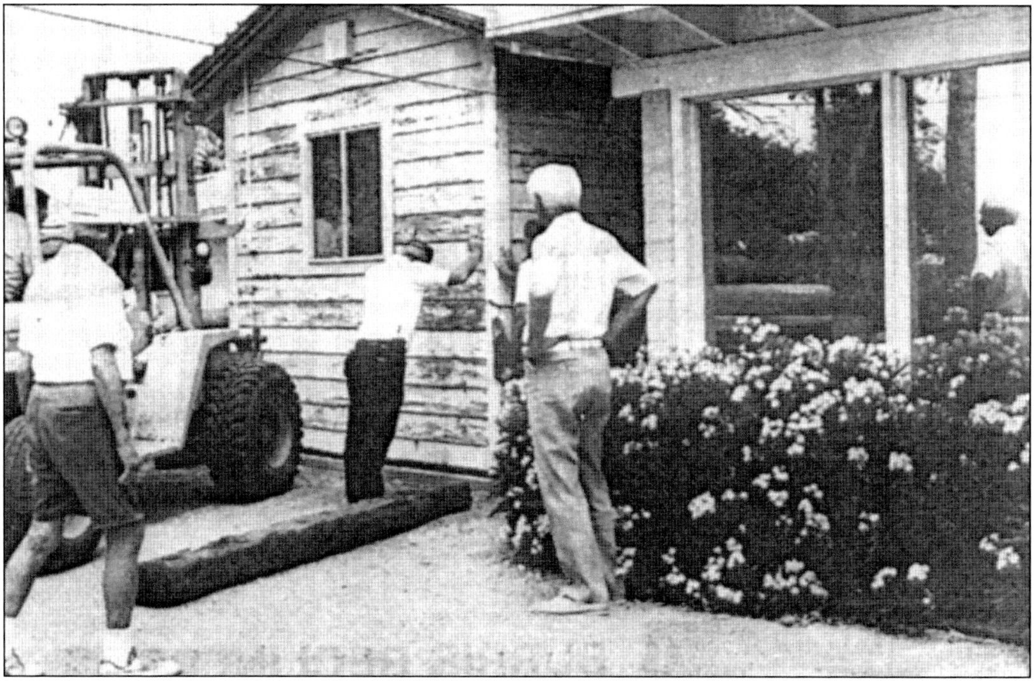

Soon after the historical society purchased the home in 1990, it also was able to secure a building that was erected by the Webb Company in 1959 to house a salesman to answer inquiries from passersby. The small office paid off as the salesman had 400 solid leads by the time the community opened in 1960. The office was attached to the home and is today part of the museum. It is the oldest building in Sun City.

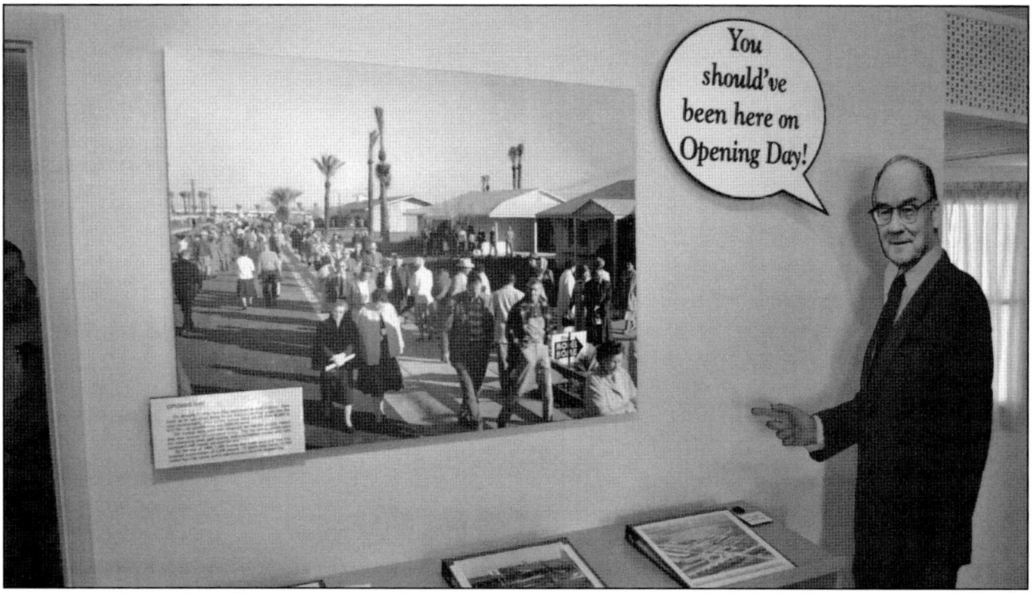


Visitors to the Del Webb Sun Cities Museum are greeted by a life-sized photograph of Del E. Webb and a large photograph of the house as it appeared on opening day in 1960. The photograph even "speaks" to visitors as a rare recording of Webb discussing his fondness for Sun City and its residents is played. (Bret McKeand.)

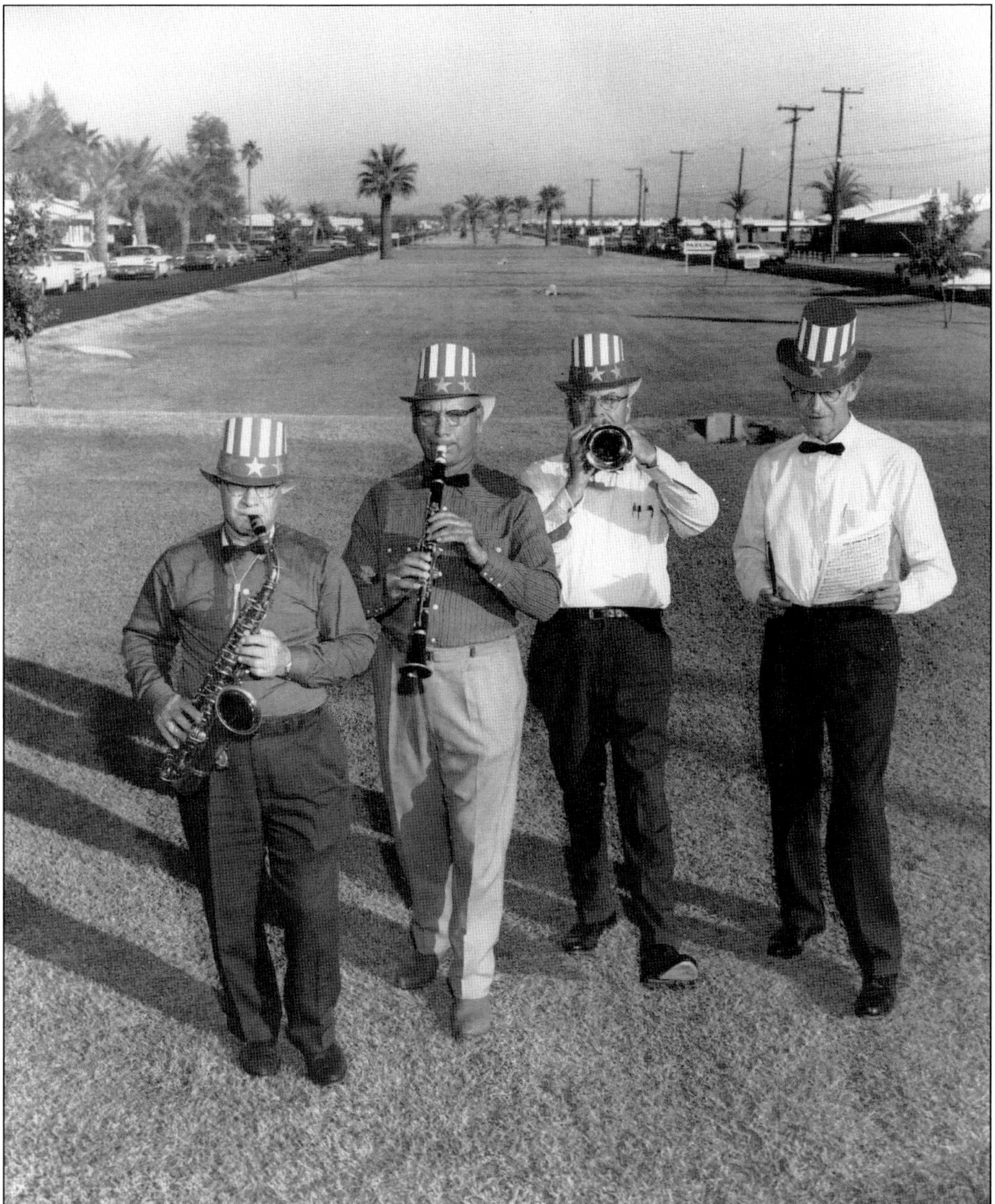

An unidentified photograph from the Sun Cities Area Historical Society archives shows a quartet of musicians in the 1960s marching along 107th Avenue near the Sun Bowl. The musicians are most likely celebrating the nation's independence on the Fourth of July, judging by the decorative hats. As Sun City enters its sixth decade, its future seems bright. The lifestyle created and fostered by the early pioneers remains as strong today as it ever was thanks to the community pride and volunteer spirit of those who followed. The community has evolved as the needs and interests of retirees have changed, and it appears evident residents are committed to making sure the nation's first active-adult retirement community remains one of the nation's most popular and attractive places in which to enjoy a life of leisure.

# About the Organization

The Sun Cities Area Historical Society (SCAHS) is a nonprofit organization dedicated to the preservation and presentation of the records and artifacts for Sun City and its sister city, Sun City West. Organized in 1986 by Jane Freeman, Glenn Sanberg, and Rita Wright, the society operates the Del Webb Sun Cities Museum.

The museum is located at 10801 West Oakmont Drive, Sun City, in one of the first five Sun City model homes opened in 1960. The home was purchased by the society in 1990 and is open to the public.

Photographs, historical artifacts, and a variety of rotating exhibits explain the interesting history of both Sun City and Sun City West. The SCAHS is managed by a volunteer board of trustees and the museum is operated by volunteer docents. SCAHS memberships are available to the general public.

Many of the photographs included in this book are available for purchase at the museum. Visit www.delwebbsuncitiesmuseum.org, or call 623-974-2568. The museum's mailing address is 10801 West Oakmont Drive, Sun City, Arizona 85351.

All author royalties from the sale of this book go directly to the SCAHS.

# About the Author

Bret McKeand is a former editor and publisher of the *Sun City Independent*, a weekly newspaper serving the community since 1960. He joined the staff in 1983 and became editor in 1985. He served as publisher from 1987 through 2009. He remains with Independent Newspapers, Inc., as vice president of the company's Arizona operations.

He is a member of the Sun Cities Area Historical Society Board of Trustees. He resides in Peoria, Arizona, with his wife and two children.

Sun City and he share the same age.

# BIBLIOGRAPHY


Allen, Edson, editor. *Sun City West Silver Celebration: The First 25 Years*. Sun City, AZ: Sun Cities Area Historical Society, 2003.

Finnerty, Margaret and Tara Blanc, Jessica McCann. *Del Webb: A Man. A Company*. Phoenix, AZ: Del Webb Corporation/Pulte Homes, 1999 (second edition).

Freeman, Jane, and Glenn Sanberg. *Jubilee: The 25th Anniversary of Sun City, Arizona*. Sun City, AZ: Sun Cities Area Historical Society, 1984.

Freeman, Jane, and Maurice Myerson. *Walter O. Boswell Memorial Hospital: An Ongoing History*, 1965. Sun City, AZ: Sun Health Corporation, 1992.

Granger, Byrd Howell. *Arizona's Names (X Marks the Place)*. Tucson, AZ: The Falconer Publishing Company, 1983.

*Reshaping Retirement in America: Sun City, Arizona, 1960–2010*. Tampa, FL: Faircount Media Group, 2009.

Sun City's 40th Anniversary: Special Commemorative Issue. Sun City, AZ: Sun Cities Independent, 2000.